IN DEFENSE OF HUMAN DIGNITY

Essays on the Just Third Way:
A Natural Law Perspective

by
Michael D. Greaney
Director of Research
Center for Economic and Social Justice

Foreword by Norman G. Kurland, J.D.
President
Center for Economic and Social Justice

Economic Justice Media
Center for Economic and Social Justice
www.cesj.org
Arlington, Virginia
2008

Text, foreword, formatting, and graphics
© 2008 Center for Economic and Social Justice (CESJ)

Published by Economic Justice Media, an imprint of CESJ
P. O. Box 40711, Washington, D.C. 20016, U.S.A.
(Tel) 703-243-5155 • (Fax) 703-243-5935
(Eml) thirdway@cesj.org • (Web) www.cesj.org

All rights reserved. No part of this edition may be reproduced, stored in a retrieval system, or transmitted, in any form, or by any means, electronic, mechanical, photocopying, recording or otherwise, without the prior written permission of the Center for Economic and Social Justice.

International Standard Book Number: 978-0-944997-02-4

Library of Congress Control Number: 2008908523

Cover design by R. L. Brohawn

Table of Contents

Author's Note i

Foreword: The Just Third Way v

1. Social Justice Betrayed 1

   Preface 3
   How to Misinterpret Catholic Social Teaching 7
   The Divine Right of Capital 23
   The Divine Right of Labor 43
   A More Excellent Way 61
   A More Excellent Way, Continued 77

2. Universal Health Care: Justice or Charity? 93

3. Social Justice Without Pius XI:
   The Triumph of Relativism 105

4. Heinrich Pesch on Property:
   Solidarism and the Just Third Way 119

   The Crisis 121
   The Solution 135

5. A Just Third Political Way:
   The Concept of Sovereignty in *Quas Primas* (1925) .. 149

   Man and Society 151
   A Personal Responsibility for the Common Good 165
   The Restructuring of the Social Order 177

6. Is Property Theft? The Idea of Property 191

7. The Only True Catholic System?
   A Critique of Social Credit 207

8. Is Distributism Socialism? 221

   An Issue of Understanding 223
   An Issue of Human Dignity 235

9. Subsidiarity and Private Property: A Catholic View 249

   The Idea of Subsidiarity 251
   The Function of Subsidiarity 273

Bibliography 291

Author's Note

While the articles in this collection have a definite "Catholic" orientation and are published by "Economic Justice Media," an imprint of the Center for Economic and Social Justice ("CESJ"), CESJ is not a Catholic organization. Nor is CESJ affiliated with any specific religion or sect. CESJ is an interfaith group, with members from many faith traditions and drawing inspiration from all philosophies and religions with a natural law orientation. As someone writing from a Catholic perspective, and the author of the articles in this collection, I have naturally expressed myself in terms of that faith tradition.

This is no way diminishes or denigrates the contributions made by other members of CESJ who do not share my beliefs or my interpretation of their applicability in implementing and maintaining the Just Third Way. It is my particular approach, and the way in which I believe I can best express myself. I assume that members of other religions will express their support for and understanding of the Just Third Way in terms of their belief systems, as I do in terms of mine.

Further, my statements reflect my understanding of the teachings of the Catholic Church and their applicability within this context. They can in no way be taken as statements of official doctrines of the Catholic Church.

A word about the articles in this collection. They were written at different times, and some were not published in the order written. Except for the final two-part article on subsidiarity (which was not published), they are presented here in the order in which they appeared in *Social Justice Review*, the official journal of the Central Bureau, Catholic Central Union of America in St. Louis, Missouri, USA. Most of the articles were composed at the special request of the late Father John H. Miller, C.S.C., S.T.D., with themes suggested by him in his capacity as editor, and scrutinized by him personally. The first five-part article was previously published as a pamphlet under the title, *Social Justice Betrayed* by the Central Bureau in 2000, appearing first as a four-part article in *Social Justice Review* under the title given by Father Miller, "Bishop Beware." When Father Miller suggested publishing the article as a pamphlet, I rewrote the final article in the series at greater length to explain CESJ's "Just Third Way" in more detail.

When CESJ decided to expand its publishing program, a reprinting of *Social Justice Betrayed* seemed in order. CESJ had run through all the copies provided by Father Miller in lieu of royalty payments. We still had a need, however, for material that explains the Just Third Way from within the framework of Catholic social teaching. We had to do this in a way that non-Catholics would presumably find accessible, and thus be more representative of CESJ. As the pamphlet format was incompatible with the general guidelines we've established, other articles requested by Father Miller and a few others on the same theme were added.

The articles do not present a complete picture of the Just Third Way. Instead, being written in response to expressed needs of a particular editor, they address certain limited aspects of the Just Third Way as applicable under certain circumstances, and from a particular perspective.

Although the articles were written from a Catholic point of view, I believe that non-Catholic readers should have no trouble reading and understanding them. Catholic social teaching is based on the natural law, which applies to every human being, regardless of religious, political, or economic beliefs. In any event, every writer must, as you would expect, write from a particular perspective. It is impossible to have a completely objective stance. Without a specific and identifiable standard against which to measure one's thoughts and behavior, the only result is pure moral relativism.

The articles have been edited slightly to clarify some of the writing that, in retrospect, seemed a little obscure in the original, and to use some possibly more appropriate words. Redundancies have not, however, been removed. To do so would have required a much more extensive editing than was perhaps warranted for the republication of a series of discrete articles.

Leaving the repetitions in place may even be of some benefit in reinforcing what seems to be a major bone of contention among social reformers: the role of private property in the social order, and as a necessary support for essential human dignity.

Michael D. Greaney
Director of Research
Center for Economic and Social Justice
June 2008

Foreword: The Just Third Way

There is an increasing roar in our day from commentators and complainers who are adept at pointing out the flaws of, and laying heavy burdens on other people. To counter the growing din, it is a pleasure to write a foreword to a collection of articles that, while based on sound philosophy and plain common sense, also point toward workable solutions to the problems that afflict modern society. Anyone can find fault, but not everyone can figure out what to do to correct those faults.

While I am not a Christian, I can appreciate the common sense embodied in the social doctrine of the Catholic Church. Catholic social teaching, as the late Father William J. Ferree, S.M., Ph.D. (my mentor in the field) informed me, is based firmly on a grounding of natural law understood within the framework of such great Aristotelians as Thomas Aquinas, Moses Maimonides, and Ibn Khaldûn. The natural law — and therefore Catholic social teaching based on the natural law — is part of "essential" human nature, meaning that the ability to understand it is part of what it means to be human. Anyone who is human (and we are all human in the same way and to the same degree) can therefore understand and agree on universal social teaching, for "catholic" means "universal."

With respect to matters of faith taught by the Catholic Church, I take the view of Alexis de Tocqueville, the insightful author of *Democracy in America*, when he said, "The sects that exist in the United States are innumerable. They all differ in respect to the worship which is due to the Creator; but they all agree in respect to the duties which are due from man to man. Each sect adores the Deity in its own peculiar manner, but all sects preach the same moral law in the name of God. If it be of the highest importance to man, as an individual, that his religion should be true, it is not so to society. Society has no future life to hope for or to fear;

and provided the citizens profess a religion, the peculiar tenets of that religion are of little importance to its interests."

For me, then, the question becomes, What is the most moral (and thus practical) way to implement the precepts of the natural law into the daily life of humanity? I answer that in terms of what we at CESJ call "The Just Third Way" of economic and personal empowerment of the human person, the dignity of which is the focus of the social doctrine of the Catholic Church, and, it is my impression, other Christian sects, as well as Judaism, Islam, Buddhism, Hinduism, B'hai, and all the other great religions and ethical systems. While the elements of the Just Third Way — a vision of the future that synthesizes the institutional design science principles of the lawyer-economist Louis Kelso and the physical world design science principles of R. Buckminster Fuller — may seem complex at first, we have to realize that is only because we are used to thinking in terms of the "same old thing" — outdated paradigms forcing us into tried and failed patterns of behavior, and unworkable solutions to world problems.

So — what are the elements of the Just Third Way?

One of the most pressing problems facing the world today is how to generate a secure and adequate income sufficient to meet common domestic needs. Most people live from paycheck to paycheck . . . or from hand to mouth. Only a tiny fraction of humanity own most of the technology, natural resources, structures, infrastructure, and other income-producing assets on Spaceship Earth that make the world of today so different from the time humans lived in caves. Most workers and most humans own none or such small portions of such productive assets that their capital incomes could not sustain their lives. If the capital assets of the world suddenly disappeared, however, most of humanity would be forced into starvation within weeks. If civilization's capital is so important, how can we grow the economy in a way that all living on Spaceship Earth could own enough productive capital to provide them a livable and secure income? The answer to how citizens without adequate savings can acquire an income-producing property stake lies in the intelligent use of credit — specifically, productive credit.

Credit is a social creation. It can only exist in a society organized to protect contracts and property rights. A central premise of the Just Third Way is that productive or capital credit is a "common good." Equal access to this good is a fundamental human right and the social key for enabling "have-nots" to become "haves."

One powerful ownership-expanding technique is known as the Employee Stock Ownership Plan ("ESOP"). The ESOP provides widespread and systematic access to capital credit to each employee in a participating company. An "empowerment ESOP" can be designed so that employees gain both a voice in corporate governance and a source of financing which does not reduce their paychecks or savings.

Traditional sources of capital funding treat loans to ESOPs the same as other corporate loans. An ESOP loan is based on the company's credit, with repayment expected wholly out of future profits of the company.

Beyond the ESOP are other credit-diffusing tools which would open up ownership and profit sharing opportunities for consumers of public utilities, residents of new or redeveloped communities, teachers and other public servants, farm families, homemakers, the disabled, professionals, frustrated entrepreneurs, and citizens generally.

Management structures and technologies can be just as or even more important than the physical technologies with which most people are familiar. Under the expanded capital ownership paradigm of the Just Third Way, the business corporation (whether a small local business or a giant multinational) can become a vehicle for transforming the world into a more free and just marketplace. The Just Third Way focuses on helping corporate managers to see that they can do their jobs more effectively by incorporating economic justice in the way they do business.

Through ESOPs and similar means for empowering corporate workers and customers, more people could legitimately acquire ownership of the growth of capital without taking from those who own existing assets. These new owners would be able to get income from capital as a supplement to their wage incomes.

Under "Justice-Based Management," employees would supplement their fixed wages or salaries with monthly and annual bonuses, stock and dividends — all generated out of profits. Each employee could automatically earn and accumulate property while working in a participatory and empowering corporate culture, thus gaining a direct, personal interest in the success and profitability of his or her employer company.

Another problem is that life-enhancing actions at the personal, family, enterprise or community level — no matter how well-intentioned — can easily be suppressed or nullified by a hostile or unjust external environment at the national or global level.

Moving from the microeconomic to the macro-economic level, the Just Third Way encompasses strategies for reshaping basic social institutions, such as tax and monetary systems, which have become barriers to human development.

A program we call the Capital Homestead Act contains reforms that are based on four interdependent pillars of economic justice:

1. Restoration of private property in the means of production
2. Restoration of free and open markets for determining just prices, just wages and just profits
3. Limited economic power of government
4. Widespread direct ownership of the means of production.

Social technologies and laws designed to advance the four-pillar approach would encourage the broad diffusion of future capital ownership opportunities — the missing link in all other strategies for transforming the economies of the world. Economic and political power would begin to be decentralized into the hands of each member of society.

The Just Third Way recognizes that the world's complex economic and social problems cannot be solved in a single stroke. There is no panacea. The concept of social justice in the Just Third Way, as developed and refined by Father Ferree, addresses the structuring of institutions (laws, systems, social organizations, *etc.*) and how they enhance or degrade the sovereignty and dignity of the individuals affected by them.

By targeting institutions in society that are defective and unjust, social justice identifies the structural cause of the problem, not just the symptoms of the problem. Through democratic processes and by combining their individual strengths, concerned individuals can act in positive ways to bring about seemingly impossible changes in the social order.

The definition of the "act of social justice" used in the Just Third Way as the moral virtue or good habit exercised when a person acts with others in an organized way to perfect the social order or any part of it within their reach.

Transforming bad laws and unjust institutions is impossible when each person acts in isolation or only for his own welfare. But together, organizing around common moral principles and a shared vision, people can convert social structures of exploitation and alienation into structures of justice.

America was born through acts of social justice. This is how racial barriers in the U.S. were lifted in the 1960s, and how the apartheid system in South Africa was overcome. And this is how communism was toppled in Eastern Europe and the former Soviet Union in the 1990s.

Implicit in any act of social justice is a recognition that improving the social order or an institution is a never-ending task. This is because human beings and human creations (including laws and institutions) are inherently imperfect. Hence, while we can never expect to achieve perfection in transforming unjust laws and institutions, we have a moral responsibility relentlessly to work with others to pursue justice. While the articles in this compendium do not, of course, detail the entire Just Third Way or even outline it completely, they nevertheless are written from that perspective, and provide a valuable resource for anyone seriously interested or involved in the restructuring of the social order.

    Norman G. Kurland, President
    Center for Economic and Social Justice

1. Social Justice Betrayed

(*Social Justice Review*, May/June 2000
through January/February 2001)

Preface

Is it possible that six popes have written so many encyclicals on social justice only to be ignored, misinterpreted or misunderstood? Yet that is a fact staring us in the face. While it is understandable that the man in the street remains ignorant of the sane and solid doctrine taught by the popes regarding social justice, how can we possibly explain Episcopal Conferences passing over in such cavalier fashion the doctrinal import of what the Chief Shepherds have so insistently taught? And what can we say about the cafeteria-style approach of theologians and Catholic economists to the corpus of papal social teaching?

For years interpretations of the Church's teachings on social justice have been distorted by a Marxist or socialist slant forced on the encyclicals, although promoters of these interpretations carefully refrain from admitting that such is the case. Even in the face of explicit warnings by Pius XI and other popes, advocates of some schools of thought in the past, such as certain forms of Liberation Theology, insisted on overweening State control or outright ownership of the means of production — socialism in all but name! As a case in point, the 1986 Bishops' Pastoral on the economy, *Economic Justice for All*, was heavily influenced by these schools of thought.

And now, directly contradicting the words of John Paul II in *Centesimus Annus*, our seminarians' minds are being deliberately inoculated with ideas about social justice that result from twisting papal teaching to support the *laissez-faire* attitude of the wealthy. Can bishops blithely overlook this abrogation of their authority and duty to see that future priests are formed according to the teaching of the highest Magisterium in the Church? I am sure that this is done innocently, just as they have innocently put their *Imprimatur* to social justice documents composed by their Episcopal Conference committees that continue to pick and choose from among the many and urgent points of papal teaching on justice.

Yes, it is innocent, I am sure. But it is innocence produced by a lack of study on their part of the Supreme Bishop's teaching. It might do all of us a lot of good, were our bishops to imitate the present Holy Father's practice of setting aside an hour for *study* in the morning before starting the customary rounds of office work in the chancery. There is a simple reason for this: Bishops cannot teach adequately unless they feed their minds on the social doctrine of the popes. There is a need for a grave submission of mind to the truth of the Catholic Faith in all its forms even to be able to compose the documents in which the bishops propose their teaching.

Perhaps what is needed is an encyclical dedicated to "economic justice," as this pamphlet suggests. "Don't we have that already?" you may be tempted to ask. No. What we have is something of far greater magnitude than mere economic justice. The thrust of the social encyclicals is not simply economics, but the whole of the common good, of the entirety of society itself. To understand how people have misinterpreted this, we need only look at the way most people refer to the encyclicals.

For example, the fact that Pope Pius XI's encyclical *Quadragesimo Anno* has a second title, clearly stated in its preamble, is rarely mentioned: "On the Restructuring of the Social Order." His Holiness was not satisfied with strictures against paying unjust wages, or approving the rights of labor to organize and urging the need for subsidiarity to function before States intervene to correct matters. His encyclical was aimed at nothing less than overhauling the entire social order, redoing it, rebuilding it and bringing it into conformity with the law of the Gospel:

> 76. What We have thus far stated regarding an equitable distribution of property and regarding just wages concerns individual persons and only indirectly touches social order, to the restoration of

which according to the principles of sound philosophy and to its perfection according to the sublime precepts of the law of the Gospel, Our Predecessor, Leo XIII, devoted all his thought and care.

Read the preamble and ask yourselves, "how will the social order ever be restructured according to the mind and spirit of Jesus Christ, if the bishops do not take the lead in teaching about and helping to achieve the 'Kingdom of Love and Justice,' so often spoken of by Pope John Paul II?" or are these just nice words to buoy up the spirits of suffering mankind? Will our bishops really do something about handing on the genuine and complete teachings of the popes?

It truly appears that what Father William J. Ferree, S.M., Ph.D. called "the great message of the encyclical" has been completely misunderstood or ignored. How, then, can anyone think that a "lesser" subject such as economic justice, firmly based on a proper understanding of social justice, has been handled with any degree of either accuracy or propriety?

Were our bishops really to internalize the popes' teaching on social justice, they would be more critical of what is placed before them for approval, especially in the area of economic justice. They could begin to exercise a strong influence on the content of their teaching documents. They would be able to discern the reasons why such-and-such an economic proposal is right or wrong. They would be in a better and stronger position to insist that the full papal doctrine shine clearly through their proposals. The workingman would no longer be left adrift in an economic system which the popes have effectively labeled "wage slavery." We would finally hear our bishops insist on one of the principal points made by so many of the popes, that true economic security comes not from wages alone, but from the workers' ownership of the means of production, from profit-sharing, from an equitable recompense for top company officials that would refuse to make them millionaires at the expense of genuine sharing. Yes, gentlemen, work is for the benefit of the worker, not to line the pockets of a chosen few with the profits of a business from which the great mass of workers are prevented from sharing in as owners.

Read the papal encyclicals on social justice; study them — but not in the manner popularized by those with a political agenda or a private ax to grind, picking and choosing which passages you want to accept or twist. No, take the entire corpus of the social encyclicals as a consistent body of teaching. If you need clarification, why not petition the Holy Father for an encyclical on economic justice, instead of relying on second-hand consultors or theologians who deliberately set themselves in opposition to the Holy See?

Let the following superb chapters by Michael Greaney be your guide to discovering the foundation of papal doctrine on justice. Then be leaders in implementing the Holy Fathers' pursuit of economic and civil peace truly founded on justice and the acknowledgment of the workers' priority over things through ownership and the fundamental right to property, as well as every human being's strict right of access to the means of acquiring a proportionate share of the good things of this earth.

    Rev. John H. Miller, C.S.C., S.T.D.
    Editor
    Social Justice Review

Part I

How to Misinterpret Catholic Social Teaching

A Conservative Call to Action

It's the eleventh hour, Your Excellency. Do you know where your seminarians are?

As you are probably aware, the magazine *Culture Wars* recently published an article criticizing the efforts of the Acton Institute to indoctrinate seminarians in its version of Catholic social teaching.[1] The Institute claims to have trained a sizable number of seminarians in its doctrines.[2] They back up their words with deeds, paying for travel, tuition, and maintenance.[3]

On the surface, there doesn't seem anything wrong with this "Call to Acton." Anyone who believes strongly enough in something should be prepared to spread the word to others. This the Acton Institute has done with exemplary skill and a sincere focus on capitalist ideology.

Again, what's wrong with that? As the Acton Institute asserts, hasn't the pope declared that capitalism is the only true Catholic economic system? Hasn't capitalism triumphed over communism? Doesn't capitalism defend and uphold what Leo XIII declared to be the sacred right of private property?[4] Also, they might continue, hasn't the pope explicitly condemned any concept of a "third way"[5] either between or beyond both capitalism and socialism? That, in their view, appears to leave only capitalism as a viable alternative, for socialism has been explicitly condemned.[6]

Your Excellency, we need to examine these rather sweeping claims promoted by the Acton Institute and its sympathizers. The fact that these beliefs are evidently held with great sincerity commands our respect. Our concern for human dignity demands that we not dismiss any belief so deeply and profoundly held without a hearing.

True, the Acton Institute, as well as most other vocal proponents of "Capitalism Triumphant," generally labeled "neoconservatives," usually dismiss criticism by ignoring it or reiterating the very assertions questioned. That, however, is unacceptable, either from the standpoint of teaching, common courtesy, or fraternal correction. When discussing an issue, we must remember to turn the other cheek to affronts, and offer the bread of explanation, rather than the stone of ignorance, or the snake of insult. Let us consider the points.

Capitalismo Triumfante

Is capitalism the only true Catholic economic system? Has the pope "endorsed" capitalism? Is capitalism even a Catholic economic system? We can answer these three questions in this way.

Is capitalism the true Catholic economic system? This is one of the few questions to which we can answer with a simple *ipse dixit*. No. Capitalism is not the one, true economic faith for the simple reason that the popes have consistently proclaimed that the Church has not made, and does not, cannot, and will not ever make any such declaration.[7]

Given what Pius XI described as "the radical instability of human affairs,"[8] any such declaration would be almost immediately nullified. Conditions that would have permitted the declaration would have changed, rendering the declaration meaningless. Such is the condition of fallen man that, even were perfection (and therefore immutability) attainable in this world, chances are most people would not complete the task of temporal perfection, whether personal or social.

A specific economic or social system is a human construct, even if society itself is divinely mandated by man's social nature. Human society cannot, by its very nature, attain perfection, and thus absolute truth. The Catholic Church, therefore, cannot and will not abuse its teaching authority to declare perfect, that which is not perfect. Capitalism, as even its supporters will admit, is not a perfect system. They sometimes paraphrase Churchill's quip about democracy into a dictum that capitalism is the worst of all possible systems — except for all the others. Capitalism cannot, therefore, ever be considered "the" one, true Catholic economic system.

The authority of the Church to teach infallibly extends only to matters of faith and morals. Economics does not fall into either category, regardless of the position it has achieved in some people's lives. The Church would be speaking outside of its competence to declare infallibly that capitalism — or any economic or political system — is "the" Catholic system.

Further, to try and find such an endorsement in anything said by Church authority is to misunderstand the teaching role of the Church. "Infallibility" does not mean that something is true because the Church or a pope in his role as teacher has said so. On the contrary, when the Church speaks, it is because she believes something is true. Maintaining that something is true because the Church (or the pope) has said so is a form of "positivism," which theologically is called "modernism," that which St. Pope Pius X called, "the synthesis of all heresies."

This is not to say, Your Excellency, that the Church does not speak with authority when commenting on applications of principles which do come under its competence in faith and morals, and which happen to occur in the realm of politics and economics. Unfortunately, people everywhere, even very intelligent people, have a strong predilection for mistaking an application for the principle itself, or the exercise of a right (the rights *of* something) for the underlying right (the right *to* something). This brings us to the second question: Did the pope endorse capitalism?

How Not to Endorse Capitalism — Or Anything Else

From the orientation and analysis of the neo-conservative position, it certainly seems that the pope did, indeed, endorse capitalism. In *Centesimus Annus*, John Paul II asks the question,

10 —In Defense of Human Dignity

> . . . can it perhaps be said that, after the failure of Communism, capitalism is the victorious social system, and that capitalism should be the goal of the countries now making efforts to rebuild their economy and society? Is this the model which ought to be proposed to the countries of the Third World which are searching for the path to true economic and civil progress?[9]

His Holiness then answers his own question.

> The answer is obviously complex. If by "capitalism" is meant an economic system which recognizes the fundamental and positive role of business, the market, private property and the resulting responsibility for the means of production, as well as free human creativity in the economic sector, then the answer is certainly in the affirmative, even though it would perhaps be more appropriate to speak of a "business economy," "market economy" or simply "free economy."[10]

That seems to settle the issue. The pope has endorsed capitalism . . . or has he? If you start by looking for an endorsement in the pope's words, you will probably find exactly what you set out to find. A sincere capitalist, however, should certainly pause at the cautious manner in which pope speaks: ". . . can it perhaps be said . . . "; "The answer is. . . complex"; "If by 'capitalism' is meant . . . "; ". . . it would perhaps be more appropriate . . . ". All this sounds very vague and should be extremely dissatisfying to the capitalist seeking an endorsement. It bears a superficial resemblance to the prevarications of politicians refusing to admit the truth and taking refuge in quibbling over definitions of words, such as, "What does 'is' mean?" What do we really have?

An "endorsement" such as the pope has presumably given to capitalism would make a starving man very suspicious of the bread he was offered. Let's rephrase the response along those lines. "Is this bread safe to eat? The answer is obviously complex. If by 'bread' we mean a type of food baked from flour and containing nothing inimical to human constitutions, then the answer is certainly in the affirmative, but perhaps it would be more appropriate to speak of 'rolls,' 'scones' or simply 'nourishment'." Anyone in his right mind would be leery of an "endorsement" phrased in such a manner — as the pope makes it very clear we should be:

> But if by "capitalism" is meant a system in which freedom in the economic sector is not circumscribed within a strong juridical framework which places it at the service of human freedom in its totality and sees it as a particular aspect of that freedom, the core of which is ethical and religious, then the reply is certainly negative.[11]

There is clearly no endorsement of capitalism as the only true Catholic economic system. On the other hand, the pope's words open up the possibility of something other than socialism, capitalism, or the unhealthy blend of the two known as the Welfare State. What about the third question? Is capitalism at least a tenable Catholic position? That gives us a significant problem before we can even begin, for there is a serious difficulty with defining "capitalism."

Is Capitalism a "Catholic" System?

As John Paul II made painfully clear in § 42 of *Centesimus Annus*, there seems to be some ambiguity about the definition of "capitalism." G. K. Chesterton, however, had no difficulties defining capitalism, a definition sufficiently clear that we can use it: "When I say 'Capitalism,' I commonly mean something that may be stated in this way: 'That economic condition in which there is a class of capitalists roughly recognizable and relatively small, in whose possession so much of the capital is concentrated as to necessitate a very large majority of the citizens serving those capitalists for a wage'."[12]

Neo-conservatives have not been slow to undermine this definition. Michael Novak "finesses" Chesterton's perorations against capitalism by stating in a foreword to a volume of Chesterton's collected works, "I find Chesterton's salvoes against 'capitalism' — keeping in mind what *he* means by it — warning shots well-fired. The essence of what *I* mean by capitalism is a system most highly valuing wit, invention, discovery — capitalism (*caput*) being the mind-centered system."[13] [Emphasis in original.]

Ignoring the fact that the *caput* referred to in "capitalism" is derived from the head of cattle,[14] not the reasoning mind of man, we can only find this deflection of Chesterton's criticisms — inserted into a foreword to Chesterton's own work — extraordinarily misleading. Mr. Novak manages to ignore every word of Chesterton's definition of capitalism, and replace the concrete realities highlighted by Chesterton with vague, "feel good" generalities that (when examined closely) turn out to mean exactly nothing.[15]

In his promotion of "democratic capitalism," however, Mr. Novak does take some cognizance of the concentration of property, and therefore power, in the hands of the few represented by capitalism as defined by Chesterton. In a singularly contradictory exercise, Mr. Novak claimed in an editorial in the *Wall Street Journal* that all Americans were rich because the government owned so much in the way of wealth, and a large number of Americans had rights in pension plans.[16] In short, "democratic capitalism" is apparently triumphant because it is indistinguishable from socialism.[17] This, remarkably, is the same claim as that of John Maynard Keynes, who declared that he could "save" capitalism by "socializing" it.[18]

Perhaps this is not so remarkable, after all. Promoters of socialism also claim to find support in Chesterton's distributism. Martin Gardner, an editor of Chesterton's works, declared that, "It is not inappropriate to describe Chesterton's economic and political opinions by a term that conservatives today abhor — democratic socialism."[19] Someone (or possibly everyone) is confused if "capitalism" and "socialism" mean exactly the same thing. There are other problems with capitalism. Capitalism in any recognizable form, especially "democratic capitalism," cannot be considered a Catholic economic system for the pure and simple reason that "democratic" is the last thing it is. As Senator Russell Long[20] put it, "the trouble with capitalism is that there aren't enough capitalists." The neoconservative stance is clear: The rich capitalist is a member of a special breed, an elite, ordained by God to supply the financing for the formation of capital which will provide the rest of humanity with wage system jobs. Because of the incidental good of job creation that results from the rich man pursuing his self interest, the effective monopoly held by the currently wealthy over the means of acquiring and possessing property is seen as a moral good.[21]

The problem is that, if the process of capital formation is carried out properly, jobs are not created, but eliminated. The whole idea of advancing technology, including skills and new ways of doing things (which some refer to under the dehumanizing label of "human capital"[22]), is to reduce the need for human labor in the production process. The solution to this seeming paradox, if you are not put off by the clever but inappropriate title, is found in Louis Kelso and Mortimer Adler's *The Capitalist Manifesto* (1958).[23] Kelso and Adler outlined a free market, private property system based on principles of economic justice. They developed practical applications for connecting people to production as owners of advancing technology that was rapidly displacing human labor in the global economy.

This creates another problem. The standard neoconservative claim is that anyone, with enough "guts and gumption," can save enough or use his entrepreneurial ability to become a "capitalist." The inability or unwillingness to do so demonstrates an intrinsic unworthiness to enter the exclusive circles of ownership. Neo-conservatives reject the possibility that there are barriers that prevent ordinary people, who by definition lack the "necessary" extraordinary ability (generally held to be a willingness to assume risk), from acquiring ownership.

The attitude that only an elite are fit to own and thereby control others is itself sufficient proof that significant barriers exist to the broad mass of people becoming direct and personal owners of an adequate stake of income-generating assets. The intent of Leo XIII in *Rerum Novarum*, generally considered the first of the social encyclicals, however, is clear: The great mass of people are to be put into such a position not only that they desire to become owners, but that means are provided to realize this desire.[24] Ownership is not just for an elite. It is for everyone, and the normal way to earn a living.[25] The assumption that capitalism of any variety is perfect or even moral is an explicit denial of Leo XIII's stated goal.

Access to the Means of Acquiring Ownership

Neo-conservatives frequently assert that, since property is the basis of civil society, and capitalism is based on property, capitalism is therefore the natural form of society, and the only workable system. This is "proved" by Panglossian[26] logic: Capitalism and socialism are the only two possibilities for the economic arrangement of society. Capitalism has triumphed over socialism. Capitalism *must* be the best of all possible systems.

The unfortunately fundamental yet widespread misunderstanding of property fosters this attitude, an attitude not countered effectively by the usual rejoinders. Many commentators insist that the true Catholic understanding of property is that property is a right that is not absolute. Moral considerations override any absolute concept of property. There is enough truth in this analysis to be extraordinarily misleading.

Taking a contrary position, neo-conservatives insist that, because property is a right that must be regarded as sacred,[27] property must be considered an absolute. The idea of putting limits on property is abhorrent and immoral. There is enough truth in this analysis also to be extraordinarily misleading.

Both positions confuse *having* a right with *exercising* a right. Property is absolute in the sense that everyone absolutely has the right to acquire and possess property. That is what Leo XIII meant when he said that property as a right must be regarded as sacred. The *exercise* of property, however, is limited by the demands of the common good and the nature of one's relations with others in society. In that sense, property cannot be regarded as absolute. It acquires, as does every other right by definition,[28] a specifically social character that subordinates to the good of all the owner's enjoyment of the fruits of ownership to some degree.

Property is, in fact, a purely social thing. Property is not the thing owned, but the natural (absolute or inalienable) right that every human being has simply because of his humanity, and the socially-determined yet strictly defined set of relationships that regulated how an owner relates to what he owns, and how the rest of society relates to the owner with respect to what he owns. Capitalists assert that the absolute character of the right to be an owner extends to its exercise, while socialists make the opposite error by declaring that the socially-determined character of the exercise of property extends to the right to be an owner in the first place. Given the correct understanding of property, both are clearly wrong, for each takes half the definition and forces it on to the other half, to the detriment of common sense.

Because capitalism thereby ignores common sense, capitalism is not a system based on a Catholic understanding of property, but on a distortion of it. The very concentration of ownership that characterizes capitalism prevents others from exercising their absolute right to property. Additionally, the absolute exercise of the rights of property, which also characterizes capitalism, represents a serious danger to the common good.

Capitalism reverses the nature of property. It does this in the first place by making its acquisition and possession dependent upon special circumstances and abilities. This negates the absolute and universal aspect of property — and contradicts both sound philosophy and legal theory by making "accidentals" (form or characteristics) determine the substantial nature of a thing.

Capitalism reverses the nature of property in the second place by asserting the absolute exercise of property once it is acquired. This negates the social nature of property. It undermines the exclusive aspect of property by exaggerating the exercise of rights all out of proportion and ignoring the demands of the common good. This gives leverage to those who would label abuses of the exclusive nature of property the rule, and therefore something to be abolished in its entirety.

Principle and Application

Your Excellency, the arguments over property are representative of the entire orientation of both the Acton Institute and its critics. Both are partly in the right, while managing to be entirely in the wrong. That is a danger of working with a partial truth. This is rooted in a fundamental misunderstanding of the idea of *principle* ("substance") and the idea of the *application* of principle ("form" or "accidental").

The neo-conservatives' greatest strength is the fact that they are clear on principle — at least on some principles, and only on their terms. This makes programs based on these principles attractive to seminarians searching for absolutes within a milieu where these principles have often been deliberately eliminated in an unconscious undermining of the Church. Where the neo-conservative runs into trouble is in the definition and application of those principles. Ironically, neither the neo-conservatives nor their critics differ on fundamental principles — only on the application.

Neo-conservatives will, in general, agree that everyone has the right to acquire and possess property — in theory. They effectively deny this in practice, however. They will not, for example, agree that everyone should have access to the means of acquiring and possessing property, or that significant barriers exist which inhibit or prevent ownership on the part of the broad mass of people. Their characterization of capitalism as the equivalent of a "free" market contradicts

How to Misinterpret Catholic Social Teaching — 17

itself. A market cannot be considered "free" if a determinant number of people are prevented from participating in the entire "package" of rights that make up the common good at that level; "human freedom in its totality," as John Paul II put it.[29]

Neo-conservatives will also insist that the rich confer benefits on society just by being rich. This echoes Keynes' opinion that great disparities in wealth were absolutely necessary for society to advance economically,[30] even to the point that the small owner is to be regarded as "functionless"[31] because he consumes the income generated by his capital rather than investing it to create jobs for others. Under the orientation of both Keynes and the neo-conservatives, the job of the rich is to be rich. They generate far more income than they can consume, necessarily investing the excess to form new capital and, presumably, create new jobs.

A different misunderstanding cripples the contrary position. Commentators on that "side" will generally be very clear on applications of principle, such as the necessity for the living wage in the current condition of society, family allowances, limits to the exercise of property, the right of workers to organize, and a multitude of other applications of the principles set out in the social encyclicals. The problem, however, is that they generally mistake the application of a principle for the principle itself.

In view of the radical instability of human affairs, both orientations and method of analyses can only result in disaster. Applications of universal principles, to be effective, are tailored to specific conditions of society.[32] Because human society is in a constant state of flux, however, changes must constantly be introduced into any system (and to any application) to bring it back into conformity with universal moral principles. Rigid insistence on a specific application designed for a former set of conditions will be ineffective, inappropriate, or disastrous.[33]

Seizing upon the inconsistencies revealed, neo-conservatives are usually delighted to point out the ultimately self-defeating nature of outdated or inappropriate applications asserted as absolute principles. This allows them to ignore or ridicule other applications which, although also ultimately self-defeating if employed as permanent solutions, are expedient under current conditions of society, and which must be implemented until appropriate changes can be introduced into the system so as to render the expedient unnecessary.[34]

The essential problem is that neither side acknowledges whatever truth the other has managed to stumble onto. Each uses the obvious inconsistencies in the other's approach to ridicule and dismiss that position. Neo-conservatives dismiss moral imperatives tailored for existing conditions of society,[35] while critics attack the neo-conservatives for insisting on the validity of certain economic principles that come into conflict with the needs of the worker in those same conditions. Both are partly right — and both are wrong. In this, the Acton Institute makes essentially the same mistake as Lord Acton himself. As one commentator put it,

> . . . he [Lord Acton] is also valuable as an example of the dangers of rejecting the more pragmatic views of men like Burke and Aristotle who were ready to make moral judgments but judged human behavior by human standards. Cicero said of his high-minded and fanatical contemporary that Cato's trouble was to think he was living in Plato's Republic instead of the dung heap of Romulus. Something like that might well have been said of Lord Acton.[36]

Your Excellency, the problem is that neither side acknowledges that Catholic social teaching is both moral, practical, and, especially, *human* in every sense. This represents a significant danger to seminarians who attend the Acton Institute indoctrination programs — and for those who don't. In either event, they are getting less than a third of the picture.

Each of the positions that has a place at the table today dismisses or ignores large portions of the Church's social teaching that they either don't understand or which they consider unacceptable, generally tossing whatever they reject as "merely prudential." One position is characterized as impracticable dreamers for ignoring economic reality, while the other is castigated as heartless fiends for neglecting the demands of charity. Since each side attacks the other's distorted truths and dismisses the rest, the result is a complete negation or abolition of authentic Catholic social teaching.

Notes

[1] Anthony Basile, Ph.D., "Selling Out Catholic Social Teaching: The Acton Institute's Misleading Message" *Culture Wars*, September 1999.

[2] "The Acton Institute's mission centers on reaching out to seminarians, clergy, and business leaders to promote a truly free society sustained by religious principles. . . . much of the Institute's outreach is accomplished through its student conferences, lectures, and publications." *Acton Notes*. December 1999, Volume 9, Number 12, 3.

[3] "I found the 'Toward a Free and Virtuous Society' conference to be very intellectually stimulating. I came to the conference with high expectations, and they were far exceeded. I must thank the Institute for an intellectually inspiring weekend. It was truly a beneficial experience, and I've taken away much food for thought." S. C., St. [X] Seminary. "From Our Mailbox," *Acton Notes*, October 1999, 2.

[4] Leo XIII, *Rerum Novarum* ("On the Condition of the Working Classes"), 1891, § 65. Some commentators assume that industrialization and capitalism are identical; that the mere employment of large, physical concentrations of capital constitutes "capitalism." This ignores the concentration of ownership of any form of productive asset that is the chief characteristic of capitalism, and is an error specifically highlighted and corrected by Paul VI in *Populorum Progressio* ("On the Development of Peoples"), 1967, § 27. "Capitalism" cannot be understood in the encyclicals as referring to large aggregations of capital or the predominance of capital as a factor of production. As Chesterton remarked, "If the use of capital is capitalism, then everything is capitalism." G. K. Chesterton, "The Beginning of the Quarrel," *The Outline of Sanity*. Collected

Works, Volume V. San Francisco, California: Ignatius Press, 1987, 43.

[5] Fr. Robert Sirico, "President's Message" *Acton Notes*. June 1997, 1.

[6] Pius XI, *Quadragesimo Anno* ("On the Restructuring of the Social Order"), 1931, § 120.

[7] Pius XI, *Divini Redemptoris* ("On Atheistic Communism"), 1937, § 34.

[8] "The fact is that precisely in those social elements which seem fundamental, and most exempt from change, such as property, capital, labor; a constant change. . . is not only possible, but is real, and an accomplished fact." Pius XI, *Discourse Commemorating the Thirty-Fifth Anniversary of Rerum Novarum*, May 15, 1926. This idea was echoed in § 132 of *Quadragesimo Anno*, ". . . *the instability of economic life*, and especially of its structure, exacts of those engaged in it most intense and unceasing effort. . . " [emphasis added].

[9] John Paul II, *Centesimus Annus* ("On the Hundredth Anniversary of *Rerum Novarum*"), 1991, § 42.

[10] *Ibid.*

[11] *Ibid.*

[12] Chesterton, *op. cit.*, 42-43.

[13] "Saving Distributism" *Ibid.*, 15.

[14] Capital, when speaking of wealth, is derived from *caput -itis*, n. (connected with the Greek κεφαλη), literally "the head," but in context a thing relating to money and capital—*de capite ipso demere* (Cicero). It is used in the sense of productive wealth, of earning a profit honestly. Compare with the parallel development of *pecunia -æ*: meaning property or wealth, from "*pecus -oris*," meaning cattle (as opposed to head [of cattle] in *caput*). "'Pecunia,' that is, property ; the original meaning of 'pecunia' being property in cattle, then property or wealth of any kind." St. Augustine, *De discipl. Christ.* 6. Also, "How elegantly they have accounted for this name! 'He [Zeus Pater/Jupiter] is also called Pecunia,' they say, 'because all things belong to him.' " *The City of God*. VII.12. *Pecunia* is used in the sense of wealth in the form of money, speculative transactions, non-productive wealth, or usury. There is a clear distinction in Latin between the two different types of wealth, sterile and productive, *pecunia* and *caput*, respectively. See *Cassell's Latin Dictionary*, New York: Macmillan Publishing Company, 1968. See also Henry George, *Progress and Poverty, Centennial Edition 1879-1979*. New York:

Robert Schalkenbach Foundation, 1979, 37 for additional commentary on the derivation of "capital." See "Life of Cato" in Plutarch's *Lives of the Noble Grecians and Romans*, as well as his essay "On Borrowing Money" for the attitude toward productive versus nonproductive wealth and borrowing. It is true that one school derives the evolution of the meaning of "capital" from the *human* head, and thus it is presumed to have referred to the native wit, intelligence, skills, and so on, intrinsic to the human person. This would appear to be an example of what philologists call "back formation" — beginning with a pre-determined conclusion as to the origin of a word that has nothing to do with the actual source. This intellectual conception of productive assets is overly sophisticated for a pastoral economy and contradicts the usual primitive perception of wealth as being what a person owns, and not the person himself or his abilities.

[15] Michael Novak has even, in blatant disregard of facts, begun asserting that the Catholic Church "invented" capitalism. Michael Novak, "How Christianity Created Capitalism" *The Wall Street Journal*. December 23, 1999.

[16] It should be pointed out that "ownership" in a pension plan or other qualified retirement trust as defined under the Internal Revenue Code in the United States is not "real" ownership, but *beneficial* ownership. That is, the participant or beneficiary has no actual ownership rights in the assets of the trust, only a statutory right to receive a distribution of benefits in a manner determined by the law and the Plan document.

[17] Cf. Peter Drucker's comments about "Pension Plan Socialism."

[18] John Maynard Keynes, *General Theory of Employment, Interest, and Money* (1936), V.24.iii.

[19] Martin Gardner, "Introduction to the Dover Edition," G. K. Chesterton, *Four Faultless Felons*, New York: Dover Publications, Inc., 1989, x.

[20] Senator Russell Long was chairman of the Senate Finance Committee, and spearheaded the initial enabling legislation for Louis Kelso's Employee Stock Ownership Plan ("ESOP").

[21] "The tale of Deere's plow illuminates another aspect of the morality of capitalism: It fosters innovation and invention." Fr. Robert A. Sirico, "President's Message," *Acton Notes*, October 1999, 1. How, exactly, "innovation and invention" are an aspect of morality is not made clear, particularly when people can invent spectacularly innovative methods of doing some very immoral things.

[22] The depersonalization of human beings in this fashion is the first step in their ultimate dehumanization. See, e.g., Binding and Hoche's *The Release of the Destruction of Life Devoid of Value* (*i.e.*, "Permission to Destroy Useless Life"), the pamphlet credited with desensitizing the German medical profession to the humanity of their patients. For a more extensive treatment of this process, see William Brennan, *Dehumanizing the Vulnerable, When Word Games Take Lives*. Chicago, Illinois: Loyola University Press, 1995.

[23] Louis O. Kelso and Mortimer J. Adler, *The Capitalist Manifesto*. New York: Random House, 1958.

[24] Leo XIII, *Rerum Novarum* ("On the Condition of the Working Classes"), 1891, § 65.

[25] Pius XII, 1942 Christmas Broadcast, "The Rights of Man" *Acta Apostolica Sede XXXV* (1943), 17.

[26] From Doctor Pangloss, a character in Voltaire's *Candide*, who declared that man had two legs in order to fit them into trousers, and two ears in order to hang eyeglasses on them.

[27] *Rerum Novarum, loc. cit.*

[28] See Wesley Hohfeld's *Fundamental Legal Conceptions* (1919, 1923).

[29] *Centesimus Annus, loc. cit.*

[30] John Maynard Keynes, *The Economic Consequences of the Peace*. London: Penguin Books, 1988, 19.

[31] John Maynard Keynes, *The General Theory of Employment, Interest, and Money*. Book VI, Ch. 24, § II.

[32] See, e.g., the specific references to applications of principles which apply "in the present condition of human society" that characterize the writings of Pius XI. *Quadragesimo Anno, op. cit.*, § 65.

[33] John XXIII, *Mater et Magistra* ("Christianity and Social Progress"), 1961, § 236.

[34] Pius XI, *Divini Redemptoris*, ("On Atheistic Communism"), 1937, § 53.

[35] *Mater et Magistra, op. cit.*, § 11.

[36] Donald Kagan, "Books: Appreciating Acton" *The Wall Street Journal*, January 11, 1988, 24.

Part II

The Divine Right of Capital

Your Excellency, we have considered the tactics of the Acton Institute and other neo-conservatives in filling the minds of seminarians and the laity with distorted versions of Catholic social teaching.[1] In common with their critics and other commentators on the social encyclicals and the Magisterium, neo-conservatives, like Adam Smith's rich man, have an almost infinite capacity to take what they please from the pile, and reject, ignore, or dismiss the rest.[2]

Perhaps the main problem with neo-conservatives is that they tend to view everything in terms of "freedom." That is not to say that freedom is not a good thing, a very important thing, or even, possibly, the most important thing — properly understood. The problem is that, because they ignore principles of justice,[3] neo-conservatives tend to define freedom more in terms of license than liberty. They make a popular mistake, and fail to realize, as Aristotle pointed out, that the most democratic behavior (and by extension, the behavior that is most free with respect to individual acts) is not always the most conducive to preserving democracy.[4]

Just the opposite is, in fact, the case. A "free market" is not a market in which anything goes, but a market to which all have equal entry and enjoy the same full spectrum of natural rights. In unrestricted competition, pure competition is the surest way to eliminate all competition through the elimination of rivals and the consequent establishment of a monopoly. Similarly, unrestricted freedom inevitably degenerates into license. The inescapable consequence is that the individual becomes the slave of sin,[5] and, finally, the political or economic slave of others who support or encourage the licentious behavior, sometimes with the deliberate intent of enslaving others.[6]

Neo-Conservatism's Classic Liberalism

Neo-conservatives and others who base their positions on the great liberal tradition of the eighteenth century tend to view any restriction or limitation of the exercise of a right as an abrogation or infringement of that right. This is based, acknowledged or not, on the liberal assumption of a "state of nature" outside society in which man has all rights (or none) against his fellow man, and a society is not acknowledged to exist or otherwise recognized until positive assent is given.[7]

In this classic liberal view, society infringes on individual rights by its very nature. The justification is that such infringement is necessary if men are to live "unnaturally" with others in society. Infringement must be tolerated for the general welfare, but careful watch kept on the State and other men in order to prevent the infringement from proceeding too far.[8] This theory is individualistic, making the existence of any particular society depend on the will of whoever is strong enough to enforce his will on others and bring them to consent to the existence of a group and participation in it. This orientation fails to take into consideration Pius XI's realization that a group *per se* has a social structure and therefore constitutes a discrete society.

Further, having justified one infringement, any new restrictions or limitations by the State necessarily are merely an increase in the *degree* of infringement, not a difference in the *kind* of limitation. This opens up the gate to complete infringement or abolition of the whole concept of inalienable rights, as Rousseau presumed in *The Social Contract*,[9] where the State takes all rights unto itself, and grants them back to individuals in whatever manner or form it pleases — which grant can be revoked at will by the State.

The truth is somewhat different. Man is social by nature, and therefore the "state of nature" is in society, not outside it. A society exists the moment there is an aggregation of individuals (even if it is only two) with some interaction among them, whether or not those individuals sit down and agree to recognize the existence of that society, and that rules exist limiting the exercise of rights so as to govern human interaction in such a way as to optimize respect for the human dignity of everyone in society.

Locke gets around this characteristic of human groups and man's natural condition in society by asserting that individuals in a state of nature are obeying God directly — private revelation of some sort combined with a kind of "personal rule" by God of the temporal order *à la* Charles I Stuart — in their relations with others. Each individual thus has full exercise of all rights granted by God. Because the individuals involved have not agreed to form a society, they cannot yet obey *human* rules that infringe on the full exercise of rights granted directly by the Creator.

Hobbes takes a different approach. He asserts that human beings in a state of nature are obeying no laws at all and have no rights. A divine right sovereign establishes society and order. The sovereign grants such rights as are consistent with the sovereign's God-given task of governing human society. Disobeying the sovereign is a religious, civil, and (ultimately) a domestic offense, as the sovereign is the "father" of the entire people.

Locke and other classic liberals were also faced with a further difficulty in that, following Hugo Grotius, they tended to base their understanding of the natural law on Revelation contained in the Bible (God's Will), as opposed to what could be discerned about God's Nature from observing what mankind has determined by general consensus constitutes "good." (The argument in the latter case being that God has created man in His own image and likeness, so that whatever mankind in general agrees is "good" must be consistent with Divine Nature.)

Understanding man as social by nature means that every human being is naturally and automatically a member of whatever society he enters or is born into, whether or not the society itself wishes to exclude him. He can, of course, remove himself from society by the commission of a crime, but society exists the moment there is more than one human being interacting with another. There is not, as Locke, Sidney, Hobbes, and others maintained, the necessity of all parties sitting down to make a formal agreement that society now exists.

Thus, the common good does not infringe on rights, but limits their exercise against others by defining them properly. In this Catholic (actually Aristotelian) orientation, the task of the politically active citizen and the participant in Catholic Action is to discern whether State action or the structuring of the institutions of society constitute a proper and necessary definition of and limitation on the exercise of rights, a bearable if illicit limitation as an expedient, or an intolerable infringement — all infringements, in this orientation, being *ipso facto* "intolerable."

Rights, in fact, cannot by definition function anywhere other than in society. Contrary to Rousseau's position, man in society does not lose all his rights, even to the State, but gains the ability to exercise the inalienable rights he possesses by nature. Since a right is defined as a duty imposed *on others*, "others" — society — are required if a right is to have meaning or even practical existence.

The Catholic Idea of Society

In a truly Catholic orientation, a limitation in the sense of defining how a right can be exercised is proper and necessary. A limitation in the sense of infringement, however, is unjust by its very nature and may be intolerable in actuality as well as in theory. If sufficiently serious (*i.e.*, intolerable),[10] infringement of rights is a justification for restructuring society to the point where the infringement ceases. The concept of "necessary infringement" is removed, obviating the implicit contradiction in the liberal position. This closes the door to the creeping tyranny that seems inevitably to occur in societies structured along the liberal orientation.

In civil society, "freedom" cannot be taken as an absolute in and of itself, but only the freedom to choose what is right. That is, in his search for the "good," man is free to choose what is acceptable under social standards or is in compliance with universal moral principles. The common good must be structured so as to make right choices possible or optimal, not coerce the right choices, as many seem to think. The common good consists of all those rights, duties, virtues, traditions, customs — in short, all the structures and institutions of society, which give a society its particular and special form. In Aristotelian terms, the common good consists of the fullness of the capacity to acquire and develop "virtue."

The task of the individual, alone or in association with others, as well as the State, is to define how rights are to be exercised so as to maximize individual freedom without harming or infringing on that of others. This is what John Paul II meant when he referred to "human freedom in its totality."[11] The "totality" of human freedom is not the exercise one's individual whims to the maximum, but the exercise of one's legitimate rights in such a manner as to gain the optimal enjoyment and benefit therefrom, while, at the same time, not infringing on the rights, needs, wants, and desires of anyone else within the institutional structure of the common good. With this in mind, we can examine the neo-conservative position on freedom and morality.

According to neo-conservatives, "capitalism" is the best of all possible economic systems because, as far as they are concerned, capitalism epitomizes economic freedom.[12] "Freedom," in a further twist in the neo-conservative lexicon, is synonymous with "justice." Justice, as understood from various neo-conservative writings, apparently constitutes the whole of morality. Obviously, there are a number of short cuts and misdirections in this orientation.

How to Misinterpret Adam Smith

The neo-conservatives' obsession with "freedom" explains their fascination with Adam Smith. Doctor Smith was an eighteenth century moral philosopher who wrote one of the early great works of political economy, *An Inquiry into the Nature and Causes of the Wealth of Nations* (1776). In common with a large number of both Smith's critics and supporters, however, the typical neo-conservative does not appear to have read or, perhaps more fairly, understood

Adam Smith.[13] It rarely occurs either to Smith's supporters or detractors, for example, that he never once used the words "capitalism" or "capitalist."

The popular perception of Adam Smith is that he is the "High Priest" of capitalism. "Adam Smith Capitalism" is somehow seen as the epitome of *laissez faire* economics, with a complete circumvention of morality. Critics assume that neo-conservatives substitute strict adherence to the presumably objective and immutable laws of economics for the subjective control of religion or morality.

This is completely wrong, and neo-conservatives are to be congratulated for realizing that fact. Unfortunately, they make a different mistake, and assume that the system described by Adam Smith in *The Wealth of Nations* is one that is automatically moral in and of itself. That, too, is completely wrong. Smith did not describe an ideal system. He made assumptions and gave the basic and necessary elements of a system that appeared to embody the essentials of justice, thus providing the minimum necessary structures of morality.

A key element in Smith's "minimal" system is that it would function even when the rich were motivated by nothing more than "selfishness and rapacity."[14] Thus, the system would operate in a moral manner even if the individuals within it were concerned with nothing more than maximizing their own enjoyment, or even indulging their own selfish appetites. One claim made with increasing frequency by the Acton Institute however is that, because good presumably results even from selfish actions, then the individual indulging his selfishness must, therefore, be virtuous!

There is also the problem that a system, *per se*, (or any other form of society) cannot be moral or immoral, as it cannot have intrinsic virtue or the inherent capacity to acquire and develop virtue.[15] It must, of course, have the "delegated" capacity to acquire and develop virtue. This can be via the establishment and maintenance of "structures of virtue." It can also, however, be immoral through the establishment and maintenance of "structures of sin." The system as a thing that is not a natural person, however, cannot have its "own" virtue or the capacity to acquire virtue. The neo-conservative assertion that capitalism is a moral system, instead of one that embodies "structures of virtue" or "structures of morality" is thus flawed on basic principles.[16] Neo-conservatives consistently ridicule the idea of "structures of sin," while assigning to "structures of virtue" more than the concept can support.

Adam Smith's thought, in contrast to the thought of the general run of neo-conservatives, is very consistent. Long before the concept was articulated, Smith based his work firmly on the idea of "structures of virtue," as any reader of his *Theory of Moral Sentiments* will discover. He posited a system based on principles of justice and applications of other "moral sentiments" which appeared to put certain absolute principles into practice. His system would therefore be quite acceptable — if his assumptions held true. The problem is that they do *not* hold true. Adam Smith relied on inserting morality, and thus a functional practicality (as a moral philosopher, Smith was well aware that morality represents the ultimate practicality) into his system indirectly and artificially. Moral structures ("structures of virtue") were thus not intrinsic to Smith's system. Morality was inserted via "the invisible hand."[17]

The invisible hand is a combination of two essential elements: 1) What Smith variously called the selfishness and rapacity or self-interest of the rich (or whoever is in the process of realizing effective demand) and 2) the distribution mechanism of human labor. The labor of the poor serves to distribute the wealth of the rich more or less evenly throughout society in order to satisfy the selfish demands, wants, and needs of the wealthy.[18]

In Adam Smith's thought, human labor was the primary (but not sole) means of production,[19] and therefore had a permanent place in the production process. Because of the presumed permanent need for human labor, the invisible hand operated to distribute the goods of society more or less equitably *in spite of* the selfishness and rapacity of the rich

— not, as the neo-conservatives misconstrue his philosophy, because of it.[20] In view of Dr. Smith's own words, the "self interest" referred to in *The Wealth of Nations* cannot be considered a moral act. Smith clearly characterized the behavior of the rich as something contrary to general morality. He modified the harshness of his language between 1759 when he wrote *The Theory of Moral Sentiments* and 1776 when *An Inquiry into the Nature and Causes of the Wealth of Nations* was published, but his negative judgment as to the objective moral quality of the behavior itself remained unchanged.

The Severed Hand of Adam Smith

Adam Smith's pivotal "invisible hand" assumption was that the rich would employ large numbers of people in preference to technology to supply one's wants. The position of employer gave immense status to the rich via the "moral sentiment" of approbation. This came from those employed (probably out of gratitude for their employment) and from others in recognition of the employer's wealth and beneficence.[21] Smith counted "beneficence" as a moral sentiment, somewhat analogous to an admixture of charity and justice. Neo-conservatives assume that Smith's system still operates in the manner he described. This assumption ignores the effect of technology.

As Louis Kelso and Mortimer Adler pointed out in their mis-titled yet profound treatise, *The Capitalist Manifesto*,[22] the whole idea of technology is to replace human labor.[23] When a human being is replaced in the production process by a machine, the income generated by the machine flows by right to the owners of the machine, not to the displaced worker.[24] The needs of the consumer are met not primarily by human agents, as Adam Smith noted in his day, and many still suppose, but by technology.

The insights of Kelso and Adler are extremely useful in examining the assumptions of classical economics. Binary economics recognizes that technology is often hyper-productive compared with human labor.[25] The owner of technology can therefore derive income to a greater degree than he would if he were purchasing or expending an equivalent value of human labor, absent a program of income redistribution.[26] One result of this is that the value of labor relative to capital is constantly declining on the market.[27] There is a consequent fall in real income to those who rely exclusively on wages for their income, again absent redistribution or coercion.[28]

Technology "amputates" the invisible hand. The goal of technology is to remove human labor from the production process. The mechanism of distribution changes from a person's ownership of his own labor to his ownership of technology. Since most people own little or no productive technology, the ownership of which provides the mechanism of distribution, they have no just or legitimate means of acquiring a fair share of the world's goods, except through almsgiving.

Kelso, Adler, and Capitalism

The solution to this dilemma, as Kelso and Adler prescribed, is to make "every worker an owner," along with, eventually, every citizen. This would reconnect the ordinary person directly to the primary means of income generation in a developed economy: Gaining an adequate and secure income by his own exertions with his own property. This would replace forcing him to rely on charity, redistribution of the income of others, or minimum wage and family allowance arrangements.

Ironically, neo-conservatives are generally opposed to the "social 'band aids'" such as welfare, minimum wage legislation, redistribution, and so on, made necessary by the system they advocate. Instead of outrage, as even Karl Marx felt against the inevitable forcing down of wages where the worker has only his labor to sell, neo-conservatives attempt to justify the situation by citing the laws of supply and demand. Frequently they make the assertion that workers are paid too little because they lack the "guts and gumption" to go out and become owners on their own. This apparently excuses the opposition to any form of "social safety net," whether the living wage, wealth redistribution, or almsgiving. This is a distorted perception of the negative effects of using a social safety net as a way of life instead of for emergencies.[29]

It is true that the laws of supply and demand will inevitably operate as the classical economists suppose. Their modern followers, however, fail to take into consideration the fact that this lowering of wages occurs *only* when wages are considered the sole legitimate form of income for the many. This results when capitalists (by definition a small elite) have an effective monopoly on the means whereby people gain income. That is, only capitalists can own capital and pay wages.

This situation is reversed when the worker has an alternative means of gaining at least a bare subsistence. In that situation, as de Tocqueville noted in *Democracy in America*, the small owner can hold his labor off the market until the price goes up to suit him.

> I shall take for example that branch of productive industry which is still at the present day the most generally followed in France and in almost all the countries of the world, the cultivation of the soil. In France most of those who labor for hire in agriculture are themselves owners of certain plots of ground, which just enable them to subsist without working for anyone else. When these laborers come to offer their services to a neighboring landowner or farmer, if he refuses them a certain rate of wages they retire to their own small property and await another opportunity.[30]

When the worker is entirely dependent on his wages for his subsistence, however, he has no such option. He must work for others or starve. Because of the monopoly power of the capitalist in such a situation, the real wage level inevitably sinks below subsistence, and the difference is made up out of charity, redistribution, and coercive wage demands of unions backed by the power of the State.

Instead of opposing this state of affairs with all the power at their command, neo-conservatives choose instead to glorify it. They ignore the seriously flawed structures of the common good, particularly economic and financial structures. The economic common good today is based firmly on outdated and inappropriate institutions that were inadequate when implemented. They have grown increasingly distorted since.

What results are the hideous discrepancies, widening every day, between the rich and the poor.[31] In the current state of society, a Bill Gates or Warren Buffett can control billions of dollars worth of wealth while others starve.[32] This is only possible when, contradicting Adam Smith's assumption of the permanent value of human labor, the value of the labor of the poor declines in utility to the rich. The "invisible hand" no longer functions. The "solution" which the rich seem inevitably to develop is to eliminate starvation by eliminating the starving.[33] It comes as no surprise, then, that the two richest men in the world have announced that they are leaving the bulk of their billions to population control.[34]

Wages and Past Savings: Modern Slavery

The neo-conservative orientation is based on two erroneous assumptions, 1) wages are the only legitimate means for the great mass of people to gain income (whether or not at a sufficient level), and 2) all capital formation *must* be financed out of past savings or reductions in current levels of consumption. In light of these assumptions, which, however, have been proved erroneous time and again, it should come as no surprise that neo-conservatives feel that a glorification of the rich is justified.

Some Catholic neo-conservatives have gone so far as to hint — and strongly, at that — that being rich is, in and of itself, moral, and an act of virtue.[35] Presumably, noting the usual orientation along the lines of the thought of Adam

Smith, these would be the virtues ("moral sentiments") of benevolence and approbation.

Catholic neo-conservatives forget, however, that Adam Smith's moral philosophy was a conscious departure from that of the classical philosophers and the scholastics. While Smith managed to come to many of the same conclusions as would a Thomist or an Aristotelian, his liberal orientation — established on a basis which assumes that society is "unnatural" — ensured that there would ultimately be a parting of the ways.

The implicit assumption that being rich is moral and a virtue in and of itself can only be accepted if we accept other assumptions. Smith himself explicitly contradicted the idea that being wealthy was a virtue when he characterized the behavior of the rich as "selfish and rapacious." We can, however, accept being wealthy as a virtue if — and only if — we accept the current state of society not only as a given, but as an ideal, God-mandated, or divinely instituted condition. Under this assumption, as Aristotle pointed out, there must be a class of persons who have the capacity to be "naturally" more virtuous (in this case, richer) than others. No Catholic — or a believer in any other ethical or religious system — could ever make such a claim, particularly since the popes[36] and even Our Lord Himself[37] have explicitly declared exactly the opposite.

A Divine Right of Capital

Are the rich a divinely-mandated elite? Are they necessary to the functioning of a well-ordered society? Is there some kind of "Divine Right of Capital"?

The fable that "the rich are different"[38] arises from the two assumptions that neo-conservatives, in common with most of society, have made about how income for the great mass of people is to be generated (wages), and how the formation of capital is to be financed (past savings). The two assumptions are very closely linked. They feed off one another like mutual parasites.

When capital formation is financed exclusively out of past savings, it requires a class of persons, necessarily small, who cannot consume the whole of their income. This is pure Keynesian economics, as any reader of either *The Economic Consequences of the Peace* or *The General Theory of Employment, Interest and Money* quickly discovers. Without getting into a discussion of the issues of market gluts, business cycles, and effective demand, we note that ownership of capital in this situation must be concentrated because the income generated by capital by right flows to wealthy owners.[39] They cannot consume at a level requisite to use up all their income, and necessarily invest it in yet more new capital.

The formation of this additional new capital presumably provides the jobs that supply average people with wage income. In view of the fact that they cannot provide labor worth what they require to receive in wages to survive, some redistribution, whether in the form of welfare, minimum wage legislation, or private charity, is absolutely necessary if the system is to operate. From the standpoint of structure, the system operates best, at least in theory, when there is one employer, such as occurs in communism or, as some put it, "State capitalism."[40] This eliminates anyone from the system who would use income from capital on consumption instead of reinvesting it to finance the formation of new capital.[41]

If this state of society is ideal, as neo-conservatives appear to assume, then the rich do, indeed, have a divinely-mandated role to fill. They are needed to finance capital formation that, although at a decreasing rate due to advancing technology, provides non-owners with jobs. In this scenario, paying workers more than a bare subsistence (which Adam Smith assumed would inevitably happen as population increased and the economy reached a stable state) becomes an injustice against the capitalist. Redistribution takes away part or all of the necessary fund for reinvestment which is so critically needed to provide jobs. Depriving the rich of the profits of their capital for the benefit of existing workers limits their ability to create additional new jobs. It thereby "robs" other workers of potential employment.

Freedom From Wage Slavery

Most people, however, do *not* have to earn their income from wages, as the popes since Leo XIII have pointed out, nor does capital formation need to be financed from existing accumulations of savings, as Kelso and Adler stated in the title of their second book, *The New Capitalists: A Proposal to Free Economic Growth from the Slavery of Savings*.[42] Capital formation, in spite of the assertions and implicit assumptions of most economists, need *not* be financed exclusively out of existing accumulations of savings, over which the rich have an effective monopoly.

In short, neither the rich nor anyone else have a "Divine Right" to be rich, in spite of the assertions of the neo-conservatives. It is not intrinsically moral to pursue one's own "self interest"[43] as defined by Adam Smith. Smith, in fact, was very explicit that "self interest" in the context of his thought was not a moral concept. It was the very opposite, regardless of the fact that pursuing one's self interest in conformity with universal moral principles may be a virtuous act, if not specifically a virtue. Further, Smith did not "endorse" what he called "self interest." He maintained that, at a minimum, society could tolerate "self interest" in order to obtain the *inadvertent* good that resulted.[44]

It is true that by pursuing their own selfish interests the rich may benefit society, even to a significant degree, but they may also harm it just as significantly. The good they do, as Adam Smith points out, is in spite of their selfishness, not because of it. The flaw in Adam Smith's thought is that the rich today do not require the poor to satisfy their wants and needs. Technology can do so with greater efficiency, higher quality, and less cost. Being rich and pursuing one's own selfish interest in and of itself cannot be construed as being virtuous for the simple fact that pursuing a selfish interest is not an intrinsically moral act. Because it does not look to the common good, Adam Smith's "self interest" is simply selfishness, as he himself stated. A moral framework is inserted into his system artificially, giving the rich license to indulge every whim at the expense of others.

No, Your Excellency, there is no "Divine Right of Capital" (or, more properly, "Divine Right of the Capitalist"). Neoconservatives perform a great disservice by their glorification of the wealthy and the presumed benefits they confer on others in the current flawed state of society. They support the continuance of injustice rather than working to overcome it and establish righteousness.

Notes

[1] Anthony Basile, Ph.D., "Selling Out Catholic Social Teaching: The Acton Institute's Misleading Message" *Culture Wars*, September 1999.

[2] "The rich only select from the heap what is most precious and agreeable. . . " Adam Smith, "Of the Effect of Utility upon the Sentiment of Approbation," *The Theory of Moral Sentiments*. Part IV, Chapter I, §10.

[3] "The love of liberty, moreover, should not be allowed to obscure humanity's other needs." Donald Kagan, "Books: Appreciating Acton" *The Wall Street Journal*, January 11, 1988, 24.

[4] Aristotle, *The Politics*, V.9.

[5] "The prime cause of slavery is sin, so that man was put under man in a state of bondage; and this can be only by a judgment of God, in Whom there is no unrighteousness, and Who knows how to assign divers punishments according to the deserts of the sinners." Saint Augustine, *Epistolæ*, 10. This is not a type of Calvinistic predestination, but a presumption by the Bishop of Hippo that "just title" slavery was the predominant form, in which the slave had either committed a crime or sold himself into slavery as the result of debt. In either event, there was a demonstrated need for the guidance of a master until such time as the slave was rehabilitated, which, admittedly, rarely seemed to happen in a truly slave society — according to the slave owners.

[6] Polybius, *The Universal History*, VI.9.

[7] This idea dates back to certain ancient Greek philosophers, but its greatest impact was made as a result of its inclusion in John Locke's *Two Treatises on Government*.

⁸ Wilhelm von Humboldt, *The Limits of State Action*. Indianapolis, Indiana: Liberty Fund, Inc., 1993, 38-39; Anthony de Jasay, *The State*. Indianapolis, Indiana: Liberty Fund, Inc., 1998, 35-38; Bruno Leoni, *Freedom and the Law*. Indianapolis, Indiana: Liberty Fund, Inc., 1991, 3-57; Johannes Althusius, *Politica*. Indianapolis, Indiana: Liberty Fund, Inc., 1995, 19-20; Jacob Burckhardt, *Reflections on History*. Indianapolis, Indiana: Liberty Fund, Inc., 1979, 63; William Graham Sumner, *On Liberty, Society, and Politics*. Indianapolis, Indiana: Liberty Fund, Inc., 1992, 8.

⁹ Jean-Jacques Rousseau, *On the Social Contract*, Book II.

¹⁰See Saint Thomas Aquinas' discussion of the necessity of rebellion and the criteria which must be met in *De Regimine Principum* ("On the Governance of Rulers"), Book I, Chapter 6.

¹¹John Paul II, *Centesimus Annus* ("On the Hundredth Anniversary of *Rerum Novarum*"), § 42.

¹²Capitalism is also confused with industrialism by some commentators, calling forth a stricture from Paul VI in *Populorum Progressio* ("On the Deveopment of Peoples"), § 27.

¹³Charles L. Griswold, Jr., "Adam Smith: Conscience of Capitalism" *The Best of the WQ*, 43-51.

¹⁴Adam Smith, "Of the Effect of Utility upon the Sentiment of Approbation," *The Theory of Moral Sentiments*. Part IV, Chapter I, §10.

¹⁵Pius XI, *Divini Redemptoris* ("On Atheistic Communism"), 1937, § 29.

¹⁶"Where the liberationists have been preoccupied with the denunciation of the 'structures of sin' (meaning capitalism), Mr. Novak has labored to piece together the scaffolding for the 'structures of virtue.' " Fr. Robert Sirico, "Free Market Morality" *The Wall Street Journal*. January 29, 1991.

¹⁷ *Ibid*.; also, Adam Smith, "Of Restraints upon the Importation from Foreign Countries of Such Goods as can be Produced at Home," *An Inquiry into the Nature and Causes of the Wealth of Nations*. Book IV, Chapter II, §9.

¹⁸ "Luxury is ever in proportion to the inequality of fortunes. If the riches of a State are equally divided there will be no luxury; for it is founded merely on the conveniences acquired by the labour of others." Charles de Secondat, Baron de Montesquieu, *The Spirit of Laws*. Book VII, Chapter 1.

¹⁹ See, for example, David Ricardo's "corrections" of the thought of Adam Smith, based on Ricardo's idea, which Marx later

congealed into an absolute dogma as the "labor theory of value," that human labor was the sole and exclusive source of all production. David Ricardo, *Political Economy, The Principles of Political Economy and Taxation*. London: Everyman's Library, 1991, 7.

[20] Smith, *Theory of Moral Sentiments, loc. cit.*; "Of Restraints upon the Importation from Foreign Countries of Such Goods as can be Produced at Home," *An Inquiry into the Nature and Causes of the Wealth of Nations*. Book IV, Chapter II, §9.

[21] Smith, *The Theory of Moral Sentiments*. Book IV, Chapter I, §6.

[22] Louis O. Kelso and Mortimer J. Adler, *The Capitalist Manifesto*. New York: Random House, 1958.

[23] Louis O. Kelso and Mortimer J. Adler, "The Role of Man as a Factor in the Production of Wealth" *The Capitalist Manifesto*. New York: Random House, 1958, 36-40.

[24] "Primary and Secondary Distribution" *Ibid.*, 46-51.

[25] For an in-depth analysis of binary economics, refer to Rodney Shakespeare and Robert H. A. Ashford *Binary Economics, the New Paradigm*. Lanham, Maryland: University Press of America, 1999.

[26] Kelso and Adler, *op. cit.*, 39.

[27] *Ibid.*, 42.

[28] *Ibid.*, 42-43.

[29] See, for example, the strictures against the various "poor laws" so endemic to *laissez faire* economists and democratic thinkers through the nineteenth century. Alexis de Tocqueville, *Memoir on Pauperism*. Chicago, Illinois: Ivan R. Dee, 1997; Henry Fawcett, *Pauperism, Its Causes and Remedies*. London: Macmillan and Co., 1871; Peter Gaskell, *The Manufacturing Population of England, Its Moral, Social, and Physical Conditions, and the Changes Which Have Arisen from the Use of Steam Machinery; with an Examination of Infant Labour*. London: Baldwin and Cradock, 1833; and, of course, Thomas Malthus *Essay on Population* (1797). Gaskell was a particularly favorite source for Karl Marx, who references him countless times in *Das Kapital*, finding in the callousness of Gaskell's position one of the best advertisements for communism.

[30] *Democracy in America, Volume II*, New York: Everyman's Library, Alfred A. Knopf, Inc., 1994, 189-190.

[31] Deborah McGregor, "Growth Fails to Close US Economic Divide" *Financial Times*, January 19, 2000.

[32] Jacob M. Schlesinger, Tristan Mabry and Sarah Lueck, "Charting the Pain Behind the Gain: Income Is Up, Poverty Down, But Overall, Wages Barely Budged Over the Decade" *The Wall Street Journal*. October 1, 1999, B1, B4.

[33] This approach is most often characterized as "Malthusian" or "Social Darwinism," but would have shocked both Malthus and Darwin. Malthus, for all his flaws and faults, relied on the voluntary "prudential constraint" to decrease population, while Darwin was adamant that his theories applied to biological evolution, not social.

[34] International Right to Life Federation, Inc., "The Gates Billions" *Newsletter*, September/October 1999, 1.

[35] "In the story of the Great Northern, we see another facet of the moral and practical superiority of capitalism: It promotes social cooperation and mutual aid. Hill's success as an entrepreneur was directly linked to the welfare of others; he therefore did what he could to help them succeed. Our future religious leaders need to understand this aspect of capitalism's morality. . . " Fr. Robert Sirico, "President's Message" *Acton Notes, The Newsletter of the Acton Institute for the Study of Religion and Liberty*. August 1999, 1.

[36] Paul VI, *Populorum Progessio* ("On the Development of Peoples"), 1967, § 30.

[37] Many of the parables hold up the rich and powerful as paragons of *immorality*, to such an extent that superficial observers assume that being rich or powerful is immoral, in and of itself. This is a conclusion as erroneous as the contrary position of the Acton Institute.

[38] As Hemmingway is reported to have said, "Yes — they have more money."

[39] See Kelso and Adler's analysis of distribution in *The Capitalist Manifesto, op. cit.*, 46-49, 67-68.

[40] Fr. William J. Ferree, *An Introduction to Economic and Social Development*. Rome, Italy: Private Printing, 1966, 15.

[41] See the discussion on the inadequacy and inadvisability of relying on past accumulations of savings to form capital in Harold G. Moulton's *The Formation of Capital*. Washington, DC: The Brookings Institution, 1935.

[42] Louis O. Kelso and Mortimer J. Adler, *The New Capitalists: A Proposal to Free Economic Growth from the Slavery of Savings*. New York: Random House, 1961. Note that in context, "savings" refers to past savings. The system Kelso and Adler developed

requires the use of "future" or "forced" savings in order to function.

[43] Sirico, "Free Market Morality" *The Wall Street Journal. op. cit.*

[44] "He generally, indeed, neither intends to promote the public interest, nor knows how much he is promoting it. . . . he intends only his own gain, and he is in this, as in many other cases, led by an invisible hand to promote an end which was no part of his intention. Nor is it always the worse for the society that it was no part of it. By pursuing his own interest he frequently promotes that of the society more effectually than when he really intends to promote it." Adam Smith, "Of Restraints upon the Importation from Foreign Countries of Such Goods as can be Produced at Home," *An Inquiry into the Nature and Causes of the Wealth of Nations.* Book IV, Chapter II, §9; "[The rich] in spite of their natural selfishness and rapacity, though they mean only their own conveniency, though the sole end which they propose from the labours of all the thousands whom they employ, by the gratification of their own vain and insatiable desires, they divide with the poor the produce of all their improvements. They are led by an invisible hand to make nearly the same distribution of the necessaries of life, which would have been made, had the earth been divided into equal portions among all its inhabitants, and thus without intending it, without knowing it, advance the interest of the society, and afford means to the multiplication of the species." Adam Smith, "Of the Effect of Utility upon the Sentiment of Approbation," *The Theory of Moral Sentiments.* Part IV, Chapter I, §10.

Part III
The Divine Right of Labor

Your Excellency, with our previous animadversions on the Acton Institute and the neo-conservative position, we may have given the impression that its critics were correct in their censures. Unfortunately, this is not so. Much of what the critics say is necessary and salutary, but their orientation is in many respects as disordered as that of neo-conservatives. We have demonstrated that a presumed "Divine Right of Capital" does not and cannot exist . . . but what about an opposed "Divine Right of Labor"?

The Laws of Supply and Demand

The article in *Culture Wars*[1] implied that all would be well if employers would simply overcome their greed and pay their workers a living or family wage. In this view, talk about economic unfeasibility is an evasion to avoid giving workers their just due. The article implied that by taking refuge behind the laws of supply and demand and asserting the immutability of economic laws, the Acton Institute is putting up a dishonest rationalization for the greed and generally immoral orientation of its members and supporters.

In this analysis, the critics commit the same error as the Acton Institute. They confuse an application of a principle with the principle itself. The laws of supply and demand as applications of the natural law *are* immutable. It is contrary to human nature to pay more for something than you think it is worth, or to accept less; a rare thing is valued more highly than that which is common. To change this would involve changing basic — that is, essential or substantial — human nature. As Pius XI pointed out,

> Even though economics and moral science employs each its own principles in its own sphere, it is, nevertheless, an error to say that the economic and

moral orders are so distinct from and alien to each other that the former depends in no way on the latter. Certainly the laws of economics, as they are termed, being based on the very nature of material things and on the capacities of the human body and mind, determine the limits of what productive human effort cannot, and of what it can attain in the economic field and by what means. Yet it is reason itself that clearly shows, on the basis of the individual and social nature of things and of men, the purpose which God ordained for all economic life.[2]

The problem (which the critics cannot see) is that they are not quibbling about the laws themselves, but the *application* of them. The issue is how economic laws function in a given state of society. It is the state of society that is subject to change, not the laws of economics.[3] *Given the current state of the economy* and the flawed financial and social structures with which society is burdened, the laws of supply and demand will operate *exactly* as the classical economists have always stated they will operate.

This gives neo-conservatives their greatest defense and surest justification. They can *prove* that, in the current state of society, the laws of supply and demand will act in exactly such-and-such a way. With some excuse they therefore conclude that disaster will occur if there is any attempt to circumvent or override them. Moral considerations cannot truly be moral, in their opinion, because greater evil than that presumably being ameliorated will inevitably result if the laws of supply and demand are ignored.

The critics counter by pointing out that, regardless of the consequences (about which they have a somewhat more optimistic view than neo-conservatives, yet still flawed), man is required to do what is right.[4] Neo-conservatives are justly accused of ignoring clear and unequivocal moral mandates to pay a living wage.

What none of those who take either position understand is that both views take many of the wrong things as absolutes

— and many of the same things, too. Neo-conservatives and their critics are in fundamental agreement with each other just where it does the most harm. Both ignore such things as barriers to participation in the common good, the real cause of the growing wealth gap, and the effect of labor-displacing technology and access to the means of acquiring and possessing property.

The Restructuring of the Social Order

What neither side realizes is that society, which they both assume to be an absolute, a given, is in fact in a constant state of flux. Pius XI referred to this as "the radical instability of human affairs."[5] The specific form of the social order is neither God-mandated, nor divinely maintained. God has mandated the fact that man must live in society, but the specific form and structure of any society is man-made.[6]

The fact that most capital is formed out of existing accumulations of savings, and most people gain their income exclusively from wages does not mean that the Creator has ordained this. On the contrary — human ingenuity, with which the Creator endows man, is equal to the task of redesigning and restructuring society so as to conform more closely to universal moral principles.

The restructuring of society so as to conform to universal moral principles *is* a mandate, as Pius XI made clear as the primary thrust of his pontificate. Neither maintaining the current elite status of the capitalist (as neo-conservatives support) nor instituting universal application of a living wage system (as many of the critics insist) meet the requirement of a restructured social order.[7]

Significantly, both neo-conservatives and their critics defend the current unjust economic system in terms that bear a chilling resemblance to defenses of slavery made through the ages. The economic necessity of slavery, for example, was brilliantly, if erroneously, defended as late as 1855 in David Christy's *Cotton is King*. Explicit papal condemnations of slavery were ignored, rejected, or "reinterpreted" since the early fifteenth century[8] in precisely the way that, *e.g.*, *Cen*-

tesimus Annus has been twisted out of shape by both neo-conservative commentators and their critics.

The Slavery of the Living Wage

These reinterpretations are understandable, considering that current economic conditions impose a state of what Leo XIII referred to as "virtual slavery" on the propertyless worker.[9] Pius XI echoed this analysis, and declared that the proletariat was in a state of "permanent bondage" (*i.e.*, slavery) to those who had property.[10] In order to justify a continuation of the current state of the economy, characterized in capitalism by great disparities in wealth, Catholic neo-conservatives necessarily reinterpret papal teachings in virtually every sphere.

Ironically, their critics, by and large, also insist that this condition of utter dependency on the part of the ordinary worker is divinely mandated. The only quarrel that they have with neo-conservatism is that capitalists are not complying with the Biblical injunction that masters treat their slaves well, that is, pay them a living wage.[11] Both sides take the "Greek" view of "inferiors": That those in the lower stations of life are in a lower station because by nature they are not quite as good as those in the higher stations.

To the ancient Greek, a man was a slave because he was inferior — an irremediable condition. To the Roman, a man was inferior because he was a slave — a condition that could be remedied by manumission; the freedman shared an equal capacity to acquire and develop virtue with the free man. To the Greek, society and the condition of man within it was therefore absolutely fixed, as they were based on nature — and nature had determined that each human being had a different capacity to acquire and develop virtue, making people permanently unequal, and some not even human (the "natural slave").

In the "Greek" view, natural law, ultimately, is not what is right because it is right. Instead, something is right because that is the way it happens to be. This was the basis of one of the great debates in the Middle Ages. The Thomists, correcting the contradiction in Greek philosophy (meaning Aristotle), argued that natural law is based on God's Nature. That is, a thing is right because it is right, and that God's Nature is reflected in human nature, with the capacity to acquire and develop virtue "analogously complete" ("equal") in every human being — whether or not a particular individual actually acquires and develops any virtue at all.

The followers of Duns Scotus, the "Dunces," maintained that natural law is right because it is a manifestation of God's Will. Unfortunately, this effectively removes the necessity of God from the equation, as Hugo Grotius admitted.[12] This acceptance of the "way things are" in the end results in the assumption that society is fixed, an assumption that becomes unquestioned, indeed, fundamental to a particular world view.

It is this blind acceptance of the current state of society as an absolute that has hampered the advance of the establishment of the Reign of Christ the King — conformity of the institutions of the social order with natural law — over the temporal order more than any other factor. This was why Pius XI insisted that the structures of society were *not* fixed, in fact, their "instability" was so marked as to be "radical."[13]

This gives us the key to understanding the role of such expedients as the living wage, family allowances, and welfare. Neo-conservatives are on solid ground when pointing out that such things do nothing to solve underlying problems of society and are, in fact, harmful in some respects. Unfortunately, they then assume that doing nothing is acceptable. They refuse to acknowledge the necessity of removing barriers to full participation in the economic common good, or even their existence, and the correlative need to restructure society.

Neo-conservatives assert that every worker has power, and thus no restructuring is necessary. This is "proved" by the fact that the worker is free to take his labor elsewhere. This is a power expressed in terms of freedom of choice of where or whether to work, but not how anyone is empowered once he is employed. This is a "take it or leave it" freedom. The obvious corollary is that, having "freely" chosen to take it, the worker must put up with anything the employer chooses to impose. This would, logically, include inadequate pay, poor treatment, and dangerous working conditions.

The critics of the neo-conservative position accurately point out that this somewhat ephemeral power through "freedom of choice" is an affront to human dignity. An employer may not have any power over whether a specific worker chooses to work for him, but the employer has some measure of control over how he treats a worker once he employs him. Just as a master owed his slaves decent treatment, an employer owes his "wage slaves" the same minimal dignity.

The critics of neo-conservatism are on equally solid ground when pointing out that everyone has a right to the means to sustain his life. In the current state of society, that means a living wage, family allowances, and welfare. These are valid because morality, which is supernatural, overrides the purely temporal, which is merely natural, when the two come into conflict.

The Reign of Christ the King

The problem is that neither side will admit that conflict between the natural and the supernatural is far from inevitable. True, *given the current state of society*, there is necessary conflict between the natural and the supernatural. Reconciliation, however, is precisely what Pius XI called for in virtually every encyclical during his pontificate. The goal of Catholic Action was to bring the natural order into conformity with the supernatural. This was to be done by removing and reconciling conflicts between the two. It could not be done on a permanent or lasting basis by overriding differences by fiat,[14] regardless of the consequences. Once we understand that the state of society is not a given, we realize that such things as the living wage, family allowances, and welfare are expedients, albeit necessary, until society can be restructured to the point where they are no longer necessary.

In the current state of society, characterized by a few owners of significant amounts of income-generating assets and great disparities in wealth, the living wage is a mandate. The only exceptions, of course, are in situations where a greater evil than not paying a living wage will result if the living wage is paid. This would be the case, for example, where an employer would be driven out of business by raising wages. No one is required to do the impossible, or that which would result in direct evil or inadvertent evil greater than the expected benefits. When that is the case, the employer is constrained to work with others in order to make payment of the living wage possible.

The mandate to pay a living wage, however, is valid only in the current, badly structured state of society. If we were to assume, contrary to Pius XI's assertion of its "radical instability," that the current state of society was divinely instituted and absolutely fixed (thus obviating the stated necessity to restructure society), then the mandate to pay a living wage in any and all circumstances would necessarily be construed as a kind of "Divine Right of Labor."

The Form of Society is Not Divinely Instituted

As any reader of the social encyclicals should be aware, however, the current state of society is not only *not* divinely mandated, instituted, or maintained, it is organized along lines that demand a restructuring of the social order, as, indeed, the title of *Quadragesimo Anno* informs us: "On the Restructuring of the Social Order."[15] The insistence of critics of neo-conservatism that the living wage constitutes the be-all and end-all of Catholic social teaching is as distorted as the insistence of neo-conservatives that the application of the laws of supply and demand in the current state of society is divinely mandated.

The neo-conservative idea is that the rich have some kind of "Divine Right of Capital." This is due to their providing financing for the formation of capital and, indirectly, jobs for the propertyless. It assumes a state of permanent dependency — effective slavery, as Leo XIII and Pius XI pointed out —

on the part of the average person. Critics not only fail to refute this conclusion, they actively support it. Indeed, they strive for its maintenance, begging the question as to whether a condition of dependency is just or even tolerable.

Just as Saint Paul urged masters to treat their slaves well, the popes mandate the payment of a living wage. The situations are exactly analogous. Both the formal slave and the propertyless worker are absolute dependents on the master or employer.[16] By the functioning of strict (*i.e.*, commutative) justice, "principals" (masters and employers) owe their dependents the means to sustain a decent standard of living in keeping with the demands of human dignity. In a sense, the employer of the propertyless worker "owns" the life of that worker just as surely as parents control the lives of their children, or a master has legal title to his slaves. Because of that "ownership" and the control he presumably has over his dependents, whether slaves, employees, or children, the principal is obligated to support those dependents in a manner consistent with human dignity.

Obviously, both chattel slavery and the condition of the propertyless worker represent an affront to human dignity at the most fundamental level. Human beings are required to act as adults. They have inalienable rights, duties, and virtues to enable them to do so. A condition of permanent dependency effectively denies or prevents this, establishing or maintaining what the popes have called a "structure of sin."

The recommendation of Saint Paul that masters treat their slaves well and the papal mandate to pay a living wage can only be understood in the context of the current or then-current state of society. Taking the state of society as a given, what is the just and moral thing to do? Since slavery exists, masters must treat their slaves well. Since the propertyless condition exists, and workers are utterly dependent on their employers for their subsistence, employers must pay a living wage, except in some narrow and explicitly-defined situations.[17]

Pius XI even addressed the situation where it is impossible to pay a living wage, or where raising wages would result in economic effects that were worse than the condition presumably being ameliorated.

> Every effort must therefore be made that fathers of families receive a wage large enough to meet ordinary family needs adequately. But if this cannot always be done under existing circumstances, social justice demands that changes be introduced as soon as possible whereby such a wage will be assured to every adult workingman.[18]

This, as Father William J. Ferree was to point out, is not a command to pay a living, just, or family wage under social justice.[19] On the contrary, it is a mandate that, if individual justice cannot function in a particular situation, the situation is to be restructured ("social justice demands that changes be introduced as soon as possible") so that individual justice can, once again, function properly.

Neither the mandate to treat slaves well, nor that to pay a living wage, however, is an admission that the existing state of society is just or even moral to any degree. These mandates are simply a means of dealing with the present situation until society can be restructured along lines more consistent with universal moral principles. They merely state what is to be done in the meantime.

A Divine Right to Be a Slave

Obviously we cannot insist that such expedients as the living wage or good treatment of slaves "prove" that the current state of society is divinely mandated. Asserting some kind of twisted "Divine Right of Labor" is itself sinful. Pius XI gave a clear mandate *under penalty of sin* to restructure society. Each of us has an absolute personal and individual responsibility to join with others and carry out acts of social justice directed toward the reform of the institutions of society in conformity with universal moral principles and consistent with human dignity.[20]

Leaving current social structures in place and unreformed without taking any action to ameliorate the situation, whatever the rationalization or justification, constitutes a complete abrogation of our responsibility and our duty to God. Paying a living wage is not a "Divine Right of Labor," but the application of a specific principle designed to accommodate the current flawed state of society until such time as the social order can be restructured.

Spinning Your Wheels

No doubt Your Excellency is by this time becoming irritated. "What," you may well ask, "have we been doing all this time, but attempting to restructure the social order? Are you suggesting that we have been spinning our wheels?"

With all due respect, Your Excellency, — that is exactly what you have been doing. Some programs you might mention, particularly Pro-Life, are absolutely necessary, regardless of the current state of society. Others, such as the Campaign for Human Development[21] and Catholic Action,[22] were originally intended to carry out the mandate of Pius XI to restructure society in conformity with universal moral principles and so establish and maintain the Reign of Christ the King, but lost their way. Some, such as protecting the interests of dependent labor (and thereby maintaining them in their condition of dependency) and promoting minimum wage legislation, may be necessary expedients given the current state of society, but are almost inevitably construed as ends in themselves. Still others, such as certain aspects of Liberation Theology[23] and Call to Action,[24] are actively opposed to the ends you seek.

The basic problem is that none of these institutions or programs, as they are currently constituted, is geared toward a restructuring of the social order along the lines commanded by Pius XI and reasserted by subsequent popes. There is no real social justice, as conceived by Pius XI, involved in any of these efforts. At the most fundamental level, this is because most people have missed the point of what Pius XI was teaching. They have not realized the profound breakthrough in moral philosophy represented by his work. This is the idea of "social virtue" itself.

The Idea of Social Virtue

Everyone is familiar with the individual virtues, or at least thinks he is. These consist of the natural or moral virtues of fortitude, prudence, temperance and, above all, justice. There are also the three supernatural or theological virtues of faith, hope, and charity. The highest of the supernatural virtues is charity.[25] The natural virtues are called natural because every human being has the natural capacity as a human being to acquire them. The natural virtues are raised to a supernatural object and facility by the infused moral virtues. The theological virtues, on the other hand, are super-natural, that is, "above" nature. They are not acquired by man's natural effort. God *infuses* the supernatural virtues into human beings as a free gift.[26]

There is, however, something more than the classic individual virtues. Based on the work of Saint Thomas Aquinas, Pius XI posited the existence of specifically *social* virtues. Social virtues are "particular" and distinct from the individual virtues. Of these he named only social charity and social justice, but with enough clarity to enable us to understand the idea of a *social*, as opposed to an *individual* virtue.

Understanding the idea of virtue through an examination of the individual virtues, we can apply the same concepts to social virtue. Just as each human being possesses individual virtues, whether naturally or by infusion, he also possesses the social virtues, presumably in precisely the same way. Whether the social virtues are present naturally or by infusion in precisely the same way as the individual virtues is irrelevant to this discussion, and need not concern us at this point. Logic and evidence would, however, indicate that such is indeed the case.

There is, however, one important characteristic of all virtues, individual or social, natural or supernatural, which is often overlooked. This characteristic is crucial to understanding the social virtues, especially social justice and its application to the proper structuring of the social order under the Divine Kingship of Christ. Social virtues (or virtues of any kind) are not, and cannot be, as Pius XI pointed out, something intrinsic to institutions or social structures, including the State or the collective.[27]

This is important. Things — and the State and the collective are, ultimately, mere things — cannot have the capacity for virtue of any kind, in and of themselves. The capacity for virtue, whether individual or social, can only be intrinsic to natural persons.[28] An institution or social structure receives virtue and the capacity for virtue only by what Aristotle referred to as "reflection." In modern terms, this is a type of delegation from natural persons, such as human beings, to whom the capacity for virtue is intrinsic by nature or by infusion. Social virtue cannot, therefore, consist of any kind of capacity for virtue or virtue possessed by an institution or social structure intrinsically, that is, by nature or by infusion.[29]

There is another important distinction to make with respect to the social virtues. Individual and social virtues are fundamentally different, and not simply because the word "social" has been appended to the front of one. The primary difference between the two is in what philosophers would call the "efficient cause," or agent, of the virtue. That is, the difference between individual and social virtue consists in who can carry out "acts" of the virtue.

This, too, is extremely important and absolutely critical to the understanding of the whole idea of social virtue. The "efficient cause" of an individual virtue is, as one might expect, the individual. That is, an individual *as an individual* carries out acts of individual virtue. This means that an individual *as an individual* is responsible under penalty of sin for carrying out such acts of individual virtue as are warranted.

The "efficient cause" of a *social* virtue, however, is not and cannot be the *individual*. As Pius XI pointed out, the individual is "frequently helpless" in social situations to effect an act of virtue.[30] Being helpless to effect an act of virtue *as an individual*, the individual *as an individual* is released from the obligation to carry out acts of individual virtue, for no one is obligated to do what is impossible.

Social Versus Individual Action

The "efficient cause" of a *social* virtue is not, however, the individual *as an individual*. Because social virtue is something specifically *social*, the "efficient cause," that is, the agent charged with carrying out acts of social virtue, is the individual *as a member of a social unit*, that is, as a member of a group. In a specifically social situation, therefore, the individual has the absolute responsibility — under penalty of sin — to come together with like-minded others into groups, whether formal or informal, and work for the restructuring of the social order in order to make the practice of individual virtue possible.

In other words, when the individual is helpless to carry out acts of *individual* virtue, he must join with others and carry out acts of *social* virtue. Social virtue does not replace the practice of individual virtue, but "enables" the practice of individual virtue upon the correction or restructuring of a flawed institution. The job of social virtue is to affect the common good so that the practice of individual virtue becomes possible, or continues to be possible within tolerable limits.

The chief difference between individual virtue and social virtue is that, while every human individual has the capacity for all the virtues, both individual and social, individual virtues may be exercised as an individual, but social virtue can only be exercised as a member of a group. Ultimately, then, the end of acts of social virtue is not to achieve a specific end result in the individual order when individual virtue fails, but to make acts of individual virtue possible. The end of social virtue is not to mandate the desired result that would have occurred had acts of individual virtue been possible without social action.

Because the individual as an individual "is frequently helpless"[31] in social situations, the current state of society can seem immutable to anyone who approaches it from the orientation imposed by purely individual virtue. The imposition of desired results, such as occurs with the living wage or redistribution, is, from the point of view of Pius XI and his concept of social virtue, an individualistic expedient that must be employed until acts of social virtue can bring about a restructuring of the social order, and people are able to gain a living income by their own efforts.[32]

The Role of the Living Wage

Neo-conservatives are therefore ill-advised to insist that the capitalist is released from his obligation to pay a living wage due to the ultimately self-defeating nature of the program or the "power" that a worker has to go elsewhere. Their critics are equally ill-advised to assert that the living wage represents the fulfillment of Catholic *social* teaching. On the contrary, the living wage represents a barely-tolerable minimum, and an individualistic (but socially-determined) expedient that the faithful are mandated — under penalty of sin — to replace at the earliest possible moment with a better way of gaining an adequate and secure income.

Your Excellency, both neo-conservatives and their critics have been pursuing the wrong course. Accusing each other of greed and envy, neither side realizes that, for all their talk of morality and practicality, they are merely being expedient. Both assume the current state of society is a given, and insist on individualistic responses to social situations. Everyone involved will continue to spin his wheels until someone realizes that something more is needed than the traditional individualistic solutions applied in the traditionally individualistic way. What is needed to address social problems is something specifically *social*: Social virtue.

Notes

[1] Anthony Basile, Ph.D., "Selling Out Catholic Social Teaching: The Acton Institute's Misleading Message" *Culture Wars*, September 1999.
[2] Pius XI, *Quadragesimo Anno* ("On the Restructuring of the Social Order"), 1931, § 42.
[3] *Ibid.*, § 132.

[4] This attitude is also an evasion from the standpoint of social justice, as Fr. William Ferree makes clear in his *Introduction to Social Justice*. Washington, DC: Center for Economic and Social Justice, 1997, 48-49.

[5] Pius XI, *Discourse Commemorating the Thirty-Fifth Anniversary of Rerum Novarum*, May 15, 1926.

[6] John XXII, *Mater et Magistra* ("Christianity and Social Progress"), 1961, § 109.

[7] The "living wage" is an expedient to address a specific condition of society, and is not a "primary" right. It is a "derived right," meaning it is subject to change to meet changing conditions of society, as Fr. John Ryan pointed out in his book, *A Living Wage*. "The source of natural rights is the dignity of the human person, while their scope is determined by the person's essential needs. A man's natural rights are as many and as extensive as are the liberties, opportunities and possessions that are required for the reasonable maintenance and development of his personality. They may all be reduced to the right to a reasonable amount of external liberty of action. Some of them, for instance, the right to live and the right to marry, are original and primary, inhering in all persons of whatever condition ; others are derived and secondary, occasioned and determined by the particular circumstances of particular persons. To the latter class belongs the right to a Living Wage. It is not an original and universal right ; for the receiving of wages supposes that form of industrial organization known as the wage system, which has not always existed and is not essential to human welfare. Even to-day there are millions of men who get their living otherwise than by wages, and who, therefore, have no juridical title to wages of any kind or amount. The right to a Living Wage is evidently a derived right which is measured and determined by existing social and industrial institutions." John A. Ryan, S.T.D., *A Living Wage: Its Ethical and Economic Aspects*. New York: Grosset & Dunlap, Publishers, 1906, 67-68.

[8] See Fr. Joel S. Panzer, *The Popes and Slavery*. New York: Alba House, 1996.

[9] Leo XIII, *Rerum Novarum* ("On the Condition of the Workers"), 1891, § 6.

[10] *Quadragesimo Anno, op. cit.*, § 59. See also John XXIII, *Mater et Magistra* ("Christianity and Social Progress"), 1961, § 109; Paul VI, *Populorum Progressio* ("On the Development of Peoples"), 1967, § 30.

[11] "If there must always be a laboring population distinct from proprietors and employers, we regard the slave system as decidedly preferable to the system at wages. . . Wages is a cunning device of the devil, for the benefit of tender consciences, who would retain all the advantages of the slave system, without the expense, trouble, and odium of being slave-holders." Orestes A. Brownson, *Boston Quarterly*, July 1840.

[12] See Heinrich A. Rommen, *The Natural Law, A Study in Legal and Social History and Philosophy*. Indianapolis, Indiana: Liberty Fund, Inc., 1998.

[13] Pius XI, *Discourse Commemorating the Thirty-Fifth Anniversary of Rerum Novarum*, May 15, 1926.

[14] Usually in the form of quasi- "acts of legal justice" (*i.e.*, passing laws which are not validations or reinforcement of prior or contemporaneous acts of social justice, and therefore ineffective or harmful), in the mistaken belief that passing a law will bring about desired results. See A. V. Dicey, *Lectures on the Relation Between Law and Public Opinion in England During the Nineteenth Century*. New Brunswick, Connecticut: Transaction Books, 1981.

[15] "What We have written thus far regarding a right distribution of property and a just scale of wages is concerned directly with the individual, and deals only indirectly with the social order." *Quadragesimo Anno, op. cit.*, § 76.

[16] Many modern translations of the scholastics obscure this point by using the words "servant," "worker," or "employee" as the English equivalent of *servitus* or *servus* — "slave." While this spares the feelings of the modern employee, worker, or servant, it militates against a proper understanding of the condition of dependency which mandates such mechanisms as the living wage, family allowances, and welfare.

[17] *Quadragesimo Anno, op. cit.*, §§ 72-73.

[18] *Ibid.*, § 71.

[19] William J. Ferree, S.M., Ph.D., *Introduction to Social Justice*. Washington, DC: Center for Economic and Social Justice, 1997, 9.

[20] *Ibid*.

[21] Paul Likoudis, *The Legacy of CHD, A Critical Report and Analysis of the U.S. Bishops' Campaign for Human Development*. Minneapolis, Minnesota: The Wanderer Press, 1990.

[22] Fr. William J. Ferree, *Forty Years After. . . A Second Call to Battle*. Unpublished manuscript, c. 1984.

[23] Sacred Congregation for the Doctrine of the Faith, *Instruction on Certain Aspects of the "Theology of Liberation,"* 1984.

[24] Brian Clowes, Ph.D., *Call to Action or Call to Apostasy? How Dissenters Plan to Remake the Catholic Church in their own Image.* Front Royal, Virginia: Human Life International, 1997.

[25] I Corinthians XIII.13.

[26] In the Aristotelian view, man either possesses or does not possess virtue. What Aristotle called a variable capacity to acquire and develop virtue, however, a Christian, Jew, or Muslim would call an "analogously complete" (*i.e.*, "equal") capacity to acquire and develop virtue. As far as Aristotle was concerned, there was no question of "acquiring" (developing) virtue for which one did not have the capacity, and an individual without sufficient virtue wasn't even human to that degree. Using Aristotelian terminology in a Christian context, therefore, everyone has the fullness of the capacity to acquire and develop all virtues simply because he is human. The task of man is to acquire and perfect all the virtues for which he has the full capacity to acquire and develop. Using Christian terminology, every individual has an analogously complete capacity to acquire and develop all virtue for for the simple reason that he is a human being made in the image and likeness of God, the realization and embodiment of all virtue.

[27] Pius XI, *Divini Redemptoris* ("On Atheistic Communism"), 1937, § 29.

[28] *Ibid.*

[29] *Divini Redemptoris*, § 29.

[30] *Ibid.*, § 37.

[31] *Ibid.*, § 53; John XXIII, *Mater et Magistra* ("Christianity and Social Progress"), 1961, § 60.

[32] *Quadragesimo Anno, op. cit.*, § 76.

Part IV
A More Excellent Way

Your Excellency, we have, up to now, concentrated on pointing out the errors that permeate the whole discussion of what constitutes a just economic order. Both neo-conservatives and their critics have managed to paint themselves into corners, as it were, by means of attempting to force individual virtues to fit social situations. The only result, aside from increased acrimony, accusation, and counter-accusation, has been a polarization of the issues along lines that have nothing to do with a viable solution. Definitions have been distorted, morality redefined, and immorality promoted, if inadvertently, on both sides of the question.

The surprising thing is that, once we examine the arguments objectively, we realize that both neo-conservatives and their critics make the same assumptions. They end up in complete agreement on the most fundamental issues. Both accept the current state of society as a given, in spite of the characterization of society by Pius XI as "radically unstable."[1] Both insist, ultimately, that only an elite have the ability and the means to rule, whether economically or politically.

The Problem of "Freedom"

In both views, society is arranged along a scale of what some call "freedom." This "freedom," however, bears a close resemblance to unrestrained license. At one end of the scale there is absolute economic and political license for the financial elite and absolute effective economic and political control of the masses. That is capitalism. At the other end of the scale there is absolute positive economic and political control of the masses by the political elite. This arrangement is sometimes referred to as "Divine Right of Kings" or of the State[2] by the more honest of the critics. That is socialism.

The only difference for the great mass of people in any of the various arrangements possible along the scale is which control group (political or economic) is doing the controlling, and whether the control is implicit, as with *laissez faire* capitalism, or explicit, as with socialism. For all practical purposes, there is no difference between capitalism and socialism — the presumed opposed ends of the scale — as far as the propertyless worker is concerned. "Often when changing rulers, nothing is changed for the poor but a name."[3]

We have a problem if we cannot get "off" this scale. On it, there is no possibility of a viable and moral solution to the problems of society, whether economic or political. Is there, however, a way to avoid trapping one's self on this "freedom scale," a way that actually respects "human freedom in its totality"?[4] We refer, of course, to genuine freedom, not the licentiousness for which it is so often mistaken. There must be, or every pope since Leo XIII would not have insisted that, yes, there is another way, a moral alternative, a "more excellent way," to the immorality and impracticality of both capitalism and socialism.

Redemption of the Propertyless Worker

To answer that question, we need to start with the realization that the basis of Catholic social teaching is respect for human dignity.[5] Respect for human dignity demands that each and every human person has the right, indeed the mandate and the personal obligation, to be free from every form of slavery. This is true whether the condition is moral slavery to sin, economic or legal slavery to a master, or political slavery to the State. Note that in a "natural law" orientation, "human person" automatically includes all human beings in all stages of development and political and economic status.

To achieve this condition of non-dependency, emancipation, or redemption (however one wishes to construe it with respect to civil, domestic or religious society), human freedom in its totality must be realized.[6] Human freedom in its totality, as John Paul II has pointed out, consists of freedom from sin, freedom from economic and political dependence, and freedom from any coercion that obviates or counters the free will of a well-formed conscience.

The common denominator of both capitalism and socialism is a condition of enforced dependency imposed on the great mass of the people through propertylessness and maintenance of the wage system. Whether ownership or control of property is concentrated in the State or in the hands of an elite few private capitalists, the effect on the propertyless worker is the same: He is utterly dependent on his employer for his subsistence. A condition of utter dependency has been recognized throughout history as tantamount to slavery — as, indeed, the popes have consistently held.

Without the means of generating an adequate and secure income independently of the beneficence or coercion of others, that is, without an adequate stake of private, income-generating property, the worker, no matter how well paid he may be, is utterly dependent on his employer. That is to say he is a slave, whether or not recognized as such by society or the legal system.

> Freedom is not an empty sound ; it is not an abstract idea; it is not a thing that nobody can feel. It means, — and it means nothing else, — the full and quiet enjoyment of your own property. If you have not this, if this be not well secured to you, you may call yourself what you will, but you are a slave.[7]

It is an affront to human dignity that anyone should be a slave, especially to sin. That does not mean, however, that other forms of slavery are at all acceptable. All forms of slavery are an abomination. A culture of slavery in any of the three societies of man, religious, civil, and domestic, has a detrimental effect on the other two. A civil or domestic slave is more inclined to the slavery of sin, just as those enslaved to sin are more likely to succumb to civil or domestic slavery.[8]

Reconciling Society

Your Excellency, the Church's primary concern in the world is the salvation of souls, that is, to free men from the slavery of sin. In order to optimize the possibility of success, therefore, all forms of slavery must be abolished, both formally and in fact.[9] Men must be redeemed from their condition of dependency, regardless of the society in which they are dependent. The process of redemption or emancipation requires a fundamental restructuring of society so as to conform it to universal moral principles and thereby establish and maintain the Reign of Christ the King. The actual redemption from slavery, especially to that of sin, is the personal responsibility of the slave. Since the individual frequently is helpless in the face of social problems,[10] however, he usually requires the assistance of others to overcome that slavery, in whatever form it manifests itself.

Because the economic order constitutes such a large and important part of temporal life, the popes in the social encyclicals have used predominantly economic examples to illustrate both the means and the goals of this restructuring of society. Pius XI made it very clear that what he spoke of with respect to economics was purely by way of example: "What We have thus far stated regarding an equitable distribution of property and regarding just wages concerns individual persons and only indirectly touches social order, to the restoration of which according to the principles of sound philosophy and to its perfection according to the sublime precepts of the law of the Gospel, Our Predecessor, Leo XIII, devoted all his thought and care."[11]

Distributive Justice or Social Justice?

The problem with using economic examples to explain the functioning of social virtues tends to confuse any commentator who already has problems with differentiating between principle and the application of principle. This tends to intermingle the specific principles of economic justice — an application of the principles of social justice — with those of social justice proper. One example of this is the confusion over the meaning of "distributive justice."

In the philosophy of Saint Thomas Aquinas, derived directly from Aristotle, distributive justice refers to distributions of all kinds (not just economic) on the basis of proportionality of inputs to the community. "Community" refers to any organized aggregation, the group as an explicitly social unit, not just the State. This is explained in Book V of Aristotle's *Nicomachean Ethics*. We have to realize, of course, that, in a significant sense, Saint Thomas' *Summa Theologica* is "merely" a commentary on Aristotle. In order to understand Thomism, we must first understand the philosophy of Aristotle. The definitions and principles of Aristotle, therefore, must be taken as normative except where Saint Thomas has somehow clarified or corrected the Philosopher.

Most commentators do not first go to Aristotle when attempting to define or explain distributive justice. Many simply assume that any distribution is somehow, *ipso facto*, "distributive justice." Once we look at Aristotle and Aquinas, however, we immediately discover that this is not the case. Most simply, distributive justice requires that each member of a social (organized) aggregation or group ("community") receive benefits in accordance with his inputs to the group.[12] This definition has been twisted to mean that each should receive according to his needs.[13] The principle "to each according to his needs" is valid for charity and for strict ("commutative") justice to a dependent — but not between mature "independent others" who possess inalienable rights and free will.

A Distinction Between Justice and Charity

Failure to make a distinction between justice and charity results in a condition that the popes have characterized as "near slavery" and "permanent bondage." It is neither justice nor charity. Maintaining distribution on the basis of need as the rule for society instead of the exception forces people into a condition of dependency. This is true whether that dependency is on the State as the grantor of largesse, or on a wealthy elite, determined to retain control over the economic, political and social lives of the great mass of people.

The three principles of economic justice, on the other hand, employ Saint Thomas' understanding of distributive justice to ensure a due respect for the dignity of the human person. These three principles are 1) Participation (everyone must be allowed the option of owning, individually or in association with others, both of the economic factors of production, human — labor — and non-human — capital — without discrimination), 2) Distribution (everyone, individually or in association with others, must have the option of employing the economic factors of distribution, both wages paid for labor and profits due to the private and individual ownership of capital, without discrimination) and 3) Harmony (the "feedback principle" wherein all social interaction should be in balance not only with respect to all parties involved in production so that "inputs" and "outputs" are in balance, but with the whole of the common good, so that every action at a particular level of the common good looks to its effect on all other levels of the common good).[14]

Louis Kelso and Mortimer Adler lay out a far more extensive treatment of these principles as they pertain to economic justice operating within the context of "full human freedom and development" in Chapter Five of *The Capitalist Manifesto*.[15] Understanding these principles, we can discern certain characteristics of an economically just society that take into consideration the basic dignity of the human person, the stated goal of the social encyclicals:

- Free and open markets,
- A limited economic role for the State,
- A restoration of the rights of private property, especially in corporate equity, and what we may call the "moral omission" of both capitalism and socialism,
- Widespread individual and direct ownership of the means of production, individually or in association with others.

Dr. Robert H. A. Ashford and Rodney Shakespeare set forth a sound basis for analysis of Louis Kelso's "binary economics" and the roles of these "four pillars" in their recent book, *Binary Economics, The New Paradigm*.[16] This book presents its case with compelling logic and concise definitions. It counters the usual excuses given by today's economists as to why the principles in the social encyclicals "cannot" be implemented. It also disabuses people of the dehumanizing concept of "human capital."

The whole point of *Binary Economics* is the establishment of a sound framework detailing the necessity and providing a means by which ordinary people could become owners of a meaningful capital stake. People are not construed or to be treated as capital themselves. The book clarifies the difference between capital and labor. It demonstrates that acquisition of *real* capital, not turning people into "human capital," is absolutely essential if the great mass of people is to have any hope of participating in a meaningful way in the economic process.

The concepts detailed in Binary Economics are put to practical use in *Curing World Poverty: The New Role of Property*. This book is a compendium of articles designed to apply papal social teachings in a consistent and integrated fashion. It can serve as a guidebook for implementing a truly just economy based on the "four pillars." Let us consider each of these in order.

Free and Open Markets

Why is the restoration of a free market a pillar of a just economy? Because a free market, regulated within the bounds of the common good, allows the forces of supply and demand to determine just prices, just wages and just profits. Neo-conservatives are very clear on this principle, and extremely insistent in their support of it, although they sometimes forget about or reject the necessity of regulation by the State or other body to ensure a level playing field.

Thus, the neo-conservatives are not so clear on what they mean by "free market," which we defined in Part II as a market that has free and equal opportunity for all to the economic process within a strong juridical order, not a market in which "anything goes." Equating "free market" with "capitalism," and "capitalism" with "democracy," however, neo-conservatives fail to realize that the structure of capitalism itself — a small number of capitalists for whom everyone else works for wages — erects barriers against the full participation of everyone in the common good. It enforces a condition of dependency on those forced into the wage system as their only means of subsistence.

What is described and supported by neo-conservatism can best be characterized as an *un*free market. There is a somewhat naive belief that the free market, in and of itself, is sufficient to ensure justice (or, more usually, "freedom"). Where workers have only their labor to sell, they are left vulnerable to technology and other workers in the global economy who may be willing to take less pay for the same work. The only solution is to provide workers with sufficient capital credit to enable them to become owners of the very technology that "endangers" their jobs.

A truly free market consists of the interplay of forces of supply and demand. This consists of a free choice regarding the subjective opinions of economic values by each party to any economic transaction. In addition, the free market, unlike current markets, assumes that every human being has the right — is free — to participate in the economic process both as an owner of human labor and as an owner of productive capital. In this understanding of the free market (as opposed to the unfree market where various classes are restricted in the means by which they participate in the economic process), the "fair market price" is an aggregate of all subjective opinion as to the value of a particular good or service. This approximates the objective "market value" for all marketable goods and services. It also serves to approximate the objective and the relative values of all forms of human contributions to the economic process, whether it is in the form of human labor, or ownership of capital.

Critics of neo-conservatism are, unfortunately, not much better than the neo-conservatives in their understanding of the free market and the functioning of the laws of supply and demand. Instinctively realizing that something is wrong with the neo-conservative definition of "freedom," they over-react and reject even legitimate concepts of freedom. The venerable idea of a socially-controlled market, along with concepts such as solidarity and subsidiarity, are re-interpreted to mean rigid State control of the market. Desired ends are to be obtained by enforcing mandated results through legislation backed up by the instruments of coercion over which the State holds a monopoly. John Paul II's call for a "strong juridical order"[17] is taken to mean absolute state control in a system that is socialism in all but name. This ignores the proviso that the "strong juridical order" was to be placed "at the service of human freedom in its totality." In common with all previous pontiffs, John Paul II's orientation was to make the State a servant rather than the master.

Clearly the approaches of both neo-conservatives and their critics obviate what John Paul II has referred to as "human freedom in its totality."[18] Because it operates within the context of a society formed by imperfect man, the free market paradoxically requires some restrictions on competition. This is so that completely free competition does not eliminate competition, which, ironically, is the natural outcome of unregulated competition. That is, in a market where "anything goes," no matter how dishonest or contrary to the common good, the end result is an economic state of society where nothing goes. The term "free market," then, means free participation of everyone to allow the optimal exercise of each one's economic rights. It does not mean the free and untrammeled exercise of economic rights on the part of an elite few, to the detriment of the great mass of others who simply don't make the grade.

Undemocratic Democracy

The functioning of capitalism of the *laissez faire* variety is similar to what Aristotle noted with respect to democracy, where the most democratic action is not always the best way of preserving democracy.[19] Pure (*laissez faire*) competition, like pure democracy, carries within itself the seeds of its own destruction. The guiding principle of a free and open market, therefore, is for participants in the market and, if necessary, the State, to keep careful watch so that unfair competition does not result in the formation of monopolies — which generally can only exist with the acquiescence of the State.

"Unfair," "unrestricted," or "unregulated" competition are all terms that have been used to describe an economic condition of society that most resembles the Hobbesian "state of nature," where life is "nasty, brutish, and short." That is, so long as an action is advantageous to a particular individual or enterprise in the short run, regardless of its effect on the community as a whole or on the enterprise or individual himself in the long run, that action will, in a *laissez faire* orientation, be taken. There will be no reference to the common good, the rights of others, or even the long term advantage to one's self. The life of the typical economic unit is "nasty, brutish, and short."

The best way to avoid or dismantle monopolies of every kind is to encourage potential competitors by opening up free access to the market. This usually translates into providing access to capital credit, the soundest and most feasible means of acquiring and possessing property. Access to capital credit allows potential competitors and entrepreneurs to develop an enterprise of optimal size and efficiency for whatever industry in which it happens to engage.

Limited Economic Role for the State

Neo-conservatives grudgingly admit a role for the State with respect to the protection of property. Their critics do not deny that this is a proper role for the State, but consider it far too limited. In general, from the viewpoint of the critics of neo-conservatism, there is a tendency to demand that the State ensure that everyone is taken care of in one form or another, usually by direct State action. The attitude usually boils down to the belief that the State must do whatever the individual cannot do for himself. If the individual cannot, for example, coerce an employer into raising his wages, the State should step in and mandate an adequate level of pay. If an individual cannot afford to raise a family, the State is obligated to provide an allowance in such an amount that it becomes possible. If an individual cannot afford to travel to work or take a vacation, the State is obligated to provide subsidized transportation and lodging. The list could go on forever.

Neo-conservatives very properly view this degree of State interference as a positive evil. The problem with the neo-conservative orientation in this matter, however, is that it does not allow the State to exercise its proper function as guardian of the common good. In reaction against intrusive State action, they have a tendency to go too far the other way. One legitimate example of State action with which the neo-conservatives generally disagree is regulating competition. Unrestricted competition raises substantial barriers against full participation in the economic common good by ordinary people because it tends to monopolization. This cuts most people off from the possibility of acquiring and possessing property by ordinary means. Extraordinary means are always available, of course, as the neo-conservatives are quick to point out, but why should it be necessary to practice heroic economic virtue merely to participate in the economic process? As we have seen in the case of some of the world's richest men, the practice of heroic economic virtue can quite easily become a moral vice.

The general neo-conservative opinion that barriers to participation in the economic common good do not exist or can be overcome with the practice of economic virtue (thrift, frugality, and the exercise of "guts and gumption"), lends credence to their critics' assertion that more State involvement is absolutely necessary. That assertion is perfectly true — to a degree. Like the neo-conservatives, however, their critics have a strong tendency to go too far too fast. The problem with the orientation of the critics of neo-conservatism is that it not only allows the State its proper role of as guardian of the common good, it insists that it is the guardian of every individual good as well.[20]

The proper orientation is a middle way not only between, but far above the two ends of the spectrum. The role of the State in the economic sphere should be to enforce contracts, protect property, punish fraud, and ensure equal access to the means to participate in the economic process. In other words, the State should be concerned solely with removing barriers to full participation in the economic common good, thereby ensuring a "level playing field."[21] Protection of private property is, of course, a large measure of this, but there is also the task of policing abuses, such as competition that tends toward monopolization.

There is, of course, a danger in misconstruing the State's role with respect to regulating competition when this is expanded beyond enforcing contracts, protecting property, punishing fraud, and lowering barriers to full participation in the economic common good. Under the guise of "regulation," the State always attempts to protect special interests and current centers of power by giving a favorable status to selected individuals, enterprises, or industries. Inevitably, unless careful watch is kept on the machinery of government and its agents, the State will protect some producers against competition by restricting entry (*e.g.*, special licenses or qualifications having nothing to do with the particular trade or industry), or actively creates special privileges or monopolies.

For example, the number of trucking licenses to engage in interstate commerce has not been increased since the 1930s when the requirement was first instituted. As a result, there are some companies or individuals who own nothing but a license, for which companies actually engaged in interstate commerce pay substantial "rental" fees. In Indiana, the number of tavern licenses is strictly regulated, so that the license itself frequently sells for more than the plant, fixtures and inventory of a restaurant — a "three-way" license is an extremely valuable commodity. In Virginia and Pennsylvania, as well as a number of other states, the government owns and operates liquor stores. State lotteries are common in places where privately-run gambling is illegal. New York's "Sullivan Law" effectively restricts ownership of handguns to former police officers and the wealthy. The number of gun licenses granted to low- or middle-income individuals, Negroes, and other minorities is infinitesimal. The waiting period (unless your last name happens to be "Trump") is years long.

Does citing these examples imply that we are advocating no regulation of interstate commerce, firearms, gambling, or liquor? Not at all. These examples, however, serve to illustrate the fact that when the State imposes a regulation (actual or effective) not directly related to the activity being regulated, the result is generally draconian in orientation. If selling liquor, running a gambling operation, or owning a handgun is either beneficial or morally neutral, why shouldn't everyone have the opportunity to apply for permission and be granted a license to participate in such an activity without discrimination?

On the other hand, if an action, good or service is morally repugnant, why should the State be involved? An action that is immoral for an individual is also immoral for the State. The State by its very nature should be more concerned with violations of the natural law and damage to the common good than any mere individual acting on his own account. The same arguments made in favor of State liquor stores and lotteries could be — and have been — made for government-supplied narcotics, licensed or State-run brothels, human sacrifice, euthanasia or assisted suicide centers, and gladiatorial combats. Government by its nature walks a tightrope, and it is very easy to fall off and into the pit of totalitarian regulation or *laissez faire* indifference.

Free markets, limited role for the State . . . so far this sounds very like the traditional neo-conservative or libertarian position. That being so, why are we criticizing that position so harshly? For the very simple reason that, while both the neo-conservatives and their critics have a portion — in some cases a very large portion — of the truth, their errors are not only in their general orientation, but in what they leave out of their programs.

Your Excellency, we have examined the principles of economic justice and the first two of the essential "four pillars" of an economically just society. In the next and final part, we will examine the two "pillars" which have been most ignored or most misunderstood: The rights of and to private property, and, the "fatal omission" from virtually every economy on the globe today: Expanded ownership of the means of production.

Notes

[1] Pius XI, *Discourse Commemorating the Thirty-Fifth Anniversary of Rerum Novarum*, May 15, 1926.

[2] In extreme cases, this results in a deification of the State, cf. Marx's "The State is God, God is the State."

[3] "In principatu commutando sæpius, nil præter domini nomen mutant pauperes." C. Iulius Phædrus c. 15 BC-AD 45 I, *Prologus*, 15, 1.

[4] John Paul II, *Centesimus Annus* ("On the Hundredth Anniversary of *Rerum Novarum*"), 1991, § 42.

[5] Pius XI, *Quadragesimo Anno*, ("On the Restructuring of the Social Order"), 1931, § 101.

[6] Paul VI, *Populorum Progressio* ("On the Development of Peoples"), 1967, § 30.

[7] William Cobbett, A History *of the Protestant Reformation in England and Ireland*. Rockville, Illinois: Tan Books and Publishers, Inc., 1988, § 456.

[8] "There are a few men whom slavery holds fast, but there are many more who hold fast to slavery." *Paucos servitus, plures servitutem tenent*. Lucius Annæus Seneca, *Epistulæ Morales*, II, 6. Seneca, of course, was a Stoic, and one who relegated all meaningful slavery to the moral realm. The legal condition of slavery did not matter to the Stoics, who strove for indifference to all worldly matters, only the moral or spiritual condition of dependency on sin.

[9] Dr. Kevin Bales supplies an immense amount of empirical data to make his case that, while slavery has been "legally" abolished in every country in the world, it is still prevalent in many countries, especially in the Third World. Slavery is absent from no

continent, with the possible exception of Antarctica. See Kevin Bales, *Disposable People, New Slavery in the Global Economy*. Berkeley and Los Angeles, California: University of California Press, 1999.

[10] Pius XI, *Divini Redemptoris* ("On Atheistic Communism"), 1937, § 37.

[11] *Quadragesimo Anno, op. cit.*, § 76.

[12] The distribution of benefits under distributive justice is to be made by the leader, leaders, or delegated authority of the leaders of the group, but, as Saint Thomas is quick to point out, every distribution by authority is not, *ipso facto*, "distributive justice." That is, the characteristic of distributive justice is proportionality (what Aristotle called a "geometric" mean), not the fact that in any group only someone in a leadership position has the authority to make a distribution. That would be to confuse an administrative function with the essence of a virtue.

[13] Distribution on the basis of need is either charity or a special type of commutative (not distributive) justice to a dependent. It is a species of justice tailored to fit an extraordinary and unjust state of civil society (although construed as the norm in domestic society), and should never be employed as a permanent solution to social problems which, as Pius XI pointed out, require a restructuring of the social order, not a temporary expedient, so that the demands of social justice may be met.

[14] See Norman G. Kurland, "Economic Justice in the Age of the Robot" *Curing World Poverty: The New Role of Property*. Saint Louis, Missouri: Social Justice Review, 1994.

[15] Louis O. Kelso and Mortimer J. Adler, *The Capitalist Manifesto*. New York: Random House, 1958.

[16] Robert H. A. Ashford and Rodney Shakespeare, *Binary Economics, The New Paradigm*. Lanham Maryland: University Press of America, 1999.

[17] *Centesimus Annus, op. cit.*

[18] *Ibid.*

[19] Aristotle, *The Politics*, V.9.

[20] The common good is not the sum of all *individual* goods, but a thing which is specifically *social*. Ferree, *Introduction to Social Justice. op. cit.*, 30.

[21] *Populorum Progressio, op. cit.*, § 61.

Part V

A More Excellent Way, Continued

Your Excellency, in the previous chapter we gave an outline of the principles of economic justice and their application in the first two of what we call the "four pillars" of an economically just society. These were the establishment of free and open markets, and a limited economic role for the State. We can now turn to the remaining two "pillars," restoration of the rights to and of private property, especially in corporate equity, and, what we consider the "fatal omission" in every economic system throughout the world today, expanded capital ownership.

Restoration of Private Property

One of the peculiarities of the capitalist orientation is that, contrary to popular belief, capitalism is not a system based on property, but on its negation.[1] That a few can control the bulk of the means of production to the exclusion of everyone else means that the common good is seriously flawed. Rights, including rights to and of property, must be open to exercise by all.

Throughout history, private property has been understood and supported as the bulwark of civilization and individual sovereignty. Property is the basis of both political and economic power. As American statesman Benjamin Watkins Leigh of Virginia stated in the Virginia Constitutional Convention of 1820 during the debates on whether the franchise should be extended to white males over the age of 21 who did not own property,

> Power and Property can be separated for a time by force or fraud — but divorced, never. For as soon as the pang of separation is felt . . . Property will purchase Power, or Power will take over Property.

When property is concentrated in the hands of a few, then, logically, so is power. That is the classic definition of "capitalism," a system endorsed so strongly by the Acton Institute and its neo-conservative allies. Ironically, for an organization named after Lord Acton, they seem to have forgotten Lord Acton's famous declaration concerning power. Echoing William Pitt over a century earlier,[2] Acton's statement is virtually a cliché today, but still true: "Power tends to corrupt; absolute power corrupts absolutely."[3]

The only way to break the current virtual monopoly on power held by the current economic or political elite is to break the near-monopoly on ownership of productive assets. Ownership of new capital follows whoever has access to capital credit. The solution, therefore, to the corrupting tendency of power is not, as Marx asserted, to concentrate it in the hands of the State. The only viable alternative to concentrated power of all kinds is to break it up. This can be done by opening up access to the ownership of new capital to all by opening up access to capital credit, the chief means of acquiring and possessing property.

What is Property?

This requires an understanding of property. Property, contrary to popular notions, is not a thing, but the rights an owner has to and over a thing. The right *to* property is universal, absolute, and inalienable. That means that every human being has the right to acquire and possess property, but not anything that already belongs to others. This is one social aspect of property, as it is one from which no human being can be excluded without violating the most fundamental precepts of human dignity. Included in the right to acquire and possess property is the derived right of access to the *means* of acquiring and possessing property. That means the right to borrow money to acquire capital, or access to the use of some other legitimate method of purchasing an adequate stake of income generating assets.[4]

Once property is acquired, however, the rights of the owner over it are exclusive. That is, the owner may restrict others from enjoying the fruits of that which he owns, and he may exercise his rights over his possessions in any way he sees fit, provided, of course, that they are not exercised in any way that harms others or the common good. That is the second social aspect of property.

The problem today is that rights of owners over their possessions, especially with respect to corporate equity ("shares"), have been eroded to the point where they are effectively non-existent. As an example, we need merely cite the double — sometimes triple — tax on corporate profits imposed by the government. Ancillary to that is the fact that the United States government (and, presumably, most other governments throughout the world) has upheld the denial of shareholder rights by the board of directors.

Henry Ford v. Natural Law

Most dramatically, erosion of the rights of private property in corporate equity is manifested by the refusal to pay out dividends except by special decree of the board of directors. Dividends, of course, are profits that belong by natural right to the shareholders of a corporation. In the landmark case, *Dodge v. Ford Motor Company*,[5] some of the shareholders of the Ford Motor Company sued over the payment of dividends. Henry Ford had changed the dividend policy of the company, reducing dividend payouts in order to use the cash to expand and improve plant facilities.

The court ruled in Ford's favor, determining that the directors of a corporation — essentially employees of the shareholders — alone have the power to declare a dividend of a corporation and determine its amount. This was a direct usurpation of the owners' property in that corporation[6] which Leo XIII had declared was sacred,[7] and an example of individual rights that were to be protected religiously and by civil authority.[8] The shareholders' rights movement, supported by various organizations such as the United Shareholders Association (USA) and the American Employees Stock Ownership Association (AESOA) is currently challenging this situation. It is also acknowledged by the popes, *e.g.*, "it is a grievous error so to weaken the individual character of ownership as actually to destroy it."[9]

The presumption of the court, of course, was that the collective ownership represented by a corporation was subject to a Benthamite "tyranny of the majority." That is, majority owners could make decisions and carry out actions to their own benefit without regard to the rights of minority shareholders or the common good. The other assumption, still present in virtually all state and federal law and tax policy, is that past accumulations of savings are the only way that capital can be formed. That being so, the property rights of shareholders, whether majority or minority, are of no consequence in view of the overriding social need to form capital in order to provide people with wage-system jobs.

When the financing of capital is restricted to past savings, the demands of the common good require that the rights of the few be overridden and they be effectively deprived of a portion of their rights of property. The problem with this is that the situation is not seen as an injustice, but as a necessary and normal manner of proceeding. No efforts are made to reform the system through acts of social justice. Individual injustices are left in place, sometimes even glorified and extolled as the best of all possible systems.

State interference, whether direct or indirect, has also been a significant factor in reducing people's civil liberties in connection with their possessions. A well-structured common good requires not only that people be permitted to own property, but that the ownership be effective or "real" ownership. As Pius XI noted, things may not be structured in such a way as to make the exercise of rights impossible, for that is the same as denying the rights.[10]

Expanded Capital Ownership

Widespread ownership of the means of production is perhaps the hardest part of the application of Catholic social teaching for most people to accept. Ever since the Reformation and the rise of capitalism,[11] the idea has become fixed in the general psyche that the only way for the great mass of people to earn a living is by selling their labor for wages. This results directly from the fact that it has been assumed for centuries that the only way to finance the formation of capital is for the rich, who are the only ones who can afford to do so, to set aside a sufficient portion of their income.

That is not, however, the only way, nor even the best way to finance the formation of capital. The truth of the matter is that, with proper use of central banking and a program of expanded capital ownership, the soundest possible economic arrangement of society can be achieved — without relying on past savings. This frees both the economic system as a whole and the poor in particular from dependence on the rich.

This can be done through the use of what is called "pure credit," as Louis Kelso advocated. Louis Kelso did not invent "pure credit," but he did set forth the principles and develop legal mechanisms that would open up this classic method of capital financing to exercise by everyone. That is, Kelso realized that central banking theory as well as practice would allow ordinary people to finance the acquisition of self-liquidating assets without the need for having accumulated savings or reducing current income. In the simplest terms, ordinary people can do this by bringing a financially feasible project to a local bank.

Banking Theory

In classic banking theory, a bank makes a loan on a financially feasible project by printing banknotes and securing its interest by taking a lien on the project. When the project makes a profit, the loan is repaid, and the banknotes are canceled. To eliminate usury from the system, a bank can only legitimately charge a fee for the service it provides in "monetizing" the project, making it possible to bring the project into existence.[12]

Implementing a "pure credit" arrangement at the local level, however, is not feasible under the banking laws current in most areas. Sound finance requires that a single bank only make loans to the amount of its existing reserves.[13] This would preclude the use of "pure credit," and force the banking system to rely exclusively on past savings. Even were the banking laws changed to allow local banks to create money by monetizing productive projects, the degree of risk entailed would be too high. Each bank's circulating notes, as in the old "Wildcat Bank" days before the United States National Bank Act of 1864, would be in danger and would fluctuate in value with the default of every loan used to back the currency.

Central Banking Theory

To regulate the value of the currency and provide a central authority and locus for monetizing the productive projects of a region, a central banking arrangement of some kind is necessary. A central bank, properly used, is not a money machine for government or a means of controlling the economy and oppressing the poor. It is an institution that is authorized to monetize eligible loans through the process of discounting. A central bank is designed to provide a "flexible currency" which expands and contracts in direct response to the needs of the economy. A "flexible currency" is neither inflationary nor deflationary, but stable when properly regulated. Discounting is the process whereby a local bank "sells" the loans it makes to the central bank at lower than face value in order to obtain more cash to lend or increase its reserves.[14] The central bank "buys" the loans by printing currency or, in these days, creating a demand deposit. This results in an asset-backed currency.

When the original borrower repays the loan to the local bank, the local bank "buys back" the loan paper it "sold" (*i.e.*, "discounted") to the central bank. The currency (or demand deposit) is canceled as it is no longer backed by the productive project represented by the loan paper. This prevents inflation. Because no past savings are involved, the rights of the owners of the accumulations of past savings need not be considered, and the currency can be lent to the local banks at the administrative cost of creating it. This avoids deflation — insufficient money for the needs of the economy. A commercial bank, in conjunction with the central bank, can create money at need and lend the money to a productive borrower, also at a very low rate. The rate charged includes a provision for a just profit and a risk premium to insure against default.

Capital Credit Insurance

Bankers are cautious people — or they should be. Banks traditionally "self insure" all the loans they make by including a "risk premium" in the interest rate. Presumably this allows the bank to recoup the losses they make from extending bad loans by forcing the riskier loans to pay for the privilege of being risky. In addition, because a risk premium can only cover a very small portion of an individual loan, bankers inevitably demand collateral to secure the entire loan against default. Collateral is inevitably composed of existing wealth or accumulations of savings. Thus we get the famous conundrum that only people who don't need money can borrow it. No one else has collateral.

To eliminate this universal collateralization requirement, Louis Kelso invented the ingenious refinement of "collateralizing" loans for people who lack collateral by means of capital credit insurance. This would replace the usual banker's "self insurance" of collateral, and turn the traditional "risk premium" contained in the interest rate into a real insurance premium. This seems so simple that it is a wonder no one else ever thought of it. (They did — but only for the already-wealthy.) Louis Kelso was the first to apply the concept where it was needed. He thereby provided a potential "preferential option for the poor" in the form of opening up access to the means of acquiring and possessing property for everyone, not just those who had the existing store of wealth to use as collateral. Thanks to Louis Kelso, a program of expanded capital ownership would be able to finance itself without reliance on the good will or purses of the already wealthy.

Property Removes the Yoke of Slavery

A program of expanded capital ownership, although not by that exact phrase, is, as Pius XI put it, "the expressed object" of the social encyclicals.[15] Leo XIII characterized the propertyless worker as under a "yoke" of "virtual slavery."[16] Pius XI reiterated this characterization, calling it a state of "permanent bondage."[17] His recommendation was that the propertyless worker be "redeemed" (language usually used for servile emancipation of some kind) by opening up opportunities and means for ordinary workers to acquire ownership. Both John XXIII and Paul VI repeated that economic as well as political dependency constituted slavery.[18]

Unfortunately, probably because of the usurious nature inherent in much of modern banking, Pius XI did not consider the use of a pure credit financing system for such a program. Hence, his recommendation was that workers be paid a living wage during the period of their "bondage." One important component of that wage was to be an amount sufficient to set aside a store of savings to be used to acquire productive assets.

This is a modern version of the ancient Roman practice of giving slaves and children a "peculium." As we see in the parable of the talents,[19] a *peculium* consisted of productive wealth or cash that could be invested.[20] While the master or *pater familias* retained legal title (slaves and children, not having rights, couldn't own anything), the slave or child was given full control. The idea was that the slave would prepare himself for manumission and the child for emancipation by managing property, being rewarded by freedom or full adult status if he exercised his (delegated) power responsibly: "Well done! You are an industrious and reliable servant.[21] Since you were dependable in a small matter I will put you in charge of larger affairs. Come, share your master's joy!"[22]

Breaking the Slavery of Past Savings

The problem with the *peculium* (as with modern corporate finance) is that it was based on existing wealth. A slave could use his *peculium* to purchase his freedom and repay his former master over time. Unfortunately, however, even if the slave had found someone with enough cash, he did not have the right to borrow money for the same purpose. It was illegal to lend money or enter into any kind of contract with a slave because a slave is not a "person" and thus has no social identity. There would be no way of enforcing the contract.[23]

The modern propertyless worker is effectively in the same position. Use of the Aristotelian term "wage slave" is not, as one commentator sneered, "silly Marxist rhetoric," but a simple statement of fact. It acknowledges that barriers exist against anyone without ownership of the means of production enjoying full participation in the common good. Legally, of course, he is a person, that is, he has rights. Lacking past savings, however, he has neither collateral to empower him to borrow, nor the cash to purchase an asset outright.

With pure credit, though, an alternative method of capital finance can be used. Pure credit breaks the reliance on past savings, which are, by definition, a monopoly of the currently wealthy. Use of pure credit releases an employer from the obligation to pay his workers extra so that they may save and thereby acquire "some property in land."[24] Land, in context, is an example and not a restriction of the type of asset that workers should strive to acquire.[25] The maintenance component of the living wage (an amount sufficient to provide a worker and his family with a decent standard of living if thrift and frugality are exercised), however, must still be considered a mandate until such time as the worker can be released from his servile condition through the acquisition of an adequate stake of income-generating assets.

Unfortunately, both neo-conservatives and their critics assume that wages themselves and the "freedom" to choose where (or whether) to work "redeem" the propertyless worker. The former do this by asserting that workers are already free, and they should be paid exactly what their labor is worth in an unregulated market, regardless of the amount of income they need to survive. The latter do this by assuming that the dependency of the workers is natural and necessary. Employers should pay workers what they need for a decent life without considering the need to lift them out of their servile condition. Both neo-conservatives and their critics insist that the current system is ideal in its fundamental principles. It only needs a stricter application of existing institutions to work perfectly. Both ignore the mandate to restructure society and foster, in the words of Leo XIII, "a state of society in which the great mass of people prefer to own property."[26]

Neo-conservatives commit a serious error by assuming that widespread ownership of productive assets will occur spontaneously, if only workers would exercise enough "guts and gumption." They ignore what the popes have to say about barriers that inhibit or prevent this from happening "spontaneously." Instead, they confuse and twist the words of the social encyclicals to support their own position.

Their critics, in some measure, fall into the trap of denigrating the expressed goal of the social encyclicals, or even, in extreme cases, attacking it. They convince themselves that they are supporting Catholic social teaching by contradicting the expressed intent of the popes. One critic went so far as to declare that the "some little property" referred to was both "prudential matter" and something only to generate a little pocket money. Such commentators, too, "support" the pope and defend "authentic" Catholic social teaching by confusing matters and bringing preconceptions to the table.

Conclusion

Your Excellency, we have examined the pronouncements of neo-conservatism and its critics. By and large, we have found that, while both promote a certain measure of the truth, there are serious discrepancies and omissions on both sides of the argument. This, in and of itself, argues that there must be something beyond what either side promotes, a "more excellent way" that resolves the contradictions implicit in both positions, and, at the same time, is in full conformity with universal moral principles.

Is there a positive solution to this problem? It seems so. Some of the confusion caused by imposing "partisan politics" on the social encyclicals might be cleared up if the bishops of the Church would exercise their teaching ministry. Requesting the assistance of the Holy Father in clarifying these matters would go a long way towards defusing a great deal of the acrimony and animosity which has been exhibited by both sides. This could be done by issuing an encyclical specifically on "economic justice." Such an encyclical would embody the principles of participation, distribution and harmony outlined in this book, or delineated in *Curing World Poverty: The New Role of Property*.[27]

Why target economic justice? The virtue of *social* justice has been covered in the majority of encyclicals issued since 1891, but the subset of *economic* justice has not been specifically addressed.[28] As Pius XI himself stated in *Quadragesimo Anno*, the economic subjects he treated were by way of example, not themselves an exposition of principles.[29] There appears, then, to be a need for an explicit treatment of this subject, if only to ameliorate the vituperation which has become a hallmark of discussions of Catholic social teaching, especially in the realm of economics.

The words that Pius XI applied to the work of Leo XIII apply equally to his own, as well as the work of subsequent pontiffs: ". . . certain doubts have arisen concerning either the correct meaning of some parts of Leo's Encyclical or conclusions to be deduced therefrom, which doubts in turn have even among Catholics given rise to controversies that are not always peaceful; and since, furthermore, new needs and changed conditions of our age have made necessary a more precise application of Leo's teaching or even certain additions thereto."[30]

Should, however, the bishops simply wait for papal action? By no means. While attempts have been made by various bishops' councils to issue joint pastorals on economic justice, such documents have been, by and large, tailored to the current condition of society. Even then the fit has not been very good. The approach has generally been to apply individual justice in a collective manner. In spite of the good will evident in such attempts, they were not truly directed toward social justice, as they did not take genuine social virtue into consideration.[31] Thus, the subset of economic justice, a social virtue, was, as might be expected, effectively ignored — even when the title specified economic justice as the subject.[32]

Taking the principles outlined in this book, any bishop could issue his own pastoral on economic justice. Rather than simply call for papal action and sit back, or increase the usual demands that individual virtues be applied more strenuously or effectively (an impossibility when the social order is in need of reform), any individual bishop can and should study the work done in the area of economic justice and prepare the ground in his own diocese for a universal treatment of economic justice by the Holy Father.[33]

Notes

[1] "One would think, to hear people talk, that the Rothschilds and the Rockefellers were on the side of property. But obviously they are the enemies of property; because they are enemies of their own limitations. They do not want their own land; but other people's. . . It is the negation of property that the Duke of Sutherland should have all the farms in one estate; just as it would be the negation of marriage if he had all our wives in one harem." G. K. Chesterton, "The Enemies of Property" *What's Wrong With the World. G. K. Chesterton, Collected Works, Volume IV*. San Francisco, California: Ignatius Press, 1987, 65-66.

[2] "Unlimited power is apt to corrupt the minds of those who possess it." Speech in the Case of Wilkes, January 9, 1770.

[3] Lord Acton, Letter to Bishop Mandell Creighton, 1887.

[4] Most often, this has been construed as a right to a living wage — as long as one component of that living wage is an amount sufficient to allow the worker to accumulate a store of savings if thrift and frugality are exercised. The derived right to a living wage, however, can (and should) be set aside if a better method of acquiring and possessing property becomes available. See John Ryan, *A Living Wage*. New York: Grosset and Dunlap, 1906, 67-68; also *Distributive Justice*, 1916.

[5] 204 Mich 459, 170 NW 668, 3 ALR 413, (1919).

⁶ *The Capitalist Manifesto, Op. cit.*, 157.
⁷ *Rerum Novarum, Op. cit.*, §17.
⁸ *Ibid.*, §54.
⁹ *Quadragesimo Anno, Op. cit.*, Part II, §1; See also *The Capitalist Manifesto, Op. cit.*, 210-213.
¹⁰Pius XI, *Divini Redemptoris* ("On Atheistic Communism"), 1937, § 30.
¹¹ Max Weber, *The Protestant Ethic and the Spirit of Capitalism.* London: Routledge, 1992; Fanfani, Amintore, *Catholicism, Protestantism and Capitalism.* New York: Sheed and Ward, 1955; Fanfani, Amintore, *Catechism of Catholic Social Teaching.* Translated by Reverend Henry J. Yannone. Westminster, Maryland: The Newman Press, 1960.
¹²Usury is not all interest, high interest, all profit, or high profit. Usury is the taking of profit (an ownership "interest") from something which does not generate a profit, or in which the profit taker has no ownership stake. See Benedict XIV, *Vix Pervenit* ("On Usury and Other Dishonest Profit"), 1746.
¹³The "100% Reserve Requirement," often known as the "Chicago Plan," has been advocated off and on since the 1930s in a move to halt the abuses of fractional reserve banking and provide the basis for a sounder currency. Unfortunately, the Chicago Plan was based on abolishing the independence of the Federal Reserve System, establishing a "Monetary Authority" that would make a subjective guess as to the amount of liquidity needed in the system, then authorize the federal government to issue bonds to that amount. As Henry Simons conceived it, the Chicago Plan would create a currency backed 100% by government debt, leaving the basic problem of a currency without an asset backing still in place.
¹⁴Discounting is a way for a bank to maintain the 100% reserve requirement, similar to what was proposed under the Chicago Plan. The Chicago Plan, however, relied on backing the currency 100% with government debt, while discounting qualified industrial, commercial, and agricultural loan paper without recourse to government debt, resulting in a 100% asset-backed currency.
¹⁵Pius XI, *Quadragesimo Anno* ("On the Restructuring of the Social Order"), 1931, § 59.
¹⁶ Leo XIII, *Rerum Novarum* ("On the Condition of the Workers"), 1891, § 6.
¹⁷ *Quadragesimo Anno, loc. cit.*

[18] John XXIII, *Mater et Magistra* ("Christianity and Social Progress"), 1961, § 109; Paul VI, *Populorum Progressio* ("On the Development of Peoples"), 1967, § 30.

[19] Matt., 25:14-30. (The parable with less detail is given in Luke 19:11-27 with a slightly different twist.)

[20] J. A. Crook, *Law and Life of Rome, 90 BC-AD 212*. (Ithaca, New York: Cornell University Press, 1967, 108-110.

[21] A more accurate translation of *servus* or *servitus* would be "slave"; in ancient times you didn't hire servants, you purchased them. Using "servant" tends to water down the effect of the parable.

[22] The sense is that the slave is to be manumitted, thereby sharing his master's joy by becoming his equal (or at least as equal as a freedman could be).

[23] It's actually much more complicated than that. If a slave entered into a contract, it would necessarily be on behalf of his master as a result of the master's delegation of what today would be called "power of attorney" — and the slave would have had to show pretty good proof that he really did have that power to exercise in his master's name. In the event of a breach of contract, the other party could not sue the slave, and could only proceed against the master, who was legally responsible for all acts by his slaves and children. If a slave entered into a contract without the knowledge of his master, the law would tend to take the side of the master if a lawsuit resulted (and the slave would probably be crucified). The other party would, under the doctrine of *caveat emptor* — "let the buyer beware" — be out of luck as a result of his failure to perform due diligence to ensure that the slave actually had power of attorney. The other party's only recourse in such a case would be to prove collusion between the master and the slave to defraud the other party. The slave would, in that case, be held innocent (being forced to obey his master in all things) while the master took the fall. Of course, the master could crucify the slave for failing to carry out the fraud successfully; a slave was a member of "domestic society," over which the Roman State — civil society — claimed no jurisdiction, and a *pater familias* could try and execute his slaves or children as he wished. The only check on the *potestas* (power) of the *pater familias* was the admittedly influential social pressure against a man who committed obvious injustices within the confines of his home. Augustus Cæsar was able to shame one such domestic tyrant into not executing a clumsy slave for the heinous offense of breaking a

goblet, while Petronius, the "arbiter elegantiarum" under Nero, gained widespread public approbation by condemning the execution of hundreds of slaves when one of them murdered a similar monster, declaring that crucifying anyone other than the actual murderer was in bad taste. The poet Martial ridiculed one master who proposed cutting out a slave's tongue for speaking out of turn by asking, in a pointed epigram, if he would then proceed to cut out every tongue in Rome to keep them from talking about his stupidity. As Pius XI points out, peer pressure is much stronger than mere laws in restructuring and maintaining the social order. See also A. V. Dicey, *Lectures on the Relation Between Law and Public Opinion in England During the Nineteenth Century*. New Brunswick, Connecticut: Transaction Books, 1981.

[24] *Rerum Novarum, op. cit.*, § 66.

[25] The insistence of some commentators that "land" is a restriction of the type of asset that can be acquired is, as noted previously, an example of confusing an application of a principle with the principle itself.

[26] *Ibid.*, § 65.

[27] John H. Miller, editor, *Curing World Poverty: The New Role of Property*. Saint Louis, Missouri: Social Justice Review, 1994.

[28] The misunderstanding is so great that at least one commentator confused social and economic justice. See Fr. William F. Drummond, S.J., *Social Justice*. Milwaukee, WI: The Bruce Publishing Company, 1955.

[29] *Quadragesimo Anno*, § 76.

[30] *Ibid.*, § 40.

[31] The 1919 and 1949 joint pastorals of the bishops of the United States were good efforts, but, inevitably, construed as individual in nature, not truly social justice.

[32] See *Economic Justice for All: Pastoral Letter on Catholic Social Teaching and the U.S. Economy*. Washington, DC: National Conference of Catholic Bishops, 1986.

[33] The preparation for such a pastoral would include reading these articles as an assist in diagnosing the problem of rampant confusion on the part of many, Chapter Five of Kelso and Adler's *The Capitalist Manifesto*, *Curing World Poverty: The New Role of Property*, and Ashford and Shakespeare's *Binary Economics*. All except *The Capitalist Manifesto* are currently in print, and Kelso and Adler's book is available in most libraries.

2. Universal Health Care: Justice or Charity?

(Social Justice Review, September/October 2003)

The health care crisis in the United States has reached epidemic proportions. In response, the American Bishops have asserted a right, under distributive justice, to universal health care, which many people interpret as meaning that the State has the obligation to provide health care to everyone at no cost. Particularly in view of the diminishing resources available for "free" health care, this claim must be given serious consideration.

What is a Right?

Does everyone have a right to healthcare? We can answer that question with a qualified affirmative if and only if we understand what a "right" is.

A right implies the functioning of the virtue of justice. It is the power a person has to force others to do or not do a specific act or acts in relation to the person that has the right. A right that one person has automatically means a duty to comply with that right imposed on everyone else, by force if necessary.

There are two kinds of rights. There are "natural rights," which in the western tradition are based on the general consensus of mankind as to what constitutes "the good," and empower each person to pursue the good. There are also "derived rights," that is, rights based on natural rights, but determined and defined by individual and social wants and needs.

There are two "parts" to every right. The first part of a right (which corresponds to all natural rights) is inalienable and absolute. An individual is not considered a "person" if deprived of an absolute or natural right. Since "personality" and "humanity" are inseparable in the human person, saying that an individual does not have one or all of the natural rights is the same as saying that individual is not human.

The fact that everyone has inalienable rights does not mean that anyone can simply exercise rights in that which accrues to another. For example, because I have inalienable rights to life and property does not mean that I can control your life or take your property.

There is a second aspect to a right. This corresponds to derived rights based on natural rights, but determined and defined by individual and social wants and needs. That is the strictly limited *exercise* of the right. Neither society nor other individuals can legitimately prevent anyone from exercising a right once a person has it, except through due process and for just cause. Society, however, can and must limit the exercise of rights to prevent harm to others or the common good, and to optimize the exercise of rights for everyone within a just social order.

Universal Health Care

We can apply these principles to health care. The popes have maintained that everyone has a right to adequate health care. Within the "language" of rights this can only mean one thing. That is, no one can be denied health care if it is, one, available, and, two, he can pay for it or persuade a health care provider to treat him out of charity.

For example, no one can be denied medical treatment on the grounds of race, sex, or age. He can, however, justly be denied treatment on the grounds that he cannot pay for it (although anyone refusing to administer a vaccination would be guilty of a grave sin in charity). If, however, the State has determined that there is an overriding *social* — not individual — need (for example) to have everyone inoculated against smallpox, then health care providers can be forced to distribute inoculations to everyone, against their will if necessary. Health care providers would, however, have the right to be compensated for their time and whatever else they might have expended in carrying out the State's orders, just as individuals receiving inoculations would have the right to

Universal Health Care — 95

petition for redress of grievances resulting from forced inoculations.

The same would not apply to broken bones or elective surgeries. An argument can be made that, yes, it is beneficial to society if everyone's broken bones were treated and no one was forced to go about with a disfigured face. Such instances, however, relate to each person's individual good. Broken bones, unlike smallpox, are not contagious. There is no automatic social benefit to be derived from across the board treatment of all broken bones.

Since broken bones are in the individual order, not the social order, the State's role is limited to allowing an individual to have his broken bones treated, not in providing treatment or paying for it. How an individual pays for treatment is his problem — but, if he can pay, and treatment is available, then he cannot be denied treatment, or he can demand that the State support his efforts to obtain treatment. This could include anything from mandating that a doctor treat a patient in return for a standard fee, to allowing the patient to solicit for alms to pay for treatment. The State cannot legitimately force a physician to treat someone for free, or force others to pay the physician, whether through direct confiscation or indirect taxation.

A Misapplied Exception

There is one exception to this, found in the philosophy of Saint Thomas Aquinas, but it is dangerous even to mention it. It is necessary to bring it up, however, because the American Bishops' argument is built on this exception. Unfortunately, people have an almost irresistible urge to turn an exception into a rule. The exception applies when a person or his dependents are in dire need — and dire need is defined as being in immediate and specific danger of death. Permanent — not temporary — disability may qualify, but is, for the purposes of this exception, a very gray area. In cases of dire necessity, a person may take what he needs from others without incurring moral guilt if, and only if, he has exhausted *all* other possibilities.

The first problem this exception, of course, is that forcing a physician to treat someone is virtually a guarantee of poor or inadequate treatment. No physician is going to function competently with a gun at his head. The second is that, obviously, Saint Thomas' exception is — an exception. It is not a blueprint for the ordinary running of society. It is a — barely — tolerable expedient to be employed as an emergency measure in dire circumstances. Saint Thomas only groups this exception under commutative justice (*not* distributive justice) to permit the State to, for example, use tax monies to carry out a program of universal inoculation against an epidemic or provide minimal emergency medical treatment for indigents who have exhausted all other recourse.

Justice or Charity?

Since the publication of Msgr. John Ryan's *Distributive Justice* (1916), the idea has seeped — flooded, rather — into Catholic philosophy that distribution on the basis of need is justice, not charity. The error has become so pervasive that it has even appeared — through human error — in the *Catechism of the Catholic Church*. Saint Thomas, however, makes it abundantly clear that, in agreement with Aristotle,[1] distributive justice concerns distribution according to a *pro rata* division of inputs to the social unit.[2] Distribution on the basis of need can only be grouped under justice as an expedient in Saint Thomas' exception.

Two errors are therefore made with respect to the claim that distribution on the basis of need is an example of distributive justice. First, of course, Saint Thomas clearly groups it — when it is grouped under "justice" at all — under *commutative* justice. Second, Saint Thomas' exception is, again, not a blueprint for society, but (to emphasize the point), a barely tolerable expedient to address an emergency situation. An emergency is, by its very nature, an extraordinary circumstance or event, not an ideal for the running of individual lives or society. Maintaining that an allowed expedient should be the rule in society is a serious error. It is analogous to a belief that because diseased organs may licitly be surgically removed from a human body, *all* organs must be surgically removed from all human bodies.

We can therefore say with certainty that, as the term is usually construed today and under ordinary circumstances, there is no *right* to universal health care. There is, of course, a serious *moral obligation* to see that our fellow men are taken care of in a manner befitting human dignity. That, however, is an obligation that comes under charity, not justice, and cannot and must not be enforced by the coercive power of the State (civil society). It is only enforceable by the moral authority of faith (religious society).

The Restructuring of the Social Order

What, however, are we to do when the extraordinary becomes the ordinary? That is, when social and economic conditions have reached the point where the abuse of human dignity is the norm rather than the exception, and social structures and institutions are such that few people can survive in a manner befitting ordinary human dignity except by the exercise of heroic effort?

That is the situation addressed by Pius XI in virtually every encyclical, allocution, and address during the whole of his pontificate. According to Pius XI, the social order has become flawed to a degree that renders conditions subhuman for most of humanity. The solution, however, is not socialism — "from each according to his ability, to each according to his needs" — but a restructuring of the social order in accordance with the philosophy of Saint Thomas Aquinas.[3] Socialism, in which the State attempts to equalize and guarantee results, is specifically condemned as contrary to human nature, and thus to natural law, which emanates from God's Nature.

Clearly many people today lack access to adequate or even minimal health care. The solution that Pius XI laid out is not, however, for the State to step in and mandate that everyone receive a desired level of health care. It is for ordinary people to gather together, study the situation, and then work to restructure and reform the necessary institutions of society so as to allow human institutions achieve the desired results in a manner consistent with the demands of human dignity. These are called "acts of social justice."

There is a substantial difference between what Pius XI called "social justice" and what many people today mean by the term. Pius XI envisioned a process whereby institutions could be reformed to the point where acts of individual virtue again become possible. The common misunderstanding today, however, is that social justice replaces, it does not enable, acts of individual virtue. (This is consistent with the view of many people today, that since the Second Vatican Council and, contrary to Our Savior's own words, charity replaces instead of fulfills justice.)

In short, Pius XI's goal was a state of society in which everyone, by ordinary effort and exertion, individually or in association with others, could achieve a state in life consistent with the demands of human dignity. He did not work for a condition of civil society in which every citizen was more or less (usually more) dependent on the State as the source of all bounty. This includes welfare, guaranteed incomes, minimum wage, family allowances, and any of the other useful but ultimately self-defeating expedients employed by the welfare State, presumably as a stop-gap on the way to a more rationally structured social order, as well as universal health care.

The Solution

We can therefore justify a program of universal health care, one that meets the minimal demands for survival (something along the lines of "catastrophic health insurance"), if — and only if — we take steps to reform society in accordance with the guidelines issued by Pius XI in *Quadragesimo Anno* (1931) and *Divini Redemptoris* (1937). This is in conformity with the principle of double effect. If steps are not taken to restructure the social order, or the formerly necessary expedients are allowed to continue after they become redundant, then a program of universal health care, as with any other redistribution program, becomes tyranny.

The initial step that must be taken to ensure that everyone has full access to adequate and reasonable health care is to restructure the medical establishment so as to put power back into the hands of patients and physicians. Currently too much power is vested in the hands of management, which tends by its very nature to look more toward cost efficiencies rather than effectiveness of treatment.

The best way to do this, of course, is, as Leo XIII pointed out, to make as many people as possible owners of productive assets so as to secure adequate incomes.[4] When people can pay for their own health care, the question of universal "free" health care becomes moot. This can best be done by following the guidelines published by the Center for Economic and Social Justice ("CESJ") as "The Capital Homestead Act." This is available as a free download on CESJ's website, www.cesj.org. A financially — and socially — feasible plan for universal health coverage can easily be worked into the framework provided by the Capital Homestead Act.

(As of the scheduled publication date of this collection of essays, the outline of such a plan — the "Doctors' Plan for Universal Health Care" — has been developed and is in the "working draft" stage. Consistent with the laws and characteristics of social justice, the formation of a new organization, "Doctors for Social Justice," is being studied, in part to promote the "Doctors' Plan" once it is finalized.)

Specifics

The first specific of a viable program of universal health coverage is that a minimum standard of health care would be guaranteed for all participants. Arranged in a manner similar to an insurance company, "premiums" would be paid by the participant. If a participant were unable to pay, he would first seek assistance from a private charity. If that failed, a State-issued voucher for health care in lieu of a welfare payment would be issued.

To become eligible as a registered provider, a plan would have to offer a nationally standardized and comprehensive package, such as the one provided to members of Congress and Federal employees. Among the mandatory eligibility criteria would be universal access and standardized co-payments, deductibles and office visit charges. "Universal access" would be construed to mean no exclusion of individuals based on pre-existing conditions, age, or any other reason.

In view of the foreseeable limited medical resources available, it might be necessary to limit to a minimum the amount of care available to individuals whose condition is directly traceable to their own voluntary actions. Such actions might include attempted suicide, smoking, venereal disease, or drug addiction. Additional costs of care for such individuals would be a personal expense of the patient, possibly from some form of secondary insurance, and not qualify under the guaranteed treatment for involuntary conditions.

There would be an individual rather than employer mandate for payment of premiums into the plan. Currently, it might be possible to use the Federal tax system to collect and disburse subscription fees. It would be necessary, however, to move to a more direct cost-benefit arrangement as soon as a determinant number of people in society were able to pay their own way without the necessity of redistribution. (A universal health care plan cannot work if it relies on redistribution as a permanent method of funding for other than a small number of indigents. For this reason, such a plan could only work in conjunction with a Capital Homesteading program.)

Individual choice on the part of patients would be guaranteed in order to ensure adequate and competent medical oversight ("second opinions") as well as provide a reasonable degree of competition.

Today's tax-free health plan benefits to employees now covered by employer-funded plans would be terminated. These were originally a way of circumventing the wage/price freeze in the Second World War, but are now viewed as entitlements. In exchange, therefore, employers would be allowed to increase employee W-2 compensation by the amount that they are presently providing as health plan benefits. This would preserve the deductibility of health care payments as tax deductions for the employer.

To cushion tax increases for employees now receiving health plan benefits, the Federal government could reduce or eliminate present FICA, Medicare and workmen's compensation payroll taxes imposed on employers and employees. In accordance with *Capital Homesteading for All Citizens*,[5] the recent CESJ study funded by the Donner Foundation, Social Security funding would change from the current surcharge on wage-based income and be financed by general tax revenues levied at a single rate on all income from whatever source derived.

Federally-standardized plan membership rates would be set wholly by competitive market forces among competing eligible plans, rather than through health alliances, state, federal or local government entities, or by any cartel. Because of generally lower health costs, a separate lower rate could be set for children. Individuals would still be free to provide for themselves supplementary benefits not provided by the standardized plans (as would be necessary for individuals suffering from self-induced conditions).

The State should encourage the formation of employee/consumer-owned, for-profit health maintenance corporations through ESOPs and CSOPs ("Consumer Stock Ownership Plans"). This would ensure that plan management is subordinate to and serves the patients and doctors through a democratically elected board of directors. This would help to preserve the unique patient-health professional relationship. Preferably, patients would hold the balance of power over the overall health care delivery system.

A reinsurance plan could be established to cover 80% of losses in the event that eligible plan providers go bankrupt. Eligible plan providers would pay the reinsurance premiums. Until a sufficient reinsurance pool was built up, the Federal government could act as the insurer of last resort.

This overall plan would force the government to reexamine the present tax system, which is overly complex and a major source of America's economic problems. It would also induce a reexamination of the CESJ proposal for a flat rate tax on all forms of income over a generous poverty level. Under this proposal, the rate would be set at whatever percentage of taxable incomes are necessary to pay for appropriated federal spending requirements in any year.[6]

Conclusion

This proposal will, obviously, raise a lot of hackles. Many people have become convinced that the proper ordering of society requires them to surrender their human dignity and have the State take care of them from the cradle to the grave. Many others have a vested interest in maintaining the *status quo*. The idea that ordinary people should be empowered with the means of taking control over their own lives is also repugnant to elitists of all varieties.

Opposition will also be seen among insurance companies and ancillary professions, such as lawyers, accountants and actuaries. The role of the insurance companies, however, will expand under this scenario, if not have anywhere near their current level of control and power. Members of the named professions will similarly find an expansion of their role, while experiencing a loss of power over the lives of others.

In addition to the obvious concern for raising both the quality and quantity of health care, the specifics of the new system will also have to be consistent with what CESJ calls the "four pillars of an economically just society." This is another way of saying that the way the system is run, as well as the desired results, should be consistent with the demands of human dignity. These "four pillars" are 1) a limited economic role for the State, 2) free and open markets, 3) restoration of the rights of private property, especially in corporate equity, and, above all, 4) expanded ownership of the means of production.

Obviously, this program will not result in the utopia desired by so many. We human beings can only change our behavior, not our nature. That is why socialism in any disguise cannot work. We can, however, consistent with Catholic social teaching and the guidelines given in the Gospels, restructure our institutions so as to conform more closely to the demands of the common good and the needs of our fellow man.

Notes

[1] *Nichomachean Ethics, op. cit.*, Book V, Chapter vi.

[2] IIa IIae, q. 61 a. 1.

[3] See *Studiorem Ducem* ("On St. Thomas Aquinas"), 1922.

[4] Leo XIII, *Rerum Novarum* ("On the Condition of the Workers"), 1891.

[5] Norman G. Kurland, Dawn K. Brohawn, and Michael D. Greaney, *Capital Homesteading for Every Citizen: A Just Free Market Solution for Saving Social Security.* Arlington, Virginia: Economic Justice Media, 2004. Also available on the CESJ website, www.cesj.org, as a free download.

[6] See the Dick Armey proposal for a 17% flat rate tax with child deduction of $5300, $13,100 as a personal allowance for an individual, $17,200 for a single head of household, and $26,200 for a married couple. Reference: *Wall Street Journal*, June 16, 1994, A16, "Review Merits of Flat Tax," by Rep. Dick Armey.

3. Social Justice Without Pius XI[1]: The Triumph of Relativism

(Social Justice Review, January/February 2004)

In certain circles, social justice is a little like the weather. Everyone seems to talk about it, but no one does anything about it. This is probably because most people don't know exactly what social justice is. While everyone seems to agree that, for good or for ill, social justice is significant, unless we know of what, specifically, social justice consists, we will never figure out why it is important.

This article will attempt a brief analysis of the current state of social justice. I will put particular emphasis on the role played by the American bishops and the bishops throughout the world in distorting, or, more properly, allowing the idea and meaning of social justice to be distorted. To do this, I will examine why social justice is important, of what social justice consists, and a brief *précis* of, as Father William J. Ferree, S.M., Ph.D., put it, "the mess we are in." I will continue with what I feel is the best explanation as to how we got into the mess, and, possibly, more important, *why* we got in it. I will conclude with a brief analysis of Pius XI's thought and his vision for the restructuring of the social order.

Why Social Justice Is Important

While the idea of social justice begins with Aristotle, the Philosopher's contribution was more in the nature of an error than a discovery. According to Aristotle and numbers of commentators down to the present day, the common good was a nebulous concept having more to do with the general welfare and collective wellbeing than anything specific. Being nebulous, it was, as one might expect, not directly accessible by the action or actions of any one individual. That is, regardless of intent, there was nothing definite in the common good on which to act directly, therefore, no direct act on the common good was possible — by definition.

This resulted in the situation where the individual was regarded as virtually helpless in social situations when it came to making any changes or improvements for the better. Only the individual with the greatest degree and broadest scope of virtue could hope to affect the common good at all, and that only indirectly. That meant the "philosopher king" was a necessity, for he was defined as being the individual with the greatest "rule virtue" in the State.

Despite this, the philosopher king — not to be confused with the similar concept developed by Plato — was as profoundly helpless as any other individual when addressing the problem of restructuring the common good. The common good was not considered a definite thing, and, therefore, nothing definite could be done to it or with it. The philosopher king or any other ruler was restricted to passing laws and hoping that things came out at least marginally the way intended.[2]

The individual was not regarded as being able to access the common good directly. This meant that he was fundamentally alienated from society itself. This in turn meant that every human being was not naturally a member of society, in spite of Aristotle's recognition of the fact that man was social by nature; someone had to qualify or meet some minimum requirement in order to be recognized as a member of society (the basis for "natural slavery," slaves not being recognized as persons, and thus cannot be members of society). This explained the problem of individual helplessness in the face of social problems, and reinforced the idea of mere existence as a condition of constant warfare.

What Is Social Justice?

All of the difficulty with attempting to affect the common good indirectly changed with Pius XI's development of a completed theory of social virtue. Pius XI started by accepting the fact and all the implications of man being social by nature. He followed this with the idea that society was intrinsically social. Society was not just a collection of individuals, but of individuals coming together and associating in groups. Groups are specifically social creations. This means that the common good, while broadly, if precisely, defined as the capacity to acquire and develop all virtue (that which all men have in common), also takes on concrete form as the aggregation of groups — institutions. These embody the ways, means, and formal "social transactions" developed within a society to assist the individual members of society in their task of acquiring and developing virtue.

The idea that only people who qualify to enter society can be members of society is abolished. Membership in society becomes unconditional, not restricted to those who meet criteria such as proper skin color, age, physical or mental condition, or stage of development. The common good is recognized as directly accessible by every human being, not just indirectly accessible by philosopher kings.

Pius XI introduced the idea of a class of virtue that was not directed at the good of the individual, but at the good of society as a whole. Social virtue is directed at the good of the common good, or, perhaps, more clearly, toward the health of those institutions of the common good which are designed to assist us in our task of acquiring and developing individual virtue. To repeat, this new class of virtue, let us call it "social virtue" (for that's what it is), is not directed toward assisting any individual in his acquisition and development of individual good or goods. Social virtue is, on the contrary, directed toward assisting the institutions of society in maintaining or reforming themselves so as to enable them to assist individuals in acquiring and developing individual good or goods.

To put it yet another way, social virtue is not directed at assisting individual members of society to acquire and develop virtue, but at helping institutions acquire and develop the structures that assist individual members of society in acquiring and developing virtue. Social virtue is, therefore, by definition, directed toward the *common* good, not the *in-*

dividual good of any member or members of society, regardless how numerous they might be.

That is a difficult concept to understand. People have been misunderstanding it since Pius XI first began teaching it. The result has been that, just as they have for thousands of years, people still attempt to reform the social order through the application, more or less intensive, of the individual virtues.

What Is This Mess We're In?

The individual virtues, while absolutely necessary for the individual and his spiritual and social health, are simply not adequate to the task of maintaining the social health of institutions. This is because individual virtues are specifically individual. Virtues that are specifically individual are not the proper "tool" for addressing problems that are specifically social.

There is a great deal of confusion over the meaning of social justice, some of which may have been intentionally caused. Nowhere is this more evident than when we consider the confusion over the difference between distributive justice (an individual virtue) and social justice (a social virtue).

Sometimes erroneously construed as "social justice,"[3] the classic notion of distributive justice, like commutative justice, is based on equality, but an equality of proportion. Aristotle defined distributive justice as a proportionality of value given and received rather than a strict equality or equivalence of value.[4] Where commutative justice is concerned with the relationship of "other to other," distributive justice deals with the relationship of the "social whole" to the "social parts." Distributive justice is therefore, but only in that limited sense, *a* "social justice." Distributive justice is not *the* social justice, for it has as its object the individual good of each of the members of a group. Social justice has as its special object the common good of all mankind. Equating the particular virtue of social justice with distributive justice is a logical "fallacy of equivocation," for the word "social" is used differently in describing the two types of justice.[5]

Demonstrating the extent to which "consultors" have managed to distort traditional understandings of principles and concepts, the *Catechism* defines distributive justice as that justice "which regulates what the community owes its citizens in proportion to their contributions *and needs*."[6] [Emphasis added.] The "and needs" add-on is directly contrary to the definition given in the *Summa*, which describes distributive justice as that virtue "whereby a ruler or a steward gives to each what his rank *deserves*."[7] [Emphasis added.] The popular commentary on the *Summa* by Msgr. Paul J. Glenn, *A Tour of the Summa*,[8] restates this passage in the following manner. "There is another type of justice, called distributive, which consists in the bestowal of good according to the *needs* of the receiver." [Emphasis added.] There is a significant difference, however, in what an individual *deserves* and what he *needs*. I may need many things, but I cannot justly receive them in distributive justice until I have offered something in equal or proportionate exchange.

To understand Aquinas, other than simply reading what he actually wrote as opposed to what commentators choose to revise or restate, we have to realize that, in a very real sense, the *Summa* is itself a commentary on Aristotle. Unless the Angelic Doctor makes it very explicit and offers substantially more commentary than a mere restatement of the Philosopher's definition, we must assume that Aquinas means exactly what Aristotle meant. When interpreting Aquinas, the thought of Aristotle, except when otherwise indicated, should be taken as normative. There is no such indication in this case.[9]

There is also the problem that many people confuse the special meanings of words used by Aquinas. "Ruler," "steward," "gives" and "deserves" all create problems if the casual reader or commentator with an agenda fail to link the passage above from the description of God's Nature with the fuller description and explanations in the discussion on "Justice" in the Second Part.[10]

Most immediately dangerous for our purposes is the confusion of the words used to describe "group" or "institution."

There is an automatic equation on the part of many commentators of "community" in Aquinas and Aristotle with "State." They presume not only that distributive justice covers all distributions from any kind of authority (not true, as Aquinas points out), but that the State is somehow the only legitimate form of civil or temporal authority. This idea is inevitably combined with the idea that the Aristotelian act of legal justice and the Thomist act of social justice are one and the same. The only possible outcome is an intense worship of the State as the sole agent for regulating and maintaining the common good not just of civil society, but of all the societies of man, civil, religious and domestic — the position of Thomas Hobbes in the totalitarian classic, *Leviathan*.[11]

The State does confer its benefits according to distributive justice. All distributions, however, are not, *ipso facto*, distributive justice. In the instance of a distribution based on need, the State is standing in for the failure of charity or *commutative* justice by individual citizens or for the sake of expedience and efficiency. This is allowed under the principle of double effect.

Distribution on the basis of need comes under a special form of commutative justice, since Saint Thomas considers extreme need to render what is ordinarily private property common property. This means that the individual in dire need has the right to exercise property in what ordinarily belongs to another. Since it is concerned with property and the exercise of a right, this comes under "proprietary justice." Proprietary justice is a type of commutative justice, not a distributive justice.

There is a caveat here, of course. Someone may be morally justified in taking what he needs from the superabundance of another (and Saint Thomas stresses that the one whose property is violated must have far more than he or his dependents could conceivably use) after exhausting all recourse, including begging, when he or his dependents are in dire need or danger of death. The State, however, would be equally justified in prosecuting as a criminal an individual who exercised such an exception to the moral law because of the bad example it would otherwise set for society.

When making a distribution based on need, the State is not functioning as the proper efficient cause of justice, but as an agent for the efficient cause — the individual on whom an individual in dire need is dependent. Simply inserting the State into the transaction does not, *ipso facto*, render it distributive justice. In addition, distributive justice can only be construed to cover a distribution based on need if "poverty" is understood as conferring a "status" that contributes to the community. On the contrary, poverty renders an individual the proper object of charity, not of justice.

How Did We Get Here?

At the risk of sounding unpastoral, I believe the blame for this state of affairs can be placed squarely on the shoulders of the bishops. The earlier encyclicals were largely addressed to the pope's brother bishops. It was and remains their responsibility to study, understand, and internalize the teachings in the documents in order to disseminate them to the faithful. The fault of the bishops as a whole is seen both in those who misinterpreted the documents, and in those who did no interpretation or teaching at all, letting things drop or their staffs take over their teaching function.

The popes obviously know what has been happening. The later encyclicals, particularly those of John Paul II, are increasingly addressed not exclusively to the bishops in their role as chief teachers in their dioceses, but to all the faithful, and even, on occasion, to everyone of good will. This demonstrates that the popes, unable to delegate effectively to those unwilling or unable to assume the burdens of teaching, have been forced to take over the role of direct teacher of the whole Church.

As John Paul II[12] has pointed out, we are faced with a plague of relativism. There is immense confusion between what constitutes principle and the application of principle. There is a lack of adequate response to various trends in modern society, selling out to the secular in most cases instead of resisting it or converting it. When there is a response, it is usually individualistic and therefore, by definition, inadequate to the task of overcoming a social problem.

There are many reasons for this confusion aside from the main one of widespread misunderstanding of the work of Pius XI in the social virtues, especially social justice. Primarily, it is because there has been a general severance of religion from daily life, as well as a consequent failure to have or use a consistent philosophy other than relativism or secularism in approaching the problems of daily life and applying specific principles to their solution.

This prevalence of relativism has infected the interpretation of the social encyclicals. The growth of relativism and expedience as the basic approach to social problems is matched only by the growth of its inevitable handmaiden in the social order — the rise of fascism in all its forms. This is understandable, for the oxymoronic "social justice without Pius XI" leads inevitably to fascism through its dependence on the State as the prime agent of all social change and maintenance of the common good. As a result, Pius XI's understanding of social virtue in general and social justice in particular has been excluded, either by design or lack of understanding, from the development of social thought and the design and maintenance of our social institutions for almost a century. Without Pius XI, we end up only in fascism. With Pius XI, we can attain the Reign of Christ the King. The condition of society throughout the world makes it apparent that we are rapidly approaching the point where any possible middle ground is disappearing.

One significant aspect of this whole problem is that various elements, for whatever reason, both misunderstood or twisted the teachings of Pius XI and seized on the vagueness that came after him to promote various agendas. This was based on a failure to understand and internalize the principles of social restructuring — which was in turn due to the failure of Catholic Action. What we ended up with is a "cafeteria-style" method of interpretation that led to a necessary vagueness. The accepted way to interpret the social teachings of the Church these days is to take them anyway you want, project your private interpretation back on Pius XI and Leo XIII, and dismiss the inevitable contradictions as "stray rhetorical fragments" or "prudential matter."

Why Did We Get Here?

The effort to undermine the true sense of the social teachings of the Church has a specific orientation. There has been a hijacking of the whole concept of social justice to meet various political agendas. Ultimately, these consist, at heart, at aiming at nothing less than control of the Church. The struggles detailed by Msgr. George Kelly in, among other works, *The Battle for the American Church*[13] and Dr. Ralph McInerny in *What Went Wrong With Vatican II*[14] reveal an unremitting effort directed at control of the Church. The goal is to make the Church not only in the world, but of it. This must be done, and done completely in order that the temporal order can force whatever current vision it has of reality on to the Church. Thus the Church will change from a censuring guide and go along with, or, more likely, offer enthusiastic approbation of every change in temporal society, no matter how greatly it may be at odds with reality, that is, with God's Nature.

The only quarrel I would have with either of these two commentators is that Dr. McInerny asserted as his premise that the Second Vatican Council was not the beginning of the institutionalization of dissent. On the contrary, according to Dr. McInerny, this move came somewhat later, with the promulgation of *Humanæ Vitæ*. I disagree. The Second Vatican Council was not the beginning of the institutionalization of dissent — we do agree there — but I consider its genesis as coming much earlier. The surge of dissent reached its height with the rapid growth of Modernism early in the twentieth century. This was ably halted, but not effectively reduced or countered, by Saint Pope Pius X. The cancer remained, although in remission, until the opportunity offered by the social upheaval coeval with the promulgation of *Humanæ Vitæ*.

The infection of Modernism joined in a synergistic alliance the lack of explicit support and iteration of both the specific thought and the precise language of Pius XI by subsequent popes. Added to this was the failure of the bishops throughout the world to carry out their teaching function effectively and properly. In support of this contention, I need only cite the change that slipped into the definition of "distributive justice," described above. This was outside of papal documents, true, but still embodied many people's understanding of the encyclicals.

The complete change in meaning from the classical understanding of distributive justice may have derived from Msgr. John Ryan, who, unknowingly, may have been infected with the attitudes of Modernism, though not the explicit doctrines of the movement. That attitude is the virtual mandate found in Modernism and other relativistic philosophies to interpret every dictum of the Church from a personal "situational" perspective based on the desire of the moment rather than eternal truth. This results in twisting the teachings of the Church in order to get what you want, regardless of the consequences.

The Social Vision of Pius XI

What was Pius XI talking about? His goal was nothing less than the complete reformation and restructuring of the social order so as to institute and maintain the Reign of Christ the King. That requires some explanation. The correct understanding of the Reign of Christ the King supersedes the somewhat simplistic ideas that have been forced onto the general understanding of the concept.

The Reign of Christ the King is the establishment of a specific state of society. Society is run in accordance with universal moral principles, as interpreted and defined — but not enforced — by the Church through the Magisterium, the bishops in communion with the pope, and the pope in his office as universal and infallible teacher in matters of faith and morals. The Reign of Christ the King is primarily civil, but includes domestic and religious society insofar as they impinge on the civil order. Attaining and maintaining the Reign of Christ the King is the goal and aim of Catholic Action, the organization and movement adapted by Pius XI to carry out his vision.

We need to realize that an interpreter and guide is not a ruler. A "Christian society" in the sense implied by "The Reign of Christ the King" does not mean control of the civil order or direct rule by the Church.[15] Nor does it mean that everyone or even a determinant number of the people must be Catholic or even Christian, however else that might be desirable for their personal salvation.

No, having the Church as guide for civil society and interpreter of the universal moral values that must underpin the social order means that there must be a single authoritative source for such interpretation and guidance. The Church, by divine ordinance, was prepared and instituted for that role in the world. This role of the Church does not mean that interpretation of natural law from a source other than the Church must therefore, *ipso facto*, be wrong or in error, as the recent document from the Congregation for the Doctrine of the Faith made clear. No one has a monopoly on the truth. As Pius XI pointed out, in the Church is found the fullness of truth in totality, not exclusively.[16]

> She has never maintained that outside her fold and apart from her teaching, man cannot arrive at any moral truth; she has on the contrary more than once condemned this opinion because it has appeared under more forms than one. She does however say, has said, and will ever say, that because of her institution by Jesus Christ, because of the Holy Ghost sent her in His name by the Father, she alone possesses what she has had immediately from God and can never lose, the whole of moral truth, *omnem veritatem*, in which all individual moral truths are included, as well those which man may learn by the help of reason, as those which form part of revelation or which may be deduced from it.[17]

Conceivably, although I think it highly unlikely, it would be possible in this sense to have a "Christian" society without any Christians. This would be possible only in the sense that a society was founded on universal moral principles as interpreted or would be interpreted by the Church. Society would be guided in such a way that the application of the principles in no wise departed from the application that would have been recommended had the direct guidance of the Church been known or sought.

Conclusion

That is the whole idea of social justice and the role it is to fill in reforming and restructuring the social order. The problem with much of what passes for "social justice" these days is clearly at variance with the intentions, both expressed and implied, of Pius XI when he made his fundamental and profound breakthrough in moral philosophy. Grasping the real idea of what Pius XI meant takes some work, however. Perhaps we should not be too surprised that man's inherent laziness, an inevitable consequence of his fallen state, kicks in and we go with what seems most comfortable for us, relatively speaking. What we end up with is social justice without Pius XI.

Notes

[1] The title of this article and the subject matter were suggested by Fr. William Ferree, S.M., Ph.D., in his unpublished manuscript, *Forty Years After . . . A Second Call to Battle* (c. 1984). The analysis which follows is based on his analysis of the social teachings of Pius XI as found in his book *The Act of Social Justice* (1942).

[2] Some commentators have seen the act of social justice in Adam Smith's "invisible hand." On the contrary, Dr. Smith in his *Theory of Moral Sentiments* (1759) and *The Wealth of Nations* (1776) outlined a theory of legal justice that removed even the good intention previous philosophers thought was necessary to effect an improvement in the common good. The invisible hand argument was a brilliant clarification of the act of legal justice, but was, in a sense, a step backwards from the whole idea of social justice.

³See John H. Ryan, *Distributive Justice*. New York: Macmillan, 1916.

⁴See *Politics* Book III, Chapter ix, §1280a21; *Nichomachean Ethics,* V.vi.

⁵Distributive justice is social in the same sense that all of the classic virtues are "social." All virtues, individual and social, require some form of an "other" toward whom the virtue can be exercised. Aristotle called this "general justice," which pervades all virtues. Virtue — the "habit of doing good" — can normally only be acquired and developed in a social context, for that is the context within which we as human beings form habits. The social virtues, on the other hand, are defined by the fact that they are directed at the common good — specifically at society. The word "social" when describing the specifically social virtues takes on a different meaning than when it is used to describe all virtues.

⁶*Catechism of the Catholic Church.* Libreria Editrice Vaticana, 1994, § 2411. The statement, taken by itself and as it stands, appears to contain the logical fallacy of "illicit contrary." It presents mutually exclusive alternatives (distribution on the basis of input and distribution on the basis of need) as being the definition of distributive justice. Both cannot be true, for that contradicts human reason. The definition violates the basic precept of Aristotelian logic that a thing cannot both "be" and "not be" at the same time. That is, distributive justice is either distribution on the basis of input ("contribution") *or* distribution on the basis of need. It cannot be both. Relying on this definition of distributive justice and asserting that distributive justice therefore covers all distributions by the State based on the need of the recipient commits an "illicit subalternation." We know from the classical definition of distributive justice as well as that found in the *Summa* (distribution to each according to his due based on his "status" within the "community"), that distributive justice does not and cannot consider the needs of the recipient, only his contribution to the social whole. The only way to make it otherwise is by redefining "need" as "due." This is another fallacy of equivocation, asserting that different words for different things actually mean the same thing.

⁷ Ia q. 21 a. 2.

⁸ Msgr. Paul J. Glenn, *A Tour of the Summa*. Rockford, Illinois: Tan Books and Publishers, Inc., 1978, 24.

⁹ These indications are relatively easy to spot. Whenever Aquinas covers a subject in far more depth than Aristotle, or uses phrases

that in effect say "what Aristotle *really* meant was. . . ," then Saint Thomas is, almost without exception, either amending or correcting Aristotle's thought or adding to it.

[10] IIa IIae q. 61.

[11] Hobbes explains in chapter 22 of his book that all organizations (which he calls "corporations," or organized bodies with a social existence) intermediate between the individual and the State must either operate with the express permission or at the order of the State, or be illegal.

[12] And now Benedict XVI.

[13] Msgr. George Kelly, *The Battle for the American Church*. San Francisco, California: Igatius Press, 1995.

[14] Ralph McInerny, *What Went Wrong With Vatican II*. Manchester, New Hampshire: Sophia Institute Press, 1998.

[15] This appears to be the orientation of many commentators on the encyclicals of Pius XI, particularly Rev. Denis Fahey, as detailed in such works as *The Kingship of Christ According to the Principles of St. Thomas Aquinas*. Palmdale, California: Christian Book Club of America, 1990, and *The Mystical Body of Christ in the Modern World*. Dublin: Regina Publications, 1987.

[16] Pius XI, *Rappresentanti in Terra* ("On Christian Education"), § 20.

[17] *Ibid.*

4. Heinrich Pesch on Property: Solidarism and the Just Third Way

(Social Justice Review March/April 2004 to May/June 2004)

Part I

The Crisis

Argument
> Father Heinrich Pesch's "three pillars of economic society" with their emphasis on the importance of private property are in substance identical to the "four pillars of an economically just society" developed by the Center for Economic and Social Justice ("CESJ"). This effective identity is demonstrated by an almost perfect congruence of means, goals, and justifications.

The interpretation and implementation of Catholic social teaching has reached a crisis. There is a profound conflict between two viewpoints. Historically and philosophically this conflict has surfaced as the Sophists versus Aristotle, the Manichees versus Saint Thomas Aquinas, the Divine Right Monarchists versus Saint Robert Cardinal Bellarmine, and the Modernists versus Saint Pope Pius X. It is, however, a constant struggle throughout all of history and in all human societies. Politically we see it as the conflict between totalitarianism and democracy, economically as between capitalism and socialism on the one hand and a just economic order on the other. The most essential point in every one of these seemingly unrelated conflicts is the nature of the human person — as the Psalmist says, "what is man, that Thou art mindful of him?"

This conflict has surfaced in the present day as two approaches to interpreting the social teachings of the Catholic Church. The first viewpoint, and seemingly the most popular, is that the social teachings of the Church mandate that the social order is to be restructured through the implementation of the living wage and other redistributive measures determined by the need of the recipient. This is combined, of necessity, with an extensive degree of State control over individuals and groups, and State control or outright ownership of the means of production.

This position supports its arguments by citing Scripture, the Church Fathers, philosophers, and papal teachings. Among the authorities cited are Saint Thomas Aquinas, Leo XIII, Pius XI, Pius XII, John Paul II, and, in particular, a neglected late nineteenth and early twentieth century scholar, Father Heinrich Pesch, S.J., Ph.D., the founder of solidarism. Father Pesch is considered by many authorities to have made the most original contribution to Central European Catholic thought before 1918.

The second viewpoint is that the social teachings of the Church mandate a restructuring of the social order so as to provide equal access to the common good and equal opportunity for all. The chief vehicle for this program is widespread ownership of the means of production by as many people as possible, individually or in association with others. Private property is recognized as a natural, primary right — a fundamental human right — with the living wage subsidiary to the right to acquire and possess property. The role of the State is to lift exclusionary barriers and ensure, as far as possible, that everyone has equal opportunity to engage in the political and economic processes.

Proponents of the second viewpoint also support their position with cites from Scripture, the Church Fathers, philosophers and papal teachings. The primary authorities cited are identical with those of the former position, with the exception of Father Heinrich Pesch and the addition of Aristotle and another neglected mid- to late-twentieth century scholar, Father William J. Ferree, S.M., Ph.D. Father Ferree is the founder of the school of thought that discerns social virtue as distinct and particular from, yet complementary to, individual virtue in the teachings of Pius XI.

Father Ferree is also a co-founder of the interfaith Center for Economic and Social Justice ("CESJ"). CESJ is an organization dedicated to examining and developing programs to implement the social and philosophical ideas of Pius XI and the economic and philosophical ideas of Dr. Louis O. Kelso and Dr. Mortimer J. Adler. CESJ claims that the two systems are both compatible and congruent to one another.

"The Beginning of the Quarrel"

Protests against CESJ's programs and proposals, whether from capitalists or socialists, seem to stem from a view of the human person and society at odds with that embodied in the Judeo-Christian tradition and in natural law. From the capitalists we have the belief that most people are incapable of owning and managing property. Thus, most people are not truly human in that they allegedly lack this necessary and inherent part of human nature, vested in the human person by God both as a species and individually, as recorded in Genesis 1:28.[1]

From the socialists we have the dogma that property is not a natural right — which means, ultimately, that man is not a human person. Since property is not a natural right, the socialists assert, no one should own. The State should own or control the means of production for the greater good. Humanity will thereby be "improved" and essential (substantial) human nature changed. Ownership of property is only prudential, not a necessary part of natural law.

This is simply a restatement of the positivist claims that resulted in the excommunication of Michael of Cessena, the Franciscan Minister General and his supporters, especially William of Ockham, in 1329.[2] Legal scholar Dr. Heinrich Rommen believed this positivist approach to natural law developed out of the reinterpretation of the basis of natural law by the followers of Duns Scotus in the previous generation.[3]

Catholic Socialism and Natural Law

"Within" Catholic social teaching (the word "within" must be used guardedly, for no one but the adherents of Catholic socialism claim that socialism is or can be Catholic) this view is most pronounced in the school of thought founded by Anton Orel. "Capitalism and communism are the individualistic and pseudosocialistic manifestations of the materialistic-mammonistic culture spirit as it manifests itself in society and economy, and are therefore incompatible with Christianity."[4]

Orel believed that only human labor, not land, capital, or anything else was responsible for production. Only labor could generate income. People could possess property, but this possession was not accompanied by actual title. Only use justified possession. Orel also rejected the concept of the living wage — wages themselves were somehow construed as robbing the worker of his production. Orel claimed that Marxism was not wrong — just the parts with which he disagreed. The labor theory of value, he declared, was true Catholic doctrine, "though not in its Marxist formulation."[5]

Orel's position was much more radical than that of *Das Katholisch-Soziale Manifest*, "The Catholic-Social Manifesto," a compendium published in 1932.[6] Contributors to the *Manifesto* were attempting to reconcile socialism with the recently published *Quadragesimo Anno*. They condemned capitalism on the grounds that, "it divided people into antagonistic classes based on wealth, that it led to the production of goods which lacked cultural value because the producers were interested only in profit, and that the workers who produced all the wealth did not receive proper compensation for their efforts."[7]

> The reform of society according to the *Manifest* would have to be based on corporative principles [*i.e.*, Fascism]. The corporate order which would result from this reform would be not only a socioeconomic system, but a moral-religious one as well. The material basis of that corporative order would be the principle of *Lehen*; that is to say, all property is created by God, man can have it for use only and must render services to God and the community for this privilege. In this way property would serve its proper dual purpose: sociocultural as well as individual ends. Nevertheless, the authors of the Manifest conceded that individuals could have title to

property, provided proper safeguards were established.
Based on property and organized on the principle of *Lehen*, economic activity would be governed by the principles of *Stand* and *Beruf*. *Stand*, in brief, was to be the community of those pursuing a common *Beruf* (vocation). By pursuing a *Beruf* under the control of a *Stand*, the individual would be assured a *standesgemässer Unterhalt* (in effect, a "family wage"). It would enable him to care for himself and those entrusted to his care, as well as pursue his cultural goals, namely, family maintenance, education, security for old age, and others.[8]

The position of these and other Catholic socialists was that private property was a prudential matter, an expedient determined by social and individual conditions. Catholic social teaching as understood and reinforced by CESJ, however, considers private property one of the most fundamental of rights under natural law.[9] This means that every human being absolutely has the right to acquire and possess property simply because he is human.

Topsy-Turvy Modernism

Asserting that the natural law right of private property is "merely prudential" and that Catholic social teaching "mandates" the man-made institution of the living wage turns the natural order upside-down. Private property is part of natural law, and therefore superior to any and all human positive law.[10] Human law must regulate the exercise of property, but it may never regulate it in such a way that it becomes a nullity. That would be to commit the wrong against which Pius XII warned in his 1942 Christmas message:

> When God blessed our first parents He said to them: "Increase and multiply and fill the earth and subdue it." And to the first father of a human family He said later: "In the sweat of thy brow thou shalt eat bread."

> Therefore the dignity of the human person normally demands the right to the use of earthly goods as the natural foundation for a livelihood; and to that right corresponds the fundamental obligation to grant private property, as far as possible, to all. The positive laws regulating private property may change and may grant a more or less restricted use of it; but if such legal provisions are to contribute to the peaceful state of the community, they must save the worker, who is or will be the father of a family, from being condemned to an economic dependence or slavery irreconcilable with his rights as a person.[11]

The limited evil of infringement on the right to and rights of property, whether of a single individual or a society as a whole, can *only* be tolerated under the "principle of double effect." This requires understanding the principle of double effect in light of the act of social justice as defined by Pius XI and systematized by Father William Ferree.

First, the principle of double effect involves performing an act that is not objectively evil in and of itself, but has evil results. Second, there must be an objectively good result intended. Third, the evil that results must be unintended — that is, you must not perform the act in order to gain the evil result. Fourth, the anticipated good outweighs the expected evil.

The Living Wage v. Property

Consider again the case of something such as family allowances or the living wage. First, paying a "living wage" or giving a family allowance on the basis of a family's needs are not objectively evil acts. They do, however, have evil results.[12] Primary among these evil results is that wages as the sole source of income or family allowances impose a condition of dependency on the part of the recipients.[13] A condition of dependency ("a yoke little better than that of slavery itself."[14]) is inconsistent with the demands of human dignity.

Second, the intent is to keep people alive and living under conditions that do not *otherwise* violate human dignity. This is the expected good. Third, the evil of imposing dependency is not ordinarily the intent in a situation in which a living wage is paid or family allowances distributed. The intent is to keep people alive in a manner otherwise consistent with the demands of human dignity. The living wage or family allowances must never be used as means of maintaining people in a condition of dependency.

Finally, the anticipated good outweighs the expected but unintended evil. Being a live "semi-slave" and dependent on another is usually better than being a proud, but dead, "independent other." In any event, the mechanism of the living wage in the encyclicals is clearly not framed as a solution to the terrible conditions afflicting the propertyless worker and his family.

> The encyclical [*i.e.*, *Quadragesimo Anno*] is severe in condemning the present condition of the propertyless wage earners. It surely calls for a change in this regard and sets forth the ideal that all workingmen should become property owners. This means more than the minimum living family wage as a recompense for their work.[15]

Private property is the chief support within civil society for human dignity.[16] Father Heinrich Pesch described private property as one of the "three institutional 'pillars' of economic society."[17] The others are "marriage and the family" and "the State as guardian of the positive legal order required by the value and rights of man."[18] The insistence of the Austrian and German Catholic socialists that property was merely prudential was not only a restatement of their traditional dogma that private property should be abolished, but, in part, a direct reaction to Father Pesch's adamantine stance on the sacredness of private property.

Because man was the center of the social system, he also was at the center of economic activity. Therefore, Pesch accepted the principle of wage labor and of the separation of labor and capital. (1, 17 – 18) He demanded, however, that the community, acting through the State, interfere to prevent capitalist excesses which might threaten the economic status of individuals, and especially their private property which they must have to be able to fulfill their function in society. (1, 188, 206 – 207)[19] [References in parentheses throughout this article are to Father Pesch's *Lehrbuch der Nationalökonomie*.]

Free and Open Markets

CESJ's "Just Third Way"[20] is based on what it calls the four pillars of an economically just society. The first of these is free and open markets for determining "just wages," "just prices" and "just profits." This does not mean markets in which "anything goes," but markets to which everyone has free and open access.[21] Market behavior is regulated by adherence to moral norms and by State policing of abuses.

This agrees with Father Pesch's approach, as explained by Father Richard E. Mulcahy, S.J., "Pesch is not opposed to competition in itself; in fact, he wishes to preserve it. In unhesitating terms he explicitly acknowledges the benefits due to competition: 'We owe to free competitive enterprise the great benefits of the last century in the field of knowledge and "know-how"; in it dwells a never-failing, animated, creative force; it is able to harness forces for the highest production, always creating new goods for the welfare of the people.' (4, 220 – 21)"[22]

Limited Economic Role for the State

The second of the four pillars of an economically just society is a limited economic role for the State. Here, too, CESJ finds itself in agreement with Father Pesch — in theory, at least — and Father Pesch's *Lehrbuch* was, by his own admission, not to be construed as a handbook for economic practice, but as a work of theory.[23]

The attainment of their private material welfare by individuals and private social units, such as families, is a matter of double causation. It must be the *immediate product* of their own self-responsible efforts and initiative. And it is, secondly, the *mediate product* of the public material welfare.

Thus, individuals and non-public social groups have the *direct responsibility* for realizing their private material welfare. (2, 289 and 316; 3, 826) To allow for self-responsibility, social economy must be organized on a basis of private enterprise and considerable freedom to compete in productive activity and in the determination of one's consumption pattern. (2, 316; 5, 123)"[24] [Emphasis in original.]

That is, the normal way of doing things is for people to secure their "private material welfare" by their own efforts. The State or other social body, "public material welfare," is permitted to offer assistance to "individuals and non-public social groups" under the principle of double effect ("a matter of double causation"). "The goal of social economy does not involve a full provision for all the wants of all the citizens. To assign such a goal to the economic system would be to demand, in effect, the very disappearance of the 'problem of economy' itself."[25]

As we have seen, the principle of double effect allows an unintended evil, in this case, the imposition of dependency status on "individuals and private social units" and a measure of degradation of human dignity, as an expedient in order to meet material needs. Thus, such mechanisms as the living wage, family allowances, health benefits, and so on, may be necessary to maintain people in a manner otherwise consistent with the demands of human dignity, but they have the unintended evil effect of undermining that same human dignity. A living wage system is still a wage system, and takes for granted the dependent status of the worker and his family.

The unintended evil is only allowed as long as the intended good outweighs it. Keeping people alive and well is more important than *how* they are kept alive and well — as long as it is not done by objectively evil means. The State cannot, for example, tax the rich to the point where the rich become poor themselves and eligible for State or private assistance,[26] or burden an employer with paying a living wage when it would drive him into bankruptcy.[27]

When the Exception Becomes the Norm

Further, any action allowed under the principle of double effect is permitted only as long as there is no other way to achieve the necessary and desired end. The State may not, for example, continue social welfare programs when there is other recourse for people to meet their "material welfare," such as widespread ownership of the means of production and access to the means of acquiring and possessing property.

Social welfare programs ("public material welfare") become morally reprehensible when the unintended evil becomes intended. That is, the intent is to keep people economically dependent on the State or their wealthy private employers. As Father Pesch states, the "social economy must be organized on a basis of private enterprise and considerable freedom to compete in productive activity and in the determination of one's consumption pattern," in order "to allow for self-responsibility."[28]

Father Pesch's idea is that the State's "mediate product" of enabling citizens to secure their own welfare is subordinate to the "immediate product" of it being the primary duty of the citizens themselves to secure that welfare. This fits in with CESJ's "limited economic role for the State."

This idea of Father Pesch's also reinforces CESJ's concept of "free and open markets," for, if markets do not offer free access to all participants, the ordinary citizen can hardly be held responsible for securing his own welfare through his own efforts. No one, after all, is obligated to do the impossible. CESJ would only add that, by means of the act of social justice as defined by Pius XI and systematized by Father William J. Ferree, S.M., Ph.D., one of CESJ's co-founders, continuing efforts must be made to organize society along the lines Father Pesch recommends.

The Role of the State Under Socialism

Father Pesch was, in part, reacting to the Germanic tendency to give too great a role to the State. This tendency was most marked in Catholics, of course, among the socialists, whom Father Pesch singled out as a special focus of instruction. Certain of his modern day disciples would disagree, particularly those who are socialists, but as Father Pesch remarked, "Socialism as a 'scientific' system is dead, but the socialists are still with us."[29] In this, however, he came up against what seemed to be an almost inherent idiosyncrasy of the German character.

> Austrian Catholics failed to devise political and social institutions which correctly expressed their basic propositions. Instead of providing for the undisturbed development of a multitude of social organs and for a reasonably clear distinction between State and society, Austrian Catholics continuously exalted the position of the State at the expense of all other social organs. This can be traced primarily to their concept of State and law as instruments for the enforcement of moral and ethical standards. A State which claims the right to enforce such standards inevitably will seriously weaken, if not destroy, the area of society, the area of voluntary action. Austrian Catholics might have recognized theoretically the right of a variety of social organs to apply these moral and ethical standards, derived from theology and natural law, but a long *étatiste* tradition predisposed them to appeal to the State and to use the State for enforcement of such standards.[30]

We can therefore conclude that a living wage system is a short-term expedient, permitted under the principle of double effect to address an emergency situation. It is not a long-term solution to the economic or social ills of society. The natural way for man to support himself and his dependents is the ancient and sacred institution of private property. In this the views of Father Heinrich Pesch and CESJ appear to be perfectly consistent with each other.

Notes

[1] Pius XI, *Quadragesimo Anno*, ("On the Restructuring of the Social Order"), 1931, § 45.

[2] John XXII, *Quia Vir Reprobus* ("That Evil Man"), 1329.

[3] Heinrich Rommen, *The Natural Law*. Indianapolis, Indiana: Liberty Fund, Inc., 1998, 30-61.

[4] Anton Orel, *Das Verfassungsmachwerk der "Republik Österreich" von der Warte der immerwährenden Philosophie aus und im Lichte von der Idee, Natur und Geschichte Österreichs geprüft un verworfen*. Vienna: Vogelsan Verlg Gmbh, 1921, 5.

[5] Anton Orel, *Kirche-Kapitalismus-Proletariat*. Vienna: Vogelsang-Verlag, Gmbh, 1928, 52-53.

[6] Studienrunde katholischer Soziologen, *Katholisch-soziales Manifest*. Mainz: Mathias Grünewald, 1932.

[7] Alfred Diamant, *Austrian Catholics and the Social Question, 1918 – 1933*. Gainesville, Florida: University of Florida Press, 1959, 68. Note that Diamant's analysis of "the social question" is colored by the fact that he apparently excludes the possibility of any system outside of the two alternatives of socialism and capitalism. Because of Father Pesch's emphasis on the importance of private property, Diamant therefore categorizes Father Pesch as a capitalist, and solidarism as a form of capitalism.

[8] *Ibid.*

[9] Fr. Thomas J. Higgins, S.J., *Man as Man, the Science and Art of Ethics*. Rockford, Illinois: TAN Books and Publishers, Inc., 1992, §§ 494-573.

[10] "Human reason is not, of itself, the rule of things: but the principles impressed on it by nature, are general rules and measures of all things relating to human conduct, whereof the natural reason is the rule and measure, although it is not the measure of things that are from nature." Ia IIae q. 91 a. 3 2m.

[11] Pius XII, *Christmas Broadcast* ("The Rights of Man"), 1942, § II.

[12] See Aristotle, *The Politics*, VI.v; Muhammad Ibn Khaldûn, *Mukaddimah*, translated by Franz Rosenthal, Vol. II, 1967, 103-109; Alexis de Tocqueville, *Memoir on Pauperism*. Chicago, Illinois: Ivan R. Dee, Publisher, 1968; William T. Thornton, *A Plea for Peasant Proprietors*. London: John Murray, Albemarle Street, 1848; Henry Fawcett, *Pauperism: Its Causes and Remedies*. London: Macmillan and Co., 1871.

[13] Michael D. Greaney, "The Living Wage (and Child Care)" *Social Justice Review*, September/October 1998.

[14] Leo XIII, *Rerum Novarum*, ("On the Condition of the Working Classes"), 1891, § 3.

[15] Dom Virgil Michel, O.S.B., Ph.D., *Christian Social Reconstruction, Some Fundamentals of the Quadragesimo Anno, Second Printing*. Milwaukee, Wisconsin: The Bruce Publishing Company, 1936, 39.

[16] Dr. Raphael Waters, Ph.D., "Freedom in the Political Order" *Social Justice Review*. November/December 2002, 165.

[17] Gustav Gundlach, S.J., "Solidarist Economics, Philosophy and Socio-economic Theory in Pesch" *Social Order*, April 1951, 185.

[18] *Ibid.*

[19] Diamant, *op. cit.*, 21.

[20] The earliest use of the term "third way" I have been able to find is in the April 1951 issue of *Social Order*. "Both Professor Briefs and Father Gundlach review the controversies in progress during these years and both show the 'third way' which Pesch developed mid-way between the opposing extremes." Richard E. Mulcahy, S.J., "Heinrich Pesch, S.J., 1854-1926" *Social Order*, April 1951, 146.

[21] Michael D. Greaney, *Social Justice Betrayed, the Misinterpretation of Catholic Social Teaching*. St. Louis, Missouri: Catholic Central Union of America, 2001, 14.

[22] Richard E. Mulcahy, S.J., "Economic Freedom in Pesch" *Social Order*, April 1951, 163. "Pesch" references in parentheses throughout this article are to Father Pesch's *Lehrbuch der Nationalöconomie*. Freiburg i. Br., Herder, 1924.

[23] Jacques Yenni, S.J., "Pesch's Goal of the Economy" *Social Order*, April 1951, 175.

[24] *Ibid.*, 172.

[25] *Ibid.*, 170.

[26] *Rerum Novarum, op. cit.*, § 67.

[27] *Quadragesimo Anno, op. cit.*, § 72.
[28] See also Rev. John Francis Murphy, S.T.L., *The Moral Obligation of the Individual to Participate in Catholic Action.* Washington, DC: The Catholic University of America Press, 1958.
[29] *Lehrbuch*, 1, 380.
[30] Diamant, *op. cit.*, 13-14.

Part II
The Solution

In the first half of this article, we saw that the urge to impose a living wage system as the solution to social and economic ills is a short-term expedient, permitted under the principle of double effect. The natural way for man to support himself and his dependents is the ancient and sacred institution of private property. We also saw that the views of Father Heinrich Pesch and CESJ appear to be perfectly congruent.

This is especially true as regards Father Pesch's "three pillars of economic society" — marriage and family, limited State interference, and private property. The first two of CESJ's "four pillars of an economically just society" (free and open markets, limited economic role for the State, restoration of the rights of private property, and expanded capital ownership) were examined in the first half of this article. Differences appeared to be largely semantic, with the exception of Father Pesch's completely understandable failure to discern the act of social justice as promulgated by Pius XI.[1] We can now move on to the remaining two pillars that CESJ posits as the foundation of an economically just society.

Restoration of Private Property

CESJ's third pillar, restoration of the rights of private property, particularly in corporate equity, also has a counterpart in Father Pesch's economic theories. There is, of course, the idea that private property is essential to the maintenance of "marriage and family" found in Father Pesch's own "three pillars" (above). When we realize that "property" is not the thing, but the rights to and over the thing, Father Pesch could not have been talking about anything other than the restoration of the rights of property — property consists of rights. Further, property rights are human rights — a "thing" cannot have rights, only persons.

Father Pesch is, however a little unclear when it comes to distinguishing the right *to* property from the rights *of* property. Property, again, is not the thing itself, but the rights an owner or potential owner has to own something, and what he may do with the thing once he owns it, including the right of control and the disposal of the income, the "fruits of ownership." Property is important in sum because, as Daniel Webster observed, "power naturally and necessarily follows property."[2]

The exercise of property, however, especially as it occurs within a social context, and including the amount of material possessions a man may legitimately accumulate, is limited; it is not absolute. Exercise of property is governed by a person's own needs and the demands of the common good.

> Private property was instituted that the goods of this earth may attain the purpose for which they were created, *i.e.*, of serving the needs of man, of all men, and giving them the opportunity to live as free and self-dependent persons. Accordingly all men have the strict right by natural law to as much of these goods as they need for attaining the purpose of their creation by God. And this in turn means a strict right to some degree of private ownership, which right no one can lawfully take away from any man against his will.[3]

No one may exercise property in such a way as to harm others or the common good, nor may anyone accumulate so much that it prevents others from exercising their rights to acquire, possess, or exercise property. We find these ideas in Father Pesch's thought as well, but it takes a little digging — and his lack of clarity leaves room for interpretations by others at variance with natural law, despite Father Pesch's firm adherence.

> An example of the application of these general principles of social organization may be seen in the

question of private property. Like individualism, solidarism recognizes the right of private ownership of property. But it is opposed to an absolute, irresponsible concept of private ownership, just as it rejects the socialistic concept of the State ownership of all the means of production or the communistic State ownership of all property. Solidarism clarifies the limits of private ownership by introducing the requirements of social duty. The central notion of property is that "the goods of the earth should serve all mankind." (2, 243) And it is recognized that this goal is best attained through private ownership, subordinate to higher rights.

Thus solidarism holds: 1. Property signifies power, but limited power, subordinate to the moral and legal order. 2. Property is a right, but not the highest right that would place the material world above the world of men. 3. Property is not an end in itself, but a means to an end — namely, the ordered providing for the needs of all men living in society. (2, 242 – 43) The social duty referred to embraces more than charity, which provides for the individual needs of the poor, or the obligation to pay taxes. It also implies the duty to use one's property for the furthering of the common welfare.[4]

There are just (barely) enough technical inaccuracies and sufficient vagueness in Father Pesch's concept of private property and the role it plays to make it relatively easy for someone to put some wonderfully heterodox interpretations on his ideas. It is, of course, also possible to interpret his words in perfectly orthodox fashion — but what fun is that? The vagueness, however, makes it easier for a less than orthodox commentator to read socialism or capitalism into them, and insert an unwarranted collectivism or individualism, depending on the commentator's orientation.

Expanded Capital Ownership

The final and fourth pillar in CESJ's set of guidelines for an economically just society is expanded ownership of the means of production. Unfortunately, the necessity of expanded ownership of the means of production in those precise words is only implicit in Father Pesch's thought — at least that available to an English-speaking audience. Instead, Father Pesch simply reiterates that it is important for as many people as possible to own property. This provides an unintentional circumlocution for those who insist Father Pesch, like Marx, meant only consumer goods[5] or, as other commentators on the social encyclicals insist, agricultural land,[6] or only sufficient property to generate a little extra pocket money.[7]

By taking into account Father Pesch's support of the free market and the importance of private property for the support of marriage and the family, we can, however, conclude that Father Pesch probably would have agreed with CESJ's fourth pillar. He may not, though, have agreed with the necessity of stating something so obvious, particularly since Leo XIII had already explicitly said as much.[8]

Father Pesch insisted that "capitalism" was not the same as the free enterprise system or even use of capital. As Chesterton agreed, "If the use of capital is capitalism, then everything is capitalism."[9] As one authority on Father Pesch's work put it, "Needless to say, Father Pesch rejected the socialist identification of capitalism with the institution of private property and with free enterprise. But he also objected to the notion that the essence of capitalism consists merely in the extensive use of capital goods (produced means of production). 'Capitalism,' he said, 'is control of the national economy through the unrestrained and uninhibited acquisitiveness of the owners of capital'."[10]

Father Pesch's views on property are fully consistent with CESJ's "Principle of Harmony."[11] The principle of harmony relates to the optimal amount of productive assets any individual should accumulate for the good of the social order without penalty or the imposition of barriers to further accumulation.[12]

> The goal of the economy according to the thought of Pesch is not simply "any kind" of provision for the satisfaction of the want-system of the community. Implicit in the goal as Pesch describes it is the demand that the legal and institutional context of the socio-economic process be such as to offer to individuals the possibility of attaining the maximum in economic benefits reasonably to be expected from the existing level of economic development. (4, 130 –31)
>
> The "economic optimum" here involved is, of course, one that is conciliable with a full safeguarding of higher moral and spiritual values. It is not the maximized "optimum" of a purely utilitarian calculus. And it is an "optimum" that is relative, obviously, to the capacities of technical knowledge and productive organization, to the existing funds of natural and human resources, of capital accumulation, *etc.*[13]

Interpreting the Social Encyclicals

There are thus three different approaches to interpreting the social encyclicals. These are based on a distortion of property, the abolition of property, or the correct notion of property. We call these approaches, respectively, capitalism, socialism, or the Just Third Way. Father Pesch and his followers called this last, "solidarism." Whatever they are called, all three relate to how power in society is vested, transmitted, and structured. Unfortunately, most commentators are locked into either socialism or capitalism. The former has been explicitly condemned, the latter implicitly by having its most basic precepts undermined by the natural law, as Father Oswald von Nell-Breuning, S.J., observed.[14]

Catholic adherents of capitalism are the easiest to critique, because they have no hesitation in declaring what they are

— however confused they may be about definitions and application of principle.[15] Catholic supporters of socialism are much harder to deal with, socialism having been explicitly condemned. In response, Catholic socialists typically hide behind barricades of illogic and bombard their opponents with volleys of hysterical accusations and irrational insinuations in order to cover up their lack of substance and failure to ground their opinions in the teachings of the Magisterium. This usually surfaces as an unreasoned defense or promulgation of the living wage as the solution to all social ills, as found in *Das Katholisch-Soziale Manifest*.

> This complex, self-contradictory definition of the just wage is evidence of the difficulties involved in finding a formula which satisfied both the just wage principle of *Quadragesimo anno* and the labor theory of value will-of-the-wisp pursued by the extreme Romantics. Apparently the moderates carried the day, and as a result the Manifest contained two important modifications of Romantic theory. It recognized the claims of private property to a greater degree than traditional Romantic theory, *e.g.*, the individual may actually retain title to property, and it rejected the labor theory of value in favor of what is essentially a family wage (*standesgemässer Unterhalt*).[16]

Unfortunately, due to the noted vagueness in Father Pesch's thought regarding private property and one fundamental omission, his work has proven to be a fertile source for socialists seeking to stamp their thought with his prestige, ironically at the same time that they are opposing his teachings. No doubt he would have found this humorous, but tragically sad as well.

The single minded seriousness, indeed, even viciousness with which socialists have pursued this line of thought on occasion would have alerted Father Pesch to something profoundly wrong in their makeup . . . if socialism itself had not already signaled it. As Franz Müller, a student of Father Pesch, recalls him saying on one occasion, "Boys, never lose your sense of humor; lack of humor almost always suggests that something is wrong with a person's religious life."[17] It is probably no mistake that communists and socialists, as well as a growing number of capitalists, seem to suffer from this lack of humor.

Further muddying the situation is an incredible confusion about what Catholic socialists actually believe. Getting straight answers or even consistent definitions of terms from a Catholic socialist is extremely difficult. Diamant lists more than a dozen major schools of Catholic socialism in Austria alone during the period 1918-1933, all of which were more or less opposed to Father Pesch's solidarism,[18] at least one, centered on Josef Eberle's periodical *Schönere Zukunft*, explicitly so.[19]

This variety is based primarily on the fact that even today much of what Catholic socialists believe is explicitly contradicted in the encyclicals themselves. To explain away inconsistencies they are forced into a species of moral, legal, and social positivism, in which logical fallacies, ranging from the straw man to *ad hominem abusive* and *circumstantial* reign supreme.

This is not conducive to rational argument or even civil discourse. According to the *Encyclopædia Britannica*, "the term positivism may be applied to any system that confines itself to the data of experience and excludes *a priori* or metaphysical speculations."[20] For modern man, this usually includes accepting the dictates of "scientists" without question. This is one of the propositions of "modernism," the "synthesis of all heresies," condemned by Saint Pius X.[21]

Within the context of this discussion, positivism could thus be described, among other things, as a philosophy in which something is "true" because someone in authority says so. This applies most particularly to "self-appointed" authority, which bows to the commentator's own opinion that something must be so, regardless of the facts, logic, explicit statements in Scripture, or the common sense of the Magisterium of the Church. The inevitable technique of this sort of positivist is to scream louder, contradict himself, and issue threats before running away when confronted with his errors in fact and logic. It is very difficult to have a debate, civil or otherwise, on these terms.

Natural Law and Human Dignity

The posivitist/modernist, therefore, actively works to undermine the truths taught as absolute by the Catholic Church. One of the more important of these with respect to man in civil society is the doctrine of individual and personal sovereignty of each and every human being. As CESJ puts it in the organization's "Core Values," "Under the highest sovereignty of God, all sovereignty begins with the human person — not social institutions such as the State, the business corporation or the labor union." Individual and personal sovereignty is thus the belief that, within the common good, that is, the embodiment of natural law, the dignity of the human person under God is of paramount importance.

Anything, therefore, that disparages, diminishes, or attacks human dignity is, by that fact alone, contrary to the Magisterium of the Catholic Church. When the attack is focused on the natural law rights of life, liberty, and property, it is also contrary to the common good, and thus the human race as a whole.

The current crisis in Catholic social teaching is thus as old as philosophy — social teaching — itself. The Church today faces the same crisis in substance that Aristotle faced with the Sophists, that Saint Thomas faced with the Manichees, and that Saint Pius X faced with the Modernists. The names change, but the issue, never. It is always a question over the nature of man, how he relates to God, and how he relates to other men in relation to God.

It is, in a very real sense, a conflict over whose will is to be supreme. On the one side is God's Will, based on His Nature and manifested in the natural law also based on God's Nature, and man's own nature created by God. This is the Law of the Gospels, a justice fulfilled and completed by charity. On the other side is man's will, based on purely human desires and the gratification of the needs and wants of the moment with no reference to any standard except, ultimately, personal opinion.

This is why the issue always seems to be about power and property. In recent centuries, power has popularly come to be understood almost exclusively in terms of power over others, almost never over one's own life. This has made power, something without which no one who lives can function at all, into a curse word. Similarly, private property, the chief and, according to some, the only means of individual and personal empowerment, has popularly come to be understood as something almost obscene.

Both power and property, then, are not something with which ordinary men should dirty themselves or assume of the risks of dealing with. Unfortunately for those who hold this viewpoint, each of us is responsible for who he is and what he does. We can never, as human beings, abdicate responsibility for our own acts, our own beliefs, or our own lives and, by extension, those of our dependents.

Charged with an individual and personal responsibility for our lives, a measure of power over our own lives is an absolute necessity. This power does not come from political rights — as human beings we have those already, and grant them to the State in order to establish and maintain a just social order. Even then our responsibility does not cease. Each of us individually and in association with others continues to be responsible for the establishment and maintenance of a just social order — we cannot simply abdicate our responsibility in that area, as Saint Thomas Aquinas made clear.

Property the Source of Power

Personal and individual power comes almost exclusively through direct and personal ownership of the means of production. It is not an accident that the most totalitarian forms of government and the most anti-human political-economic theories always posit a diminution or elimination theories always posit a diminution or elimination of private property in one form or another. This can be the violent abolition of the communists, the slower and more benign takeover of the socialists, or the alternately crude and subtle monopolization of the capitalists, but it all ends the same way. Ordinary people, whom the elite consider as not sufficiently responsible, or responsible at all, must be stripped of power and thus property, or property and thus power. In the end it makes little difference.

Twenty-five centuries or so ago Aristotle declared that a meaningful property stake was necessary for the "good life," that is, for the acquisition and development of virtue, at least of the elite. With the Thomist revolution and the redefinition of human nature along Judeo-Christian lines, it became increasingly apparent that private property was necessary for the mere acquisition of virtue, let alone the development, by everyone. With the Industrial Revolution and the increasing importance of the capital input to production, widespread ownership of the means of production became not only a personal and political necessity, but a social and economic necessity as well. It is no longer possible to argue that all production comes from labor, or even primarily from labor — not when newspapers trumpet exponential increases in productivity as workers by the tens of thousands are laid off in response to improvements in productive technology.

In spite of this, the urge to control others continues to inspire a great many people. The Catholic Church, while run by a great many fallible human agents, has never erred in matters of faith or morals. It is a matter of faith that some men should not control the lives of others. "It is not meet that man redeemed by Christ should serve other men."[22] The Catholic Church has therefore consistently come forth as the defender against concentrated ownership or control of the means of production, whether through the private system called capitalism, or the public system called socialism.

The Rejection of Reason

Yet, in the end, matters such as property and power are symptoms of a deeper crisis, not only in Catholic social teaching, but in the whole of modern life. The real crisis, of which such things are only symptoms, remember, is that men have forgotten how to think. This has been going on for so long that, in the twentieth century and at an increasing rate in the twenty-first, men are even beginning to forget why they should think.

The neglect of thought, of logic, is a crisis. That is why is was necessary for both Leo XIII and Pius XI to recommend the last great philosophy that was based not on human emotion, but on human reason, for study before they issued their greatest encyclicals: that of Saint Thomas Aquinas. Thomism is the philosophy of Christian common sense, just as Aristotelianism is the philosophy of pagan common sense, and just as the binary economics of Louis Kelso is the economics of common sense.

> Since the modern world began in the sixteenth century, nobody's system of philosophy has really corresponded to everybody's sense of reality; to what, if left to themselves, common men would call common sense. Each started with a paradox: a peculiar point of view demanding the sacrifice of what they would call a sane point of view. That is the one thing common to Hobbes and Hegel, to Kant and Bergson, to Berkeley and William James. A man had to believe something that no normal man would believe, if it were suddenly propounded to his simplicity; as that law is above right, or right is outside reason, or things are only as we think them, or everything is relative to a reality that is not there. The modern philosopher claims, like a sort of confidence man, that if once we will grant him this, the rest will be easy; he will straighten out the world, if once he is allowed to give this one twist to the mind.[23]

And that is what many interpreters of the social encyclicals demand today, whether they are capitalists or socialists, but particularly supporters of the idea that the living wage is the quintessence of Catholic social teaching. "Only accept the idea that a man should receive more or less than he actually contributes to the productive process," they say, "and all will be well. We know this flies in the face of common sense, against the laws of supply and demand, but it must be this way because we will have it so. The case is closed."

The case is closed? By no means — but their minds are, for they have forgotten how to think, or even failed to remember that thought is necessary.

Notes

[1] Rev. William J. Ferree, S.M., Ph.D., *The Act of Social Justice*. Washington, DC: The Catholic University of America Press, 1942.

[2] Daniel Webster, "Speech Before the Massachusetts Constitutional Convention of 1820."

[3] Michel, *op. cit.*, 20.

[4] Mulcahy, *op. cit.*, 166.

[5] "The distinguishing feature of Communism is not the abolition of property generally, but the abolition of bourgeois property. But modern bourgeois private property is the final and most complete expression of the system of production and appropriating products, that is based on class antagonisms, on the exploitation of the many by the few." *The Communist Manifesto, op. cit.*, 96.

[6] National Conference of Catholic Bishops, *Economic Justice for All: Pastoral Letter on Catholic Social Teaching and the U.S. Economy*. Washington, DC: United States Catholic Conference, 1986, § 19.

[7] "Pay a man a just wage and he can buy stock with his extra income, or tools or rental property, or he can simply put extra money aside in liquid savings accounts that is his business, and there is nothing especially sacred about owning stock, even in the company where he happens to work." Dr. Rupert J. Ederer, Letter to Father John H. Miller, C.S.C., S.T.D., August 4, 1993. This declaration flatly contradicts Leo XIII's explicit statement in *Rerum Novarum* (§ 46) that private property is, in fact, to be regarded as "sacred."

[8] *Rerum Novarum, op. cit.*, § 46.
[9] G. K. Chesterton, "The Beginning of the Quarrel" *The Outline of Sanity, Volume V, Collected Works*. San Francisco, California: Ignatius Press, 1987, 43.
[10] Franz H. Müller, "I Knew Heinrich Pesch, the Formative Influence of a 'Human Scholar'" *Social Order*, April 1951, 149.
[11] Formerly the "Principle of Limitation."
[12] Norman G. Kurland, "Beyond ESOP: Steps Toward Tax Justice" *Curing World Poverty, the New Role of Property, John H. Miller, C.S.C., S.T.D., editor*. St. Louis, Missouri: Social Justice Review, 1994, 155-156.
[13] Yenni, *op. cit.*, 171.
[14] Rev. Oswald von Nell-Bruening, S.J., *Reorganization of Social Economy*. Milwaukee, Wisconsin: Bruce Publishing Company, 1936.
[15] *Social Justice Betrayed, op. cit.*, 8-9.
[16] Diamant, *op. cit.*, 68.
[17] Franz H. Müller, "I Knew Heinrich Pesch" *Social Order, op. cit.*, 150.
[18] "The dominant type of socialism in Pesch's lifetime was Marxism. In his day, however, it was no longer a unified creed. There were communists of various shades, such as the Austro-Marxists and the 'revisionists' of the E. Bernstein dispensation." Briefs, *op. cit.*, 157.
[19] Diamant, *op. cit.*, 19-73.
[20] *Encyclopædia Britannica*, "Positivism."
[21] Pius X, *Pascendi Dominici Gregis* ("On the Doctrines of the Modernists"), 1907, § 6. See also the Apostolic Constitution, *Lamentabili Sane* ("Syllabus of Errors Condemning Modernism"), 1907, esp. §§ 3, 5, 19, 26, 32, 40, 52, 53, 57, 58, 59, 61, 63, 64, 65.
[22] Pius XI, *Quas Primas* ("On the Feast of Christ the King"), 1925, § 19.
[23] G. K. Chesterton, *Saint Thomas Aquinas, "The Dumb Ox."* New York: Image Books, 1956, 145-146.

5. A Just Third Political Way: The Concept of Sovereignty in *Quas Primas* (1925)

(Social Justice Review, March/April 2005 to July/August 2005)

Part I

Man and Society

Pius XI's 1925 encyclical instituting the Feast of Christ the King, *Quas Primas*, "On the Feast of Christ the King," is possibly one of the most misunderstood and ignored encyclicals of all time. This is doubly ironic, for not only is *Quas Primas* easy to understand once we grasp the encyclical's basic Thomist orientation, it is the cornerstone of Pius XI's concept of individual sovereignty in the temporal order. *Quas Primas* is the political foundation of Pius XI's revolutionary breakthrough in moral philosophy represented by his theory of social virtue.

The most politically significant passage in the encyclical is Paragraph 19, in which the pope sets out a precise explanation of the interrelationships between individuals in civil society, the State (in the persons of "princes and rulers"), and God.

> When once men recognize, both in private and in public life, that Christ is King, society will at last receive the great blessings of real liberty, well-ordered discipline, peace and harmony. Our Lord's regal office invests the human authority of princes and rulers with a religious significance; it ennobles the citizen's duty of obedience. It is for this reason that St. Paul, while bidding wives revere Christ in their husbands, and slaves respect Christ in their masters, warns them to give obedience to them not as men, but as the vicegerents of Christ; for it is not meet that men redeemed by Christ should serve their fellow-men. "You are bought with a price; be not made the bond-slaves of men."[1] If princes and magistrates duly elected are filled with the persuasion that they rule, not by their own right, but by the mandate and

in the place of the Divine King, they will exercise their authority piously and wisely, and they will make laws and administer them, having in view the common good and also the human dignity of their subjects. The result will be a stable peace and tranquility, for there will be no longer any cause of discontent. Men will see in their king or in their rulers men like themselves, perhaps unworthy or open to criticism, but they will not on that account refuse obedience if they see reflected in them the authority of Christ God and Man. Peace and harmony, too, will result; for with the spread and the universal extent of the kingdom of Christ men will become more and more conscious of the link that binds them together, and thus many conflicts will be either prevented entirely or at least their bitterness will be diminished.[2]

A Lack of Understanding

Much of this passage seemed obscure and confusing when *Quas Primas* was issued, and has become more so with the passage of time. This is not, however, due to lack of clarity or precision in the language itself. Lack of understanding can be traced directly to two factors. The first is that, by and large, people have ignored the explicit instructions by two popes, Leo XIII in *Æterni Patris* (1879)[3] and Pius XI in *Studiorum Ducem* (1923).[4] Both of these encyclicals contain a clear mandate to interpret the papal encyclicals in strict accordance with the philosophy of Saint Thomas Aquinas, that is, in conformity with a "Christianized" Aristotelian analysis — or, if you prefer, ordinary common sense illuminated by the revelation of the Gospel.

The second factor limiting understanding of Catholic social teaching in general and *Quas Primas* in particular is a lamentable aspect of modern society that has become increasingly prevalent, almost by the day. That is the refusal of the intellectual elite to think in any logical or consistent fashion. This has seeped out into the general culture. The result is that many people not only refuse to think, they have forgotten how to think.

Nowhere is this more evident than in the analysis of the above passage. Astonishingly, a number of commentators, many of them otherwise far from unintelligent, have interpreted Paragraph 19 as mandating a divine right monarchy as the only legitimate Catholic form of government.[5]

Is "Divine Right" Catholic?

The exact opposite is true. The Catholic Church has declared on more than one occasion that it has no competence in the civil sphere, other than as a moral guide. There can be no "Catholic form of government," as the following passage from *Divini Redemptoris* makes clear:

> Thus even in the sphere of social-economics, although the Church has never proposed a definite technical system, *since this is not her field*, she has nevertheless clearly outlined the guiding principles which, while susceptible of varied concrete applications according to the diversified conditions of times and places and peoples, indicate the safe way of securing the happy progress of society.[6] [Emphasis added.]

To understand this, we need to examine exactly what Pius XI says in Paragraph 19 of *Quas Primas*. Perhaps the single most important word in this passage from the point of view of political analysis is "reflected." This is the same word used by Aristotle in Chapter V, Book I of *The Politics* to describe how a thing (in Aristotle's example, a slave) becomes an artificial person so as to enable something that is not a natural person to function in society.[7]

With that single word Pius XI completely obviates the idea that God grants political sovereignty directly to any particular individual in civil society, bypassing the rest of humanity. The State only gains the "rule virtue" as the instrument or tool of the group. This is exactly analogous to the way that

Aristotle claimed slaves acquire virtue in order to carry out their functions in society. This is by a process that we would call "delegation" but which in Aristotelian and Thomist philosophy is called "reflection."[8]

The Servant Leader

Thus, Pius XI embodied in his thought the idea of the "servant leader." This is not, however, a "warm and fuzzy" catch phrase, but a hard and practical description of the transmission and exercise of the sovereign power for the benefit of the group. The leader or ruler in the thought of Pius XI is philosophically the slave of those whom he rules. Jesus Himself signaled this understanding of the role of the leader when He washed the feet of the Apostles at the Last Supper.[9]

The leader as leader has no authority to act in his own personal interest, except that which he has as just another member of the group — in which case he is not acting as the leader. As a "slave," the leader may not under any circumstances act materially contrary to the best interests of his "masters," or the general sovereign political power with which he has been vested will be revoked.[10]

The Problem of the Collective

There is, however, a problem with the cited passage. Paragraph 19 apparently leaves in place Saint Robert Cardinal Bellarmine's idea from *De Laicis* ("On Civil Government") that God grants general political sovereignty not to individuals, but to the collective.[11] The collective then transmits sovereignty to the chosen representative via a revocable grant. This theory inserts a "thing" — the collective — between God and man, and between the human person and his chosen representatives in the temporal order.

Pius XI, however, had already overcome that difficulty. It is probably not coincidental that he beatified Saint Robert Bellarmine and announced his reconciliation of Saint Robert's political thought with the social teachings of the Church in the same year, 1923. This reconciliation was announced, again probably not coincidentally, in the encyclical *Stu-*

diorum Ducem, "On Saint Thomas Aquinas," already noted above in connection with the same matter. In *Studiorum Ducem* Pius XI gave a clear indication of his thought and intentions when he pointed out that legal justice and social justice were not simply different names for the same thing.[12] The pope thus signaled rather plainly his revolutionary breakthrough in moral philosophy — the idea of social virtue, and social justice especially, as a *particular*, not a *general* species of virtue.[13]

It was, however, necessary to remove Saint Robert's insertion of the collective between man and the State and, of course, between man and God. "Only man, the human person," Pius XI declared later, "and not society in any form is endowed with reason and a morally free will."[14] It is thus impossible, in Pius XI's view, that God could grant anything directly to the collective — or to a leader *qua* leader, for that matter. The collective had to be removed from the equation.

Pius XI and Social Virtue

Pius XI accomplished this seemingly impossible task through his realization that there exists a type of particular virtue — social virtue — fundamentally different from the classical Aristotelian understanding of virtue. This "social virtue" has as its directed object not the good of any individual human person (as is the case in the traditional understanding of virtue), but the good of the institutions of society, the common good of all mankind.[15]

This is easy to understand once we get away from the idea that the act of a virtue can only be directed to the human person or other natural persons.[16] According to Pius XI, there are certain virtues (and thus rights) that are, as is the case with all virtue of whatever kind, acquired and developed by individuals, but — and this is the essence of social virtue — which can only be exercised by individuals as members of groups.

Traditionally it was thought that only individuals as individuals could exercise ("carry out") acts of virtue. Pius XI, however, realized that man is not solely an individual, but an individual who is a member of many groups. Man as a human being is a member of a consciously-structured society by nature — as Aristotle said, "a political animal."[17] This caused Pius XI to develop Saint Thomas Aquinas' seminal idea of a class of virtue specifically directed toward the social structures — the institutions — of groups.[18] The idea that an act of a particular virtue could be directed at something other than a natural person was a profound breakthrough in moral philosophy.

For example, being nice to a dog doesn't mean that you are directing an act of a virtue to the dog, except in a colloquial sense. No, you are directing your act of virtue (kindness) to the owner, via the owner's rights in the dog, and to God, via God's rights in His creation. You are kind to animals not because an animal has a right to be treated kindly, but because God and the animal's owner (if any) have a right that you will treat an owner's property and God's creation with proper respect and deference. You are also developing your own virtue by building the habit of being kind to animals. (It is in this sense that "virtue is its own reward.") The dog is, philosophically speaking, only the indirect object of your act of virtue.

How to be Virtuous to a Thing

Man therefore has the capacity to acquire and develop individual virtues, and thus possesses inalienable individual rights as an individual to assist him in his acquisition and development of individual virtue. These acts of individual virtue, however, while they have a direct effect on persons, have only an indirect effect on things. Pius XI's breakthrough consisted, in part, in this: that man also has the capacity to acquire and develop social virtues. Social virtues are directed at the common good — a thing, although a very special kind of thing. A thing, according to Pius XI *can* be the directed object of an act of virtue!

Not unnaturally this requires a little explanation. The common good consists of institutions. Institutions are organized aggregations, traditions, customs, laws, and so on, that have received a delegation of virtue (and thus rights) from natural persons. This delegation occurs "automatically" whenever human persons come together in an organized manner — an "institution" could not otherwise exist; all you would have otherwise is a non-organized aggregation. This delegation may be either explicit or implicit, but the mere fact of organization gives positive evidence that the delegation has been carried out. The institutions of society have thereby become, in a sense, "persons" themselves (sometimes legally so, as with a business corporation or a court of law) — but *artificial*, that is, man-made, not God-made persons . . . but God participates in this creation, as He does in all other acts of creation.

The Role of the Corporation

This is an important aspect of the social thought of Pius XI. The process of creating an artificial person is embodied in the very act of organization. Legally this is referred to as "incorporation," that is, "putting into a body" — making something into a "person." An association of natural persons, while remaining a "thing," thereby acquires the ability to be the direct object of the act of a virtue — it acquires "personality."

> If, therefore, We consider the whole structure of economic life, as We have already pointed out in Our Encyclical *Quadragesimo Anno*, the reign of mutual collaboration between justice and charity in social-economic relations can only be achieved by a body of professional and inter professional organizations, built on solidly Christian foundations, working together to effect, under forms adapted to different places and circumstances, what has been called the Corporation.[19]

In today's society the general meaning of corporation is restricted to the business corporation, the most widespread creature of positive law in civil society. It also, on rare occasions, refers to an incorporated town or city that gives a municipality legal existence. This is simply an accommodation the State makes to reality and the complexity of the common good. It would not be expedient to require that every organization be legally incorporated and under the direct control of the State, although that is what the totalitarian philosopher Thomas Hobbes demanded. The State therefore usually restricts this "privilege" to organizations that have a material or significant effect on the natural persons involved, the common good at their level, or the common good as a whole. Requiring virtually universal legal incorporation would also, to a great extent, interfere with the right of free association, although the idea has been used to comic effect as satire.[20] Pius XI was, in part, responding to Hobbes in *Leviathan*,[21] who would prohibit all organizations ("corporations") other than those specifically authorized by a divine right monarch, thereby abolishing the right of free association.

The right of free association is of paramount importance in social justice. In a single paragraph in *Quadragesimo Anno*, Pius XI states it specifically seven times by count, and countless times by implication throughout the encyclical:

> Moreover, just as inhabitants of a town are wont to found associations with the widest diversity of purposes, which each is quite free to join or not, so those engaged in the same industry or profession will combine with one another into associations equally free for purposes connected in some manner with the pursuit of the calling itself. Since these free associations are clearly and lucidly explained by Our Predecessor of illustrious memory, We consider it enough to emphasize this one point: People are quite free not only to found such associations, which are a matter of private order and private right, but also in respect to them "freely to adopt the organization and the rules which they judge most appropriate to achieve their purpose." The same freedom must be

asserted for founding associations that go beyond the boundaries of individual callings. And may these free organizations, now flourishing and rejoicing in their salutary fruits, set before themselves the task of preparing the way, in conformity with the mind of Christian social teaching, for those larger and more important guilds, Industries and Professions, which We mentioned before, and make every possible effort to bring them to realization.[22]

Inasmuch as the pope repeatedly references the right of free association and stresses over and over that these associations (often poorly translated as "vocational groups") must be *free*, it is truly baffling how anyone could possibly conclude that this right of free association is, on the contrary, "not strictly speaking voluntary."[23] Yet that is precisely what has happened in more cases than not![24]

Recognition by the State as a legal entity imposes certain obligations on an organization. These can become overweening, sometimes to the point that the organization forgoes all or part of its original mission in its anxiety to comply with governmental regulations. Is it necessary to cite the fact that certain U.S. corporations are forced to provide permanent office space for IRS staff as they undergo continuous audit, or that an annual corporate tax return can exceed the equivalent of 45,000 pages of text?

Clearly Pius XI, due to the immediacy of the economic common good, put most of his focus on reforming the business corporation as a vehicle for restructuring the social order, as we will see in Part III of this article. The passage (above) from *Divini Redemptoris*, however, gives just as clear an indication that the corporate form itself is integral to his social thought. The pope expands the scope of the corporation into "forms adapted to different places and circumstances." He thereby indicates that the concept has applications beyond its admittedly crucial role in the economic common good.

The Moral Philosophy of the Corporation

The important breakthrough that Pius XI made, however, is not an expansion of the role of the corporation beyond business and today's limited understanding of "politics." It is that a social entity, a "thing," can become, within the constraints of the common good, a "person." It is this fact of personality, whether natural or artificial, that allows an entity to be the directed object of an act of virtue. In the case of a natural person, the entity is the object of a directed act of individual virtue. In the case of an artificial person, the entity is the object of a directed act of social virtue.

For Christians, there is an interesting "twist" that Pius XI put on this concept via his idea of the "Reign of Christ the King." One of Jesus' sayings in the New Testament is that, "For where two or three have gathered together in My name, there I am in their midst."[25] Now Jesus as God shares His substance with the Father, and therefore partakes of the Nature of God. This makes Jesus a sharer in the basis for natural law, those universal moral virtues that underlie a just social order, as well as the structure of every just organization (formal group or institution) within the social order.

This means that the act of organization itself, when carried out in conformity with universal moral virtues — that is, the natural law — does not merely "create" a person as described above. It also, in a certain sense, brings God Himself, via the natural law based on His Nature as manifested in His Son, into the process as "co-Creator." The personality of the institution is not simply created out of nothing, but out of a sharing in the personality of Jesus, transmitted to the organization by means of a delegation of virtue — legal justice — from those making up the group.

Does this mean that a group has to be specifically Christian in order to participate in the common good? Of course not. As Saint Thomas Aquinas pointed out, the natural law is inherent in each and every human being, and consequently every individual has the same capacity to acquire and develop virtue as every other individual. Each and every human being is equal ("analogously complete") in this respect.

Whether or not a particular individual actually does acquire and develop virtue is a different issue — all have the same capacity to be virtuous, and thus all have equal rights and the exercise thereof until some crime has been committed in punishment for which the exercise of some or all rights is abrogated.

Similarly, as Father William Ferree points out in his "Discourse on Social Charity" (1966), all groups — that is, organized aggregations of persons — have the same capacity to acquire and develop social virtue simply because they are groups. The act of organization itself vests a group with this capacity, meaning that any group can be either the object or agent of social virtue. Any group, therefore, can be reformed; destruction is (in theory at least) not a viable option. Of course, whether any particular group actually does acquire and develop social virtue is, as with individual human persons, another issue altogether. The potential to be a "structure of virtue" is inherent in any group by the mere fact of its being a group; man's inherent social nature makes his creations — institutions — as fully subject to the natural law as he is himself.

This understanding of Pius XI's thought has the added benefit of making the concept of the "Reign of Christ the King" more palatable to non-Christians, as well as secularists and other non- or even anti-religious individuals. Jesus "reigns," but only through the natural law, inscribed in the hearts of men, and by having a sound interpretation of natural law embedded in the institutions of a just social order. Within the temporal sphere, it can be considered a matter of opinion under freedom of conscience whether the Nature of the Christian God is the basis of natural law. For civil purposes, what matters is a sound interpretation of natural law, not the recognized basis.

Man therefore possesses inalienable social rights as a member of society in order to assist him in his acquisition and development of social virtue. Man possesses at one and the same time the character of an individual and that of a member of society. Logically, then, we as human beings possess both individual and social rights.

General and Particular Virtue

The social virtues are of two kinds. These are "particular" and "general" virtues, terms that have specific meanings in philosophy. A "particular virtue" has a specific object toward which its act is directed. That is, the act of a particular virtue has a direct effect on whatever constitutes its object. A "general virtue," however, does not have a specific object toward which its act is directed. The effect of a general virtue is *always* indirect.

The "act" of a general virtue consists of the act of another particular virtue altogether, which act has a kind of "ripple effect" on something else. That "ripple effect" or "fallout" is the indirect "act" of the general virtue. In the philosophy of Aristotle and in Scholastic philosophy before Aquinas, philosophers by and large considered it was only necessary to add a good or general intention that the indirect object be beneficially affected by the act of the particular virtue.

The most important of these social virtues after social charity is (as we might expect) justice. In the philosophy of Aristotle, who seems to have invented the term,[26] legal justice is a general justice. The Philosopher used the term to describe the beneficial effect that passing and obeying particular laws (applications of commutative and distributive justice) had on the common good. Unlike Aristotle, however, who saw legal justice solely as a general virtue, Saint Thomas Aquinas differentiated between a *particular* and a *general* legal justice.

The second part of this article is concerned with the implications of Saint Thomas' discernment of a particular legal justice. The idea that the common good can be acted on directly has a profound impact on our understanding of the role of the State — and, most especially, on the role of the sovereign individual as a member of society.

Notes

[1] I Cor.vii,23.

[2] Pius XI, *Quas Primas* ("On the Feast of Christ the King"), 1925, § 19.

[3] "On the Restoration of Scholastic Philosophy."

[4] "On Saint Thomas Aquinas."

[5] A few of the many commentators to hold this opinion are Rev. A. Phillipe C.SS.R., *Christ, King of Nations* (Kansas City, Missouri: Instauratio Press, 1992); Rev. Fr. A. Roussel, *Liberalism & Catholicism, the Great Betrayal* (Kansas City, Missouri: Angelus Press, 1998); Solange Hertz, *Utopia: "NOWHERE" — Now Here* (Santa Monica, California: Veritas Press, 1992), *The Star-Spangled Heresy: Americanism* (Santa Monica, California: Veritas Press, 1992).

[6] Pius XI, *Divini Redemptoris* ("On Atheistic Communism"), 1937, § 34.

[7] "Politikos bios" — the life of a citizen in the *polis*.

[8] "Delegation" is a Roman concept, derived from the temporary grant of the Legatine power to someone who wasn't a Legate. It rapidly came to mean the temporary grant of any kind of power or duty.

[9] Jn. 13:1-11.

[10] *De Regimine Principum*, I.vi.

[11] *De Laicis*, VI. A serious logical flaw in Bellarmine's argument is that "rule virtue" as exercised through acts of legal justice is a general virtue, yet a grant to the State even by the collective is a particular act. The same holds true for God's presumed particular grant of a general virtue in divine right theory.

[12] *Studiorum Ducem*, § 27; Father William J. Ferree, S.M., Ph.D., *The Act of Social Justice* (Washington, DC: The Catholic University of America Press, 1942), 96-97.

[13] *Ibid.*, 36-76.

[14] Pius XI, *Divini Redemptoris* ("On Atheistic Communism"), 1937, § 29.

[15] *Summa*, Ia IIae q. 61 a. 5 4m; Ferree, *op. cit.*, 83.

[16] Christian belief, God and the angels are also "natural persons."

[17] *The Politics*, I.ii.

[18] Ferree, *op. cit.*, 193-211.

[19] *Divini Redemptoris*, § 54.

[20] Incorporation of an individual and universal incorporation of everything were used to comic effect by W. S. Gilbert (of

"Gilbert and Sullivan" fame) in *The Gondoliers* and *Utopia, Ltd.*, respectively. Gilbert was trained as a lawyer, and well knew the bizarre conclusions that could be drawn when a seemingly reasonable proposition was taken to its *reductio ad absurdum*.

[21] Thomas Hobbes, *Leviathan, op. cit.*, 285-286.

[22] *Quadragesimo Anno*, § 87.

[23] As one commentator put it, "If a true distributist order were ever instituted, there would be less government, not more, than we have today. This is because many tasks which are now performed directly by the government would be performed by intermediate bodies which, while not strictly speaking voluntary associations, would neither be governmental organs nor departments." Thomas Storck, *Catholic Men's Quarterly*, Fall 2007, 36.

[24] See virtually any recommendation to institute the Industry Council Plan, which is described as "voluntary" . . . except when people refuse to go along with it: "Decisions approved by the councils would be binding on all workers and employers and would become part of the law of the land, to be enforced by government if self-enforcement failed." Mary Lois Eberdt, C.H.M., Ph.D. and Gerald J. Schnepp, S.M., Ph.D., Industrialism and the Popes. New York: P. J. Kenedy & Sons, 1953, 4. This particular work also carefully removes the word "free" from the right of association when it is mentioned.

[25] Matt. 18:15-20.

[26] Aristotle, *Nicomachean Ethics*. Book V, Chapters I and II (1129a-1130b30). Lessius attributes the first use of the term to Aristotle in his *De Justitia et Jure*, Cap. I, Dub. III, 10.

Part II

A Personal Responsibility for the Common Good

In the first part of this article we examined the popular interpretation of *Quas Primas*, Pius XI's 1925 encyclical that instituted the Feast of Christ the King. We discovered that, contrary to the impression that many people have, Pius XI was far from mandating a divine right monarchy as the only legitimate Catholic form of government.

Further, not only is a divine right monarchy (or any other specific form of government) not mandated in *Quas Primas*, it appears that Pius XI presents a definite theory of individual sovereignty. If anything, taking the political philosophy of Saint Robert Cardinal Bellarmine as our lead, we must construe the encyclical as "mandating" a form of government that is democratic in substance.

From the point of view of Pius XI, however, Bellarmine's political philosophy had a few difficulties. These were overcome when Pius XI obviated Bellarmine's insertion of the collective between God and man, and between man and the State. The pope did this by substituting a completed doctrine of social virtue in place of Bellarmine's perceived necessity for the collective.

That is, formerly it was believed that only the State in the person of the leader had access to the common good (and that was necessarily indirect), and that certain rights were delegated to the leader after being vested by God in the collective. Using hints given by Saint Thomas Aquinas, however, Pius XI posited a theory of social virtue by which each human person — not the people as a whole — gains direct access to the common good.

Within the context of social virtue as the concept was developed by Pius XI, the implicitly or explicitly chosen leader changes from an authoritarian to a "servant leader." The leader is not the servant of God (in the way that all human beings would be were it not for Christ's redemption of us on the Cross), but the servant of those on whose behalf he exercises the functions of government.

The function of government is to care for and maintain the common good as a whole. This is a general function. The specific care of each level of the common good, however, is the particular responsibility of the people who subsist within that level of the common good.

How Pius XI reconciled these two seemingly incompatible areas of responsibility can be found in how Aquinas treated legal justice — the justice that Aristotle claimed was the only virtue that had anything to do with the common good. The Angelic Doctor did this almost casually. He merely noted that there are two types of legal justice. (Of course, this could also be due to the fact that Saint Thomas never finished the *Summa*. It was completed after his death by others working from his notes. They might not have understood the significance of calling legal justice particular as well as general, and failed to develop the thought.)

One of these types of legal justice is a general virtue, just as Aristotle had claimed. The other, however, is a particular virtue. This is a concept directly contrary to Aristotle's whole idea of general justice and its application to the common good in the form of legal justice.

The Role of the State

Saint Thomas restricted the general type of legal justice to what Aristotle meant by the term, that is, the passage and enforcement of laws by the State — an identifiable (though not particular) application of Aristotle's conception of "general justice" or "virtue entire." Passing and enforcing laws (the most obvious way in which society regulates itself) are acts of distributive and commutative justice. These have a direct effect on individuals, but only an indirect effect on the common good.

Saint Thomas' reformulation of Aristotle, however, included the idea of a particular virtue directed at the common good — and calling it, too, legal justice. He didn't get into this *particular* type of legal justice very much, except to say that it had a direct effect on the common good: "Legal justice *alone* directly looks to the common good."[1] The implications, however, are profound. This means that every human being has the capacity to acquire and develop the virtue of particular legal justice.

Obviously using the same term for something completely different is a little confusing. Pius XI went to work and tightened up Saint Thomas' terminology. General legal justice *per se* he "gave back to the lawyers" by restricting the term legal justice to mean only "general legal justice" — Aristotle's term applied to Aristotle's concept. Particular legal justice he renamed "social justice."

The capacity to acquire and develop legal justice is delegated to the chosen representatives of the people as a political entity. This is to ensure that society — which is naturally hierarchical, consisting of many levels of the common good — is properly run and due attention paid to the maintenance of the whole of the common good. Because this is a general function, it is perfectly appropriate that the capacity to acquire and develop legal justice — a general virtue — be delegated to the State or some other institution.

The common good is maintained through direct acts of commutative and distributive justice that also constitute indirect "acts" of legal justice via their indirect effect on the common good. These are the exercise of rights, such as declaring war, keeping the peace, passing laws, and collecting taxes, that Saint Robert Bellarmine assumed were granted to the people as a whole, not to individuals, and then delegated to the State by the collective consent of the people.[2]

On the contrary, as Pius XI clearly pointed out, these rights are granted to individuals, but cannot be exercised by individuals as individuals.[3] They can only be exercised by agents of the State on behalf of the individuals who make up society. Even then this is only when the agent of the State is acting as the legitimate representative of the people — as a member of the group carrying out his delegated role.

The State does not, therefore, possess this sovereign power in its own right, but only because the group has selected representatives to act on its behalf, and the group consents to those representatives, implicitly or explicitly. Leaders are entrusted with the exercise of specific indirect social rights in order to ensure that the common good as a whole is properly maintained and protected.

A Personal Responsibility

The fact that certain social rights are delegated to the State does not mean that individuals retain no social rights. Very much the contrary! The State has the job of reconciling the interests of all the different levels of the common good and ensuring that everything operates harmoniously together. This is why the State has the job of passing and enforcing laws, as well as adjudicating disputes between individuals and groups, levying and collecting taxes, setting standards for weights and measures, declaring war, and so on. The leader or governing group of any other institution within a particular level of the common good is similar, within its own purview, to that of the State over the whole of the common good.

Passing and enforcing laws and regulations and so on are all social goods. They must be regulated and reconciled in some fashion or society will not be in harmony. Imagine trying to carry on trade when every individual decides for himself how long a foot is, or sets his own private standard of value for the currency — or what specific words mean in a legal context, or even whether a specific act constitutes a crime. Similarly, try and imagine running a business if no one follows procedures to which everyone has agreed. A system of accounting or internal control would be impossible.

A Personal Responsibility for the Common Good — 169

The individual levels of the common good are another matter. These are effectively infinite, resulting, as they do, from the effectively infinite relationships between individuals and individuals, individuals and groups, and groups and groups. They are the *personal and individual* — direct — responsibility of the members of society who subsist within or at those levels,[4] and only secondarily (indirectly) the general responsibility of the leader. This is why each individual as a member of a group retains the capacity to acquire and develop social justice, a particular virtue.

Each individual has a *personal and direct* responsibility for the care and maintenance of the common good at his own levels. We need to specify *levels* for a very good reason. Each of us subsists within an almost unlimited variety of "milieux," as the different levels of the common good can be termed. These milieux change from day to day, even from moment to moment, as we become involved in the almost infinite variety of social transactions that make up daily life.[5]

Each of these milieux is therefore our personal responsibility. It so happens, though, that, as Pius XI observed, we as individuals are often helpless when confronted with the seemingly impossible task of caring for and maintaining the common good at our level.[6]

The Act of Social Justice

To try and make this clearer, let's look at the role that social justice can play in a badly structured social situation — a business enterprise in which no one does his job. This is adapted from the illustration Father Ferree used in his pamphlet, *Introduction to Social Justice*, that of a society in which no one is honest.

The first mark of social justice is that it cannot be performed by individuals as individuals, but only by individuals *as members of groups*. When a member of the company performs his work, he is also continuing a laudable tradition in his company that tasks are carried out when assigned. By doing his job promptly he contributes to the conviction that is prevalent in his company that tasks are to be carried out promptly. He not only performs his individual task, but he also contributes the performance of a task which he owes to his company, namely, support of the principle that at the proper time tasks are to be carried out. He also knows that when he assigns a task to somebody else, it will be carried out as well.

Now this "tradition," this "confidence" are *social* things. They are marks of the society as a whole. These acts then, insofar as they contribute to the health of that company, are *indirect* "acts" of legal justice[7] (promoting the corporate common good) although they are *directly* acts of individual responsibility.

What about *direct* acts of social justice? Suppose the company has a long tradition of people *not* doing their jobs without somebody standing over them with whips, chains, or threats of dismissal. As a result, everybody is suspicious of everybody else. No one will do his job without coercion even in an emergency where the survival of the company is at stake. To do your job in a holistic sense without coercion in such an environment is to be taken advantage of.

Emergencies, however, have a habit of coming up, and people as well as companies suffer. Likewise, all jobs that are too big for one person go undone because no one will trust another sufficiently to ask for assistance or go into even informal partnership with a co-worker. The consequence is that the economic life of the company as a whole is suffering more and more; and the company is being driven out of business.

The solution? First of all, we as *individuals are helpless* before the accumulated evil of the unjust *system in force*. We need help. If we are wise we will not tackle the whole company at once, but will look around among our co-workers and try to find other people who are as dissatisfied as we are with the condition of their company.

With these fellows in misfortune we sit down to study the sad condition of our company and to see what can be done about it — we *organize*. We determine the cause of the badly structured social order in our company, and set out to

A Personal Responsibility for the Common Good — 171

correct it. The first step is to bring others into the group in solidarity with its new principles.

We will make it a condition of joining our group that the newcomers study the necessity of doing one's job as much as we studied it when we started out. In other words, we will attempt to *form* our new members to the habit of industry. Actually we are setting up a new "social conscience" to take the place of the old falsified "social conscience" that made shirking a normal thing.

In this *social way of action* — this *organization of the company* — something can really be done. We as organized human persons are going to show to our disorganized company an example, not of individually trying and failing, but of arriving at a viable and competitive company by the operation of industry as a group.

Subsidiarity

This is the basis of the principle of subsidiarity. The essence of subsidiarity is that care of the common good is entrusted not to those at the highest level, not to those at the lowest level, but to those at the most *appropriate* level. That is, matters pertaining to the care and maintenance of the common good as a whole (that is, in general) are the proper purview of the State. Matters pertaining to the care and maintenance of the common good at a particular level are the purview of those subsisting within or at that level.

When problems occur and the members of a specific milieu are unable to carry out their task of caring for and maintaining the common good at their own level, a "higher" level may step in and provide assistance.[8] This assistance can take one of two forms, frequently both. Where emergency aid is necessary, the "higher" level can provide for immediate subsistence of the members of the flawed milieu. This aid should be provided in a manner consistent with the demands of human dignity when possible, but sheer survival is the real issue and the justification for such assistance.

The assistance must never stop there, however. Keeping people alive in a manner consistent as far as possible with the demands of human dignity is a matter of the highest importance, and certainly the most immediate.[9] It is not, however, the only important matter, nor is it the highest matter, even in the temporal sphere.

In temporal matters that place is reserved for restructuring the social order at a particular level of the common good so as to enable the human persons within that milieu to carry out the functions themselves, without further assistance from a higher level. The primary assistance from a higher level *must*, therefore, take the form of removing barriers to the effective functioning of the people within the lower level so as to be able to carry out the operation of that level themselves.[10]

The Right of Free Association

As noted above, our direct and personal responsibility for the common good at our level means that each of us retains certain social rights. The single most important of these social rights is that of free association — the right to organize. Unless we can organize and thereby become members of groups, exercise of our social rights and development of our social virtue becomes impossible. Remember, acts of social virtue are carried out and social rights exercised *only* by members of groups.

Sadly, this right of free association has frequently been limited to simple encouragement of the related right of labor to organize.[11] It is, as should now be clear, far more than that. The right to organize does not apply merely to the rather narrow task of restructuring the economic milieu of wage workers, but to the whole of the common good at all levels. Wherever flaws exist in the common good at any level, it is the individual and personal responsibility of everyone at that level to organize in order to correct those flaws. This personal responsibility takes precedence over the responsibility of higher levels to assist lower levels.[12]

Constant Vigilance is Necessary

Further, individuals within a particular milieu must continue to associate in an organized manner so as to keep a constant watch on the common good at that level.[13] This means not only correcting obvious flaws as they appear, but changing and improving the institutions at that level of the common good to meet the changing conditions of society. As Pius XI noted, the whole of society is in such a state of flux as legitimately to be termed "radically unstable."[14]

Changes must therefore constantly be introduced into the system so that institutions can continue to meet human wants and needs in the most effective and efficient manner possible. This requires organization and the exercise of social rights, which affect the common good directly, for the practice of individual virtue and the exercise of individual rights can only affect the common good *indirectly*, as Aristotle noted.[15]

The indirect "acts" of legal justice carried out by the State are direct acts of commutative and distributive justice. These acts, whether construed as indirect "acts" of legal justice or direct acts of commutative or distributive justice, are generally insufficient for the task of restructuring the social order at any level. As de Tocqueville noted,

> The first of the duties that are at this time imposed upon those who direct our affairs is to educate democracy, to reawaken, if possible, its religious beliefs; to purify its morals; to mold its actions; to substitute a knowledge of statecraft for its inexperience, and an awareness of its true interest for its blind instincts, to adapt its government to time and place, and to modify it according to men and to conditions. A new science of politics is needed for a new world.[16]

This anticipated Pius XI's statement that, "The pastoral theology of another day will no longer suffice."[17] It also gives a hint that Pius XI may have been familiar with de Tocqueville's work — particularly its emphasis on individual sovereignty and the whole idea of groups. No one can read de Tocqueville's *Democracy in America* or Pius XI's

Quadragesimo Anno without being struck by just how many times each one emphasizes the right of free association.

Solidarity

What is the role of "solidarity" in all this? We hear a lot of talk about it, but very few people ever seem to get down to specifics. Solidarity is actually quite a simple concept.

Solidarity, often mistaken for social charity, is merely a characteristic of groups *per se*. It is an inherent and integral part of all social virtue. This is because without solidarity "the group" simply would not exist.

Solidarity consists of acceptance and internalization by the members of a group of the principles and goals that define a group as that particular group. One of the "acts" of social charity — the virtue that commands us to love our institutions as we love ourselves (and structured groups are institutions) — is accepting and internalizing the principles and goals that define the group. This can lead to the understandable confusion between solidarity and social charity.

Solidarity is thus the "glue" that holds groups together, but it is not a virtue in the philosophical sense of the term. Some very unvirtuous groups, for example, can have a high degree of solidarity, such as street gangs and Nazis. We cannot carry out acts of any kind of social virtue without solidarity, and may even, in a limited sense, understand solidarity as an act of social charity — perhaps even the act of social charity. Solidarity is not itself, however, a virtue in the classic sense.

Where Do We Go From Here?

What we've analyzed of Pius XI's political thought so far gives us the basis to understand his specific recommendations for restructuring the social order, and for putting them in their proper order. That is, consideration for the dignity of the human person is paramount within the temporal sphere. This requires recognition of each human being's individual and personal sovereignty.

This Pius XI did with his careful correction of the political thought of Saint Robert Cardinal Bellarmine, and his equally careful exposition of this correction in his encyclicals, most notably *Quas Primas*. This was the foundation for Pius XI's completed doctrine of social virtue, a development from the hints given by Saint Thomas Aquinas. In the third part of this article we will move on to specifics, as well as develop an orientation for understanding Pius XI's plan for a more just ordering of society, both economically and politically.

Notes

[1] 1-2: 61: 5, 4m.
[2] *De Laicis*, VI.
[3] Ferree, *op. cit.*, 193-211.
[4] Rev. John Francis Murphy, S.T.L., *The Moral Obligation of the Individual to Participate in Catholic Action*. Washington, DC: The Catholic University of America Press, 1958; Ferree, *op. cit.*, 186-187.
[5] Ferree, *ibid.*, 177-178.
[6] *Divini Redemptoris*, § 53.
[7] Father Ferree used the term "indirect social justice," which didn't make complete sense, given his thesis that social justice was a particular virtue. I believe he meant legal justice, which can, in a certain sense, be understood as "indirect social justice."
[8] *Quadragesimo Anno*, § 79.
[9] *Ibid.*, § 63.
[10] Rev. Heinrich Pesch, S.J., *Lehrbuch der Nationaloeconomie*, 2, 316; 5, 123.
[11] Mary Lois Eberdt, C.H.M., Ph.D., Gerald J. Schnepp, S.M., Ph.D., *Industrialism and the Popes*. New York: P. J. Kenedy & Sons, 1953, 53 *et seq.*; Fr. Thomas J. Higgins, S.J., *Man as Man: The Science and Art of Ethics*. Rockford, Illinois: TAN Books and Publishers, 1992), §§ 962 – 975; Raymond J. Miller, C.Ss.R., *Forty Years After: Pius XI and the Social Order, A Commentary*. St. Paul, Minnesota: Radio Replies Press, 1947, §§ 22.4, 30.15, 110.3.
[12] Pesch, *loc. cit.*
[13] Rev. William J. Ferree, S.M., Ph.D., *Introduction to Social Justice*. Washington, DC: Center for Economic and Social Justice, 1996, 49-50.
[14] Discourse to Diocesan Congress of Catholic Youth, May 16, 1926; *Catholic Action*, 107-112.
[15] *Ethics*, 1129b26

[16] Alexis de Tocqueville, *Democracy in America*, "Author's Introduction to the First Part."

[17] Pius XI, *Discourse to the Ecclesiastical Assistants of the U.C.F.I.*, July 19, 1928. Quoted in Civardi, *Manual of Catholic Action*. New York: Sheed and Ward, 1936, 178.

Part III

The Restructuring of the Social Order

In the first two parts of this article we saw that Pius XI supported the Judeo-Christian concept of individual and personal sovereignty with the rigorous development of a new theory of social virtue. Based soundly on the lead provided by Saint Thomas Aquinas,[1] the pope's theory of social virtue corrected the error that Saint Robert Bellarmine committed by his insertion of the collective between God and man, and between man and his chosen representatives.

What resulted was a theory of individual and personal responsibility for the whole of the common good by direct action on the part of each person on each person's particular level of the common good. Individuals acting alone cannot fulfill this responsibility. It can only be effected by sovereign individuals acting in solidarity and free association with like-minded others.

The role of the State is not forgotten or ignored in Pius XI's analysis. On the contrary, the role of the State is extremely important — but nowhere near as significant as some people appear to believe.[2] The primary responsibility for particular levels of the common good rests through acts of social justice on those subsisting within or at each particular level. The role of the State, on the other hand, is the care and maintenance of the whole of the common good.[3] This is a general responsibility through indirect "acts" of legal justice. Care of the common good is not a particular responsibility of the State through direct acts of social justice, except in instances where those at particular levels of the common good cannot carry out their responsibilities without the assistance of a higher level.

We are now in a position to examine specifics of what Pius XI meant by his mandate to restructure the whole of the social order. A significant measure of this can be found in his treatment of an extremely important institution in civil society, that of private property.

Private Property

First we need a brief definition of property. "Property" is not the thing owned. Property is the bundle of rights an owner or potential owner has to own a thing, and what he can do with that thing once he owns it. Primarily this means that every human being by nature has the right to acquire and possess things, without let or hindrance, unless other individuals or the common good are thereby harmed in some manner.

It also means that the owner has the right to receive the benefits of ownership once a thing is owned. For productive things, this means the right to receive the income generated by the thing. It also means the right to dispose of the thing as the owner wills, and to treat it as he sees fit. Unlike the right to own, however, these rights of property are not absolute or unlimited. An owner cannot in any way harm others or the common good in his exercise of his rights, and the exercise itself must be consistent with the needs of a well-ordered society.

Property and Politics

Political commentators through the ages have always assigned great importance to the institution of private property. Some, like John Locke, have declared that private property is the sole foundation for the whole of civil society.[4] Others, such as Karl Marx, have blamed all the troubles of the world on the existence of private property, and advocated its abolition.[5] Until the aberrations of capitalism and socialism infected most of human society, however, no one thought that private property was negligible in its effect, however much they might argue whether it was beneficial or harmful.

Concepts such as liberty, sovereignty of the people, dignity and freedom are inextricably linked with the idea of property. This is clear from the sources the Founding Fathers of the United States drew upon to design a government of the people, by the people and for the people. Sidney,[6] Locke,[7]

Montesquieu[8] all relied on a theory and philosophy of property which enhanced the sovereignty of the individual and protected the family from the encroachments of the more powerful.

For Pius XI, private property provides the most effective and intimate connection with our milieux.[9] Nothing else gives the individual the same natural degree and kind of control. From both a social and an individual standpoint, then, private property is essential to the maintenance of a stable and moral social order.[10] As Pius XII was to observe later,

> Therefore the dignity of the human person normally demands the right to the use of earthly goods as the natural foundation for a livelihood; and to that right corresponds the fundamental obligation to grant private property, as far as possible, to all. The positive laws regulating private property may change and may grant a more or less restricted use of it; but if such legal provisions are to contribute to the peaceful state of the community, they must save the worker, who is or will be the father of a family, from being condemned to an economic dependence or slavery irreconcilable with his rights as a person.
>
> Whether this slavery arises from the tyranny of private capital or from the power of the State makes no difference to its effect; indeed under the oppression of a State which controls everything and regulates the whole of public and private life, which encroaches even upon the sphere of thought, conviction, and conscience, this lack of freedom may have consequences even more disastrous, as experience shows.[11]

The Means to Acquire and Possess Property

This is all very well, but how are ordinary people without savings supposed to become owners of productive assets? As everyone knows, it takes money to make money — and the poor, by definition, don't have money.

Access to the money and credit systems in modern society is severely restricted. Since the means to acquire and possess property is concentrated, it follows, then, that ownership itself will be concentrated. This turns out to be the case. Pius XI reminds us that,

> ... not only is wealth concentrated in our times, but an immense power and despotic economic dictatorship is consolidated in the hands of a few ... who, since they hold the money and completely control it, control credit also and rule the lending of money. Hence, they regulate the flow, so to speak, of the life blood whereby the entire economic system lives, and so have firmly in their grasp the soul, as it were, of economic life that no one can breathe against their will. This concentration of power and might ... [is] the character mark ... of contemporary economic life .... [12]

If capital credit became as universally accessible as the political ballot, another "social good," capital assets could become a growing source of independent capital ownership and thus incomes for everyone. What makes capital credit special is that by nature it is procreative or "self-liquidating." That is, capital credit is restricted to the purchase of assets that are expected to pay for themselves out of the revenues generated from the capital project which it financed, and thereafter these assets are expected to earn a continuing flow of profit for whoever owns the assets. Capital credit is inherently counter-inflationary. Consumer credit, on the other hand, does not generate its own repayment, and any repayment must come out of the user's other resources. When used to any significant extent, consumer credit greatly reduces the purchasing power of the user.

Power and property go together, and how money and credit flow into society determines who has property, and thus power. This is not to say that the power that derives from property is the only kind of power that exists. It is, however, the single most important kind of power in the temporal order, for it is through property that the human person is connected to the economic process in a way that guarantees the opportunity for full participation in the common good at his levels of the common good. "Equal opportunity" includes equal access to the means to exercise that opportunity, and access to capital credit determines who has access to property.

An Economically Just Society

We are now in a position to understand what Pius XI intended by his mandate to restructure the social order, at least in the economic sphere. When we understand that, however, we will also have an understanding of the application of the term to the whole of civil society — the subject is, after all, *political* economy. As astute political theorists and practitioners through the centuries have noted, political power and private property are inextricably linked.[13] One will not last without the other.

Society — whether political or economic (or political *and* economic) — must be based on universal moral virtues. In Pius XI's concept, these virtues must be interpreted and applied in a manner consistent with the principles taught by the Catholic Church. The Catholic Church is thus the principal guide — a conscience (although not the sole conscience) — of civil society. As a discrete society of its own, however, neither the Church nor any other religious society has the competence to enforce its interpretations of universal moral virtues in the civil order. Maintaining the civil order is the job of the "princes and rulers of men"[14] — the State.

Obviously this understanding of the role of the Catholic Church precludes a theocracy. Separation of Church and State, properly understood, is a given, and has been from the establishment of the Church. "Render therefore unto Cæsar that which is Cæsar's, and unto God that which is God's."[15] This understanding also obviates the takeover of the Church by the State, creating an "established church" as a government bureau, with the ministers of religion construed as civil servants.

Nor, finally, is it necessary that everyone on earth become a Catholic — at least not for the purpose of establishing and maintaining a just economic and political order in the temporal sphere. (Personal salvation and attainment of heaven is another matter, but one that does not concern us in this analysis.) It is not necessary in this respect that everyone on earth even be aware of the existence of the Catholic Church. It is only necessary that whatever form of civil society is adopted be based on universal moral virtues as interpreted — or would be interpreted — by the Catholic Church. Effectively, in "Catholic language," this means that the interpretation and application of universal moral virtues in civil society not be contrary in any material way to the Magisterium.

The Four Pillars

Economically, then, the arrangement of civil society that Pius XI had in mind is characterized by what the interfaith Center for Economic and Social Justice calls "the Four Pillars of an Economically Justice Society."[16] In no particular order, these are as follows:

1. A Limited Economic Role for the State

A limited economic role for the State conforms to the principle of subsidiarity as explained in the first part of this article. It is most improper, indeed, a violation of the most basic principles of civil society, that any level of the common good, high or low, usurp or "pirate" the functions of any other level of the common good.[17] Where the people at a "lower" level of the common good can meet their economic needs without the interference of the "higher" levels, the higher levels have no excuse to intervene. When the necessity of intervention exists, it must be limited to giving immediate and necessary assistance, and helping to arrange matters so that the people at the lower level can once more take care of matters themselves.

2. Free and Open Markets

"Free and open markets" does not mean the traditional *laissez faire* economy so dear to today's "neo-conservatives." It is, rather, an economic order characterized by free and full access by everyone, and one in which the State confines itself to keeping order and policing abuses.[18] Within this "strong juridical framework," the market operates to determine justice in prices, wages and profits. This is achieved through free association within a structured framework that also fosters choice and efficiency. The free market is the economic application of Pius XI's demand for the right of free association in all matters relating to the common good.

3. Restoration of the Rights of Private Property

Restoration of the rights of private property, particularly in corporate equity, is integral to Pius XI's program of restructuring the social order, as any objective reading of *Quadragesimo Anno* reveals. The need to restore individual rights of private property is obvious from the importance Pius XI placed on the institution. What is not so obvious is the role that the pope assigned to the business corporation.[19] While some authorities dispute this interpretation,[20] Pius XI saw a reformed business corporation conformed to universal moral virtues (principally justice) as a primary vehicle for restructuring the economic order. The business corporation is designed specifically to enable many people to own a single asset or group of assets. Thus, in our technologically advanced age in which things, not people, carry out the bulk of production,[21] a mechanism that allows ordinary people to own and control the means of production — the business corporation — exactly fills the bill.

4. Expanded Direct Ownership of the Means of Production

Expanded ownership of the means of production is simply Leo XIII's mandate from *Rerum Novarum* that, "The law, therefore, should favor ownership, and its policy should be to induce as many as possible of the people to become owners."[22] The emphasis on this "pillar" reinforces Pope Leo XIII's declaration earlier in the same encyclical that, "It is surely undeniable that, when a man engages in remunerative labor, the impelling reason and motive of his work is to obtain property, and thereafter to hold it as his very own."[23]

The Restructuring of the Social Order

This, then, is why Pius XI, faced with the decay, even dissolution of society throughout the world, focused all his attention on establishing and maintaining a social order based on a sound interpretation of absolute and universal moral virtues. It emphasizes the importance of *Quas Primas*, the encyclical that instituted the Feast of Christ the King, a day intended to celebrate a sound restructuring of the social order. The "Feast of Christ the King" does not mean that Christ acting through His vicegerent the pope is the rightful or supreme temporal ruler of the entire world. Nor does it mean that everyone on earth must become a Catholic so that the civil order can be properly maintained and advanced. As Jesus said in response to Pilate's question as to whether He was a king, "That is your word for it."[24]

Pilate's question was very important. This was not just for his personal comfort (he could not allow an unauthorized king to arise in opposition to Cæsar, after all[25]), but for all ages that followed. The Romans had a very specific idea of kingship, one that lasted, again in theory at least, until the Reformation. That is, a king was an elected or appointed representative of a tribe or nation. He could be elected by his own people and confirmed by the Augustus, or simply appointed by the Senate and the People of Rome . . . and confirmed by the Augustus.[26]

In reality, while the theory was that a king's power came from the people whom he ruled on their behalf and for the benefit of the whole Empire, it was the Augustus — Cæsar — who held the real power. The power of the Augustus was presumed to come from the people of the Empire, confirmed by the Senate and enforced by the Legions. We may look down on the Romans' general failure to conform reality to theory, but then, how close does our contemporary American society come to the vision of the Founding Fathers? People without property, even Roman citizens, may not have had much effective political power, but at least they paid lip service to the ideal.

Are You a King?

Within a specifically Christian orientation, Jesus is therefore a "king," but not in today's usual civil meaning of the term, nor even the pre-Reformation sense. The Reformation made matters worse, merging civil and religious society and promoting the divine right of kings . . . a theory developed out of the *potestas* of the *pater familias* who ruled domestic society. "Divine right" is, essentially, the idea that the State and its agents receive their authority directly from God.[27]

God the Father — the Augustus of the universe — appointed Christ as King. The Father thereby delegates religious and personal power over the world to His Son, as Jesus Himself acknowledged — ". . . the Son cannot do anything by Himself — He can do only what He sees the Father doing."[28] That is, Jesus acts "automatically" in accordance with natural law, which is God's Nature, which (as the human person is made "in the image and likeness of God") is also "analogously complete" ("equal," loosely) in every human being, although, being "fallen" and in possession of free will, we do not act automatically in accordance with our own nature.

In the Christian view, Christ therefore rules over the whole world, but without prejudice to the established civil rulers of men, and not in the same way that they rule. Christ rules morally, individually, and religiously through adherence to the natural law by individuals and institutions (including nations), not politically or civilly. According to Pius XI's formulation, even non-Christians live within this framework when they order their private and public lives in accordance with a sound interpretation of natural law. In Catholic theology, it is possible to reject Christ's moral authority explicitly and still be in material conformity with it.[29]

Civil rule is distinct from the religious and personal rule of Christ. The "catch" is that the authority of chosen representatives and even the legitimacy of the State itself are based, ultimately, on the authority given to Jesus by God the Father. Jesus in turn grants a measure of this sovereignty directly to the human person, from which a portion of it (the general virtue of legal justice) is delegated[30] to the chosen representatives of the people.[31] The State then exercises indirect control over the common good through "acts" of legal justice — passing and enforcing laws, supporting custom and tradition, and encouraging generally moral behavior. Passing and enforcing laws, of course, are direct acts of distributive and commutative justice, which, as Aristotle and Aquinas observed, have a direct effect on individuals, and an indirect effect on the common good.

Individual Sovereignty and the Act of Social Justice

The human person retains the larger and by far the most important portion of the sovereignty of the human person, that which is exercised through acts of social justice. Individuals exercise social justice by coming together in groups in free association, thereby gaining and maintaining direct control over the common good at their particular levels.

The authority of "Christ the King" is moral, but none the less real for that — "Render therefore unto Cæsar the things which are Cæsar's, and unto God the things which are God's."[32] Jesus is concerned with the acquisition and development of virtue and the practice of these universal moral virtues on the part of individuals.[33] Christ "rules" as "king" only indirectly over society, that is, the common good, via His sovereignty transmitted through the individuals who participate fully in the social order.

Christ's dominion exhibits itself through a proper interpretation of natural law — something that exists in every human being, at least in essence. He rules over the hearts of men, explicitly or implicitly (it doesn't matter for the purposes of civil society) by human acquisition, development, and exercise of virtue, not as a political representative. Virtues are to be understood and interpreted in a way that does not contradict the interpretation of the Catholic Church.

Men are to acquire and develop virtue as the means of attaining heaven, their true end. To assist them in this, the institutions of society are to be structured through acts of social justice in such a way as to assist individuals to the optimal level in their task of acquiring and developing virtue. This structuring (or restructuring) is not the job of "Christ the King," but of individual men, each of whom has a personal responsibility for the common good. Each individual's power to do this comes directly from God. Jesus through His Church guides each individual in his efforts, but is not the only guide — the Catholic Church claims a fullness of truth, not a monopoly on it. The individual effects the actual work himself, in free association with others as members of society.

In Conclusion . . .

What Pius XI had in mind, then, is a state of society based on universal moral virtues interpreted in a manner that is not contrary to the Magisterium. Politically this means that a State that embodies the substance of democracy, which best respects the dignity of the human person, and is, as Saint Robert Bellarmine says, "the more useful form of government,"[34] is the Catholic ideal — but without prejudice to any specific arrangement or form of government. Economically, it means that society must embody the "Four pillars of an economically just society."

In short, in contrast to civil leaders and all members of society, who are concerned with the common good, "Christ the King" is concerned with the individual good of each member of the human race. It is therefore impossible that He should be "king" in the sense many people understand the term — He has no direct authority over the common good's institutional structure, a human construct. Rather, it is His concern that each of us gain heaven, our true end and home. Without that, everything else is meaningless. With that, everything acquires the most sublime and profound meaning. The perfection of the temporal order is completely meaningless unless it assists us in our individual perfection and final attainment of our true end.

This is valid for non-Catholics, even atheists, who (if rational) assume that life has a purpose, and that purpose is to become more fully human. The definition and understanding of what it means to become more fully human may be a matter for discussion among various religions and ethical systems, but the fact that man's "job" on earth is to become more fully what he is by nature should be obvious. We therefore have a personal and individual responsibility to see that our network of institutions — the common good — supports and assists us in our job of becoming more fully human.

This means that we may not ignore the flaws and imperfections in the common good. On the contrary, it is our personal responsibility to take care of matters in conformity with universal moral virtues. Restructuring the social order is our problem, not God's, and we shall be held accountable for our success or failure. That is why each of us has been granted an individual and personal sovereignty by God, and how we are to use it.

Notes

[1] Father William J. Ferree, S.M., Ph.D., *The Act of Social Justice*. Washington, DC: The Catholic University of America Press, 1942.

[2] *E.g.*, "The state is the sole intercessor available to the poor." Rupert J. Ederer, Ph.D., "Solidaristic Economics" *Fidelity* magazine. July/August 1994. This belief is flatly contradicted not only in the New Testament, but *Quadragesimo Anno*, § 78 as well.

[3] Higgins, *op. cit.*, § 859.

[4] John Locke, *Second Treatise on Government*, §§ 94, 124.

[5] ". . . the theory of the Communists may be summed up in the single sentence: Abolition of private property." Karl Marx and Friedrich Engels, *The Communist Manifesto* (London: Penguin Books, 1967), 96.

[6] Algernon Sidney, *Discourses Concerning Government*, III.16.
[7] Locke, *op. cit.*, § 201.
[8] Charles Louis de Secondat, Baron de la Brède et de Montesquieu, *The Spirit of Laws*, V.14.
[9] *Quadragesimo Anno, op. cit.*, §§ 59-60.
[10] *Ibid.*, § 61.
[11] Pius XII, Christmas Broadcast, 1942, "The Rights of Man."
[12] Pius XI, *Quadragesimo Anno* ("On Restructuring the Social Order"), 1931, §§ 105-107.
[13] Daniel Webster, Massachusetts Convention of 1820, Benjamin Watkins Leigh, Virginia Convention of 1820, William Cobbett, *A History of the Protestant Reformation in England and Ireland* (1827).
[14] *Quas Primas, loc. cit.*
[15] Mt. 22:21.
[16] Norman G. Kurland, "Beyond ESOP: Steps Toward Tax Justice" *Curing World Poverty: The New Role of Property, John H. Miller, C.S.C., S.T.D.*, ed. St. Louis, Missouri: Social Justice Review, 1994, 159.
[17] Rev. William J. Ferree, S.M., Ph.D., *Forty Years After . . . A Second Call to Battle*. Ms., c. 1984
[18] John Paul II, *Centesimus Annus* ("On the Hundredth Anniversary of *Rerum Novarum*"), § 42.
[19] Rev. William J. Ferree, S.M., Ph.D., *Administration and Social Ethics*. Ms., c. 1980, § 163.
[20] See, *e.g.*, Rev. Edmund Cahill, S.J., *The Framework of a Christian State*. Dublin: M. H. Gill and Son, Ltd., 1932, 419, 421, 473, 481.
[21] Robert H. A. Ashford, "The Binary Economics of Louis Kelso" *Curing World Poverty, op. cit.*, 112.
[22] Leo XIII, *Rerum Novarum* ("On the Condition of the Working Classes"), 1891, § 46.
[23] *Ibid.*, § 5.
[24] Lk. 23:3.
[25] Jn. 18:37, 19:15. In a bit of historical irony, the man who is believed to have been the Senatorial governor of Syria at the time of Jesus' birth, Publius Quinctilius Varus, is reported by Flavius Josephus as making an attempt to set himself up as king in opposition to Cæsar. (Publius Sulpicius Quirinius, the one named as governor of Syria in Luke, seems to have been Augustus Cæsar's personal representative, acting as governor to get the work done, while Varus collected graft. Varus was related to

Augustus by marriage and appears to have been utterly incompetent — he was responsible for the destruction of three Legions and the loss of Germania at the Battle of Teutoburgerwald in A.D. 9 . . . an unnecessary battle for which he was personally culpable. Quirinius was a friend of the family, and by all accounts an excellent soldier and administrator, often being charged with "cleaning up" the messes left by Varus.)

[26] J. B. Bury, *The Invasion of Europe by the Barbarians*. New York: W. W. Norton, 1967, 13.

[27] James VI/I, *The Trew Law of Free Monarchies* (1598), *A Speech to the Lords and Commons of the Parliament at White-Hall* (1610); Sir Robert Filmer, *Observations Upon Aristotle's Politiques* (1652), *Patriarcha* (1680), and others too numerous to list. The official position of the established Church of England is published in its *Constitutions and Canons of the Church of England*: "The most sacred order of kings is of Divine Right."

[28] Jn. 5:19.

[29] Mt. 21:28-31.

[30] "Reflected" as Pius XI puts it in § 19 of *Quas Primas*, using Aristotle's terminology.

[31] The "princes and rulers of men." *Ibid*.

[32] Lk. 20:20 – 25.

[33] Igino Giordani, *The Social Message of Jesus*. Boston, Massachusetts: The Daughters of Saint Paul, 1977, 19.

[34] *De Ecclesiastica Monarchia*, I.

6. Is Property Theft? The Idea of Property

(*Social Justice Review*, January/February 2006)

Many people make a seemingly unimportant error about the institution of private property. Concerned about growing economic and consequent political disenfranchisement of increasing numbers of people, they assert with Proudhon that, "property is theft."[1] Liberal political philosophy, however, declares that the State was organized by men agreeing to enter society from a "state of nature" in order to obtain protection of property. If "property is theft," then the State, government, and everything relating to them are necessarily illegitimate.

The claim that "property is theft" also contains an inherent contradiction from the Judeo-Christian perspective. The Decalogue clearly states, "Thou shalt not steal." As any lawyer can tell you, the existence of a proscription implies the legitimacy of the thing against which a proscribed act is directed. It otherwise makes no sense to forbid an act. Theft is a violation of the right to and rights of private property; ultimately Proudhon's little jibe ends up meaning that "property is a violation of property" — an obvious contradiction, and therefore nonsense.

The Foundation of the Social Order

The liberal orientation, while containing a measure of the truth, is not completely sound. This provides a "wedge" for anyone intent upon promoting his own concept of property. The liberal error lies primarily in the view of society itself. That is, society does not exist until individuals, by their explicit consent, enter or form a society and bind themselves and their descendents. Prior to this, relations among individuals are not social, but individual interaction.

From the traditional Christian perspective, best explained by Saint Thomas Aquinas[2] and Saint Robert Cardinal Bellarmine,[3] however, men do not agree to "enter" society for any reason. As Aristotle claimed, man is political by nature. We don't agree by any kind of compact to *enter* society. Instead, the human person is *automatically* a member of society, but makes a compact, express or implied, as to his membership in a particular social order and his consent as to how it is structured. The structuring of the system becomes the issue, not the mere fact of the system itself. "The system" is not a given, but (as Pius XI hinted in the title and stated in the text of *Quadragesimo Anno*) is a thing under our direct care. The system is subject to restructuring the better to meet man's wants, needs, and the demand to respect the dignity of each human person.

This does not, however, negate the significance of private property. On the contrary, it emphasizes the importance of the institution. "Power," as Daniel Webster observed, "naturally and necessarily follows property."[4] Every human being needs power in order to exist in a manner befitting human dignity. Man needs power over his own life in order to keep himself alive. That is, he needs power to obtain the means of production in order to produce goods and services so that he may live. This power we derive from something we call "property." Man also needs a certain amount of power to protect himself from domination by others. This is not to control others' lives, but to prevent others from controlling him. This power, too, we derive from what we call "property," and the ordering of "property" must be systematic, that is, part of the overall social system, or it becomes meaningless. This may be confusing, but we can clarify it as follows.

What is Property?

First, it must clearly be understood that property is not a thing, but the bundle of rights a person has to or over a thing. Second, there are two categories of rights of property, as we have already noted. The first is the right that everyone has to become an owner — the right of access in order to obtain the means of production to produce goods and services so that he may live. The social system must first be arranged so that this right is operative for the maximum number of people.

This right of access to property is natural, sacred, and universal. No one may be deprived of the right to own property, any more than he may be deprived of life or liberty. This is a generic right, what the popes have referred to as "the generic right of dominion." That is, being "generic" and relating to the structure of society, it must be an integral part not only of human nature, but of the system structured in conformity with human nature.

This right to property does not apply to possessions that are already owned by others, except in extremely limited circumstances. It refers only to the fact that everyone and anyone must be allowed to become an owner, and that individuals, government, or society as a whole may not place or maintain barriers — a system of exclusion — against any who desire to become owners. This right to property is *inclusive*.

The second kind of property consists of the bundle of rights that an owner has over his possessions — the right to control others to a limited extent. This kind of property is also part of the social system, but in an exclusionary way because it is not generic, but individual. As one legal text on property puts it,

> Property as a social institution implies a system of relations between individuals. Like other social institutions it involves rights, duties, powers, privileges, forbearances, etc., of certain kinds. It differs essentially from other social institutions — familial, political, religious, and so on — because in addition to the relations between the individuals involved, there are always relations of a certain kind to a wide range of objects of various categories (or infrequently, people who function as objects in a particular system of property relations). As Cairns formulates it, "the

> property relation is triadic: 'A owns B against C,' where C represents all other individuals; . . ."[5]

This "type" of property is the owner's rights of possession, control and disposal of the thing owned, or the fruits of whatever is owned. These rights of property are *exclusive*, that is, the owner may exclude others from enjoying the fruits of ownership. This type of property is, by its very nature, limited by the demands of the common good. In general, an owner may not use his possessions to harm himself, others or society.

Unlike his right to become an owner, a person's control over his possessions is not unlimited, although, as Saint Thomas pointed out, it is derived from the natural right to property, and alienable only through due process and for just cause. There are, then, circumstances in which the amount and kind of possessions owned or controlled by one individual, a group, or even the whole of society must be limited for the common good, but without prejudice to the underlying right to become an owner. This could be the case when an actual or effective monopoly prevents or inhibits others from exercising their rights to and of property — the system is distorted due to concentration of economic power in the hands of a few.

To try and make the nature of this type of property clear, we can again quote from the same legal text cited above.

> First of all it is necessary to consider the nature and the kinds of rights exercised and their correlative duties and obligations. What sometimes has been considered the essence of the property relation in western society, viz., exclusive use, enjoyment and disposition of an object for an unlimited period of time, is only one specific constellation of property rights, a limiting case, as it were. As a matter of fact, absolute control of property by an owner is non-existent in our society and according to Seagle "in no legal system have rights of property been absolute." . . . In

all societies, then, property comprises a "bundle of rights," not a single right, nor an absolute right. These rights may be of different kinds.... [6]

No Paradox in Property

Here we seem to have a contradiction. To resolve it, we need only realize that *having* a right is not the same as *exercising* a right. A right — such as property — can be *possessed* in its entirety. It must be regarded as both sacred and inviolate, that is, inalienable, a natural right or part of human nature. Possession of such a right cannot be abrogated without negating, denying, or destroying human nature itself.

What cannot be unlimited, especially in light of the above quoted analysis, is the *exercise* of a right. Unless we carefully and precisely distinguish between the two meanings of "property," we will never understand that, far from being "theft," private property is an essential, almost cosmically important pillar of civil society.

The liberal errors lie in maintaining, one, that man is not social by nature, and two, that the *sole* justification for society is protection of property. Protection of property is an extraordinarily important aspect or feature of man's social nature, but it is not the reason for society's existence, which is the perfection of the human person in his relationship with God.

Man needs power in order to function as a human person in society, and that power is rooted in private property. As Benjamin Watkins Leigh declared, "Power and Property can be separated for a time by force or fraud — but divorced, never. For as soon as the pang of separation is felt. . . Property will purchase Power, or Power will take over Property."[7]

Medieval Social Teaching

With this clarification of property we can understand what Saint Thomas had to say. He asks the question, "whether it is natural for man to possess external things?"

> External things can be considered in two ways. First, as regards their nature, and this is not subject to the power of man, but only to the power of God Whose mere will all things obey. Secondly, as regards their use, and in this way, man has a natural dominion over external things, because, by his reason and will, he is able to use them for his own profit, as they were made on his account: for the imperfect is always for the sake of the perfect, as stated above (Question [64], Article [1]). <u>It is by this argument that the Philosopher proves (*Polit.* i, 3) that the possession of external things is natural to man</u>. Moreover, this natural dominion of man over other creatures, which is competent to man in respect of his reason wherein God's image resides, is shown forth in man's creation (Gn. 1:26) by the words: "Let us make man to our image and likeness: and let him have dominion over the fishes of the sea," *etc*.

In response to other objections, the Angelic Doctor goes on to say,

> Augustine says (*De Haeres.*, haer. 40): "The 'Apostolici' are those who with extreme arrogance have given themselves that name, because they do not admit into their communion persons who are married or possess anything of their own, such as both monks and clerics who in considerable number are to be found in the Catholic Church." Now the reason why these people are heretics was because severing themselves from the Church, they think that those who enjoy the use of the above things, which they themselves lack, have no hope of salvation. Therefore it is erroneous to maintain that it is unlawful for a man to possess property.

> Two things are competent to man in respect of exterior things. One is the power to procure and dispense

them, and in this regard it is lawful for man to possess property. Moreover this is necessary to human life for three reasons. First because every man is more careful to procure what is for himself alone than that which is common to many or to all: since each one would shirk the labor and leave to another that which concerns the community, as happens where there is a great number of servants. Secondly, because human affairs are conducted in more orderly fashion if each man is charged with taking care of some particular thing himself, whereas there would be confusion if everyone had to look after any one thing indeterminately. Thirdly, because a more peaceful state is ensured to man if each one is contented with his own. Hence it is to be observed that quarrels arise more frequently where there is no division of the things possessed.

Thus, Saint Thomas distinguished between the right *to* and the rights *of* property. The former is to be considered, in the words of Leo XIII, as "sacred and inviolable," that is, inalienable, and not subject to any limitation at all, construing "limitation" in the sense that you limit who may become an owner and in what degree that owner may enjoy the socially-defined exercise of the right possessed.

(In this sense, the "beneficial ownership" that participants in qualified retirement plans in the United States have instead of direct ownership and title is a serious abrogation of the natural right to private property. Ownership through a trust — beneficial ownership — is imposed on incompetents and children because they presumably are not capable of exercising the rights of property properly. That is, they are either not fully human, or have not acquired and developed a sufficient degree of virtue to be able to administer their own property competently.)

The exercise of property — the rights of property — is limited to the extent that others would be excluded from enjoying the same right, or when others or the common good would be materially harmed. The exercise of property, including at times the amount that any individual may acquire, is limited by the demands of the common good and the needs of other individuals. Property in its exercise and its acquisition is an individual, not a collective right.

It is, in fact, impossible for any natural right to be a right of the collective. As Pius XI pointed out, "only man, and not society in any form, has a morally free will."[8] The collective, a form of society, can only have rights that are delegated to it by the individual members of the collective who are "natural persons" with "morally free wills" and thus natural rights.

This was the very point on which John XXII issued the Bull *Quia Vir Reprobus* ("That Evil Man") in 1329, excommunicating the then-Father General of the Franciscans, Michael of Cesena. Michael of Cesena was asserting that access to property was not a natural right, and that use alone, determined by man's law, was the sole justification for ownership. Michael of Cesena refused to accept correction and, in fact, circulated insulting pamphlets about the pope and Saint Thomas' teachings on property.

Deciding that the ultimate power of correction and rehabilitation should be invoked to bring the *reus* ("criminal") to a more reasonable frame of mind, the pope excommunicated Michael of Cesena. The pope exhaustively detailed the justification for the traditional teaching that access to private property is a natural right, and that the exercise of private property, while not a natural right, is derived therefrom and can never be defined in any way that undermines the underlying natural right.

Paragraph 27 of the Bull, for example, states that "the heretic" is incorrect in his essential premise. Genesis relates that God explicitly gave personal, not common, ownership to Adam before our "first parent" was expelled from Eden. The right to property, antedating the Fall, is therefore a natural right. The use thereof, while subsequent to the Fall, was derived from and inextricably linked to the natural right to be an owner, with specific exercise determined and limited by man's social nature, the needs and rights of other individuals, groups, and the demands of the common good as a whole.

Modern Social Teaching

Leaping quickly to the modern age, we come to *Rerum Novarum*, considered by many authorities to be the first social encyclical. The following extracts were taken from the official English edition on the Vatican website.[9] Careful readers will note that certain words have been deleted from a number of other editions in ways that tend to water down or confuse the issue.

> 9. Here, again, we have further proof that *private ownership is in accordance with the law of nature.* Truly, that which is required for the preservation of life, and for life's well-being, is produced in great abundance from the soil, but not until man has brought it into cultivation and expended upon it his solicitude and skill. Now, when man thus turns the activity of his mind and the strength of his body toward procuring the fruits of nature, by such act he makes his own that portion of nature's field which he cultivates — that portion on which he leaves, as it were, the impress of his personality; and it cannot but be just that he should possess that portion as his very own, and have a right to hold it without any one being justified in violating that right. [Emphasis added.]

> 22. . . . The chief and most excellent rule for the right use of money is one the heathen philosophers hinted at, but which the Church has traced out clearly, and has not only made known to men's minds, but has impressed upon their lives. *It rests on the principle that it is one thing to have a right to the possession of money and another to have a right to use money as one wills.* Private ownership, as we have seen, is the natural right of man, and to exercise

that right, especially as members of society, is not only lawful, but absolutely necessary. "It is lawful," says St. Thomas Aquinas, "for a man to hold private property; and it is also necessary for the carrying on of human existence." [Emphasis added.]

46. . . . *We have seen that this great labor question cannot be solved save by assuming as a principle that private ownership must be held sacred and inviolable.* The law, therefore, should favor ownership, and its policy should be to induce as many as possible of the people to become owners. [Emphasis added.]

Pius XII restates this in his pivotal 1942 Christmas broadcast, "The Rights of Man." The pope clearly construed this address as a response to the terrors of Nazism. The Nazi concept of landed property has been stated thus:

In its underlying theory Nazism denied the absolute character of property, and imposed obligations conditioning property tenure. Property without function was to be abolished.[10] The acquisition of legal title was a continuous process, of which legitimate use was the essence. Ownership was not a right that stood by its own virtue, but a trusteeship for the discharge of the aims of the community. "All property is common property. The owner is obliged to administer it."[11]

Pius XII, carefully distinguishing between the inalienable and the limited characters of property, declared that,

The dignity of the human person, then, requires normally as a natural foundation of life the right to the use of the goods of the earth. *To this right corresponds the fundamental obligation to grant private ownership of property, if possible, to all.* Positive legislation regulating private ownership may change and more or less restrict its use. But if legislation is to play its part in the pacification of the community, it must prevent the worker, who is or will be a father of a family, from being condemned to an economic dependence and slavery which is irreconcilable with his rights as a person. [emphasis added]

National Socialism is True Socialism

Ironically, the Nazi position is virtually indistinguishable from that of Fr. Charles Curran, former professor of Catholic Theology at the Catholic University of America. In his book, *Moral Theology, A Continuing Journey* (1982), Fr. Curran states,

> It appears there is still a tendency to give absolute rather than relative or instrumental value to the right of private property understood in the strict sense. GS [*Gaudium et Spes*] and PP [*Populorum Progressio*] made more clear the distinction between the generic right of dominion which belongs to all human beings and the right to private property in the strict sense. After affirming the principle of the universal destiny of the goods of creation, PP maintains that all other rights including that of private property and free commerce are to be subordinated to this principle.

Fr. Curran's position, regardless what he or his disciples may choose to call it, is socialism, an approach explicitly condemned by Pius XI:

> If Socialism, like all errors, contains some truth (which, moreover, the Supreme Pontiffs have never denied), it is based nevertheless on a theory of human society peculiar to itself and irreconcilable with true Christianity. Religious socialism, Christian socialism, are contra-dictory terms; no one can be at the same time a good Catholic and a true socialist.[12]

In preceding sections of *Quadragesimo Anno*, Pius XI made clear that at least part of the erroneous "theory of human society" to which he referred was the notion of the common ownership of the goods of the earth and the theory that private property is prudential matter rather than coming under the virtue of justice. Any right, in fact, automatically implies the functioning of justice, just as the *exercise* of any right also implies not only justice, but prudence, temperance, fortitude, and (as revealed by Jesus in the New Testament) charity as the fulfillment and completion of the temporal virtues.

Completely ignoring this, and based on a faulty or twisted understanding of human nature and the fact that human beings are naturally more important than material things,[13] Fr. Curran's misinterpretation of the preeminence of man leads to the conclusion that everyone can exercise property in anyone else's material goods. To put it another way, it generates a claim that a right of participation exists in the property of others to the complete abrogation of the owners' rights of property. This confusion was clarified and the premise demolished by Fr. Matthew Habiger, O.S.B., Ph.D. when he explained,

> Curran mistakes [the pope's] insistence upon the absoluteness of man's right to own property, for the right of an owner to have absolute control over its use. [The pope] could not be more clear in keeping this distinction complete. Curran wishes to diminish the private dimension of all private property. The distinction which Curran does not make is that "the generic right of dominion" does not refer to ownership, but to use. The basic right of the individual to own property is left intact by these documents. The subordination of private property and free commerce to the universal destiny of the goods of creation in no way rules out private property; it only qualifies how the right is to be exercised.[14]

So — Is Property Theft?

The late lawyer-economist Louis O. Kelso would have described the idea that "property is theft" as the logical outcome of what he called "one-factor thinking." That is, the assumption that the single factor we call labor is responsible for all production. According to this theory, capital — productive property — only contributes to production because of the original labor that went into producing the capital. The results of this assumption are profound. As Kelso pointed out,

> The significance of the labor theory of value is more than academic. If labor is the source of all value created in the productive process, then labor has a valid moral claim to all wealth created through production. Then the only moral claim of the owner of capital is to have his capital restored to him, *i.e.*, to get back the value of his capital with compensation for the effects of wear, tear, and obsolescence. Honestly to reach his conclusion that the capitalist was thieving from the laborer, Marx had only to believe that labor did in fact create all economic value (*i.e.*, the values added to raw materials found in nature).[15]

What is property, though, but the right to the profits derived therefrom — the "fruits of ownership"? If, therefore, labor is the sole source of all value, then all profit is due to labor, not to the purported "owner" of any capital used in production. Anything else would be theft from the worker. Leo XIII would have been completely wrong when he declared that the right to property is "sacred and inviolable," for a thing cannot be construed in any way as "sacred and inviolable" if by its very definition it is the commission of an act of injustice. Further, if all property and hence profit is theft, it would have been foolish of Benedict XIV to distinguish between legitimate and unjust profits in his 1746 encyclical *Vix Pervenit* — "On Usury and Other *Unjust* Profit." [emphasis added]

Conclusion

As can be seen, then, confusion over property results from a failure to distinguish an individual's right to acquire property from that same individual's right to exercise the property he has acquired. The former is a natural right, and thus absolute or inalienable, while the latter, while not a part of the natural law is derived from the natural right to property, is necessarily limited — although never in any way that effectively abolishes the underlying right to property. From the time of the early Church Fathers there has been a clear distinction between "ownership" and "use."

What is clear is that the generic right of dominion — the universal destination of the earth's goods — which refers to use, includes the right to acquire property by those who lack ownership of productive assets, although it mainly affects how property is to be exercised once it is acquired. The right to property is inalienable, inviolable, and sacred. That is, every single individual has the right to acquire property, and no one can be constrained from the opportunity that is his by right. The dominion over the world demonstrates the essential autonomy of man, albeit exercised within the common good.

In short, the right to property is a natural right, and inalienable. The exercise of property is derived from that natural right, with specifics of its exercise defined by current conditions and social needs. Specifics concerning the exercise of property thus fall under the purview of civil authority (as well as custom and tradition), but only to the extent that civil authority does not define the underlying right to property out of existence by making its legitimate and necessary exercise impossible.

Notes

[1] Pierre Joseph Proudhon, *What is Property? An Inquiry into the Principle of Right and Government* (1841), Ch. I.
[2] *De Regimine Principium* ("On the Governance of Rulers").
[3] *De Laicis* ("The Treatise on Civil Government").
[4] Massachusetts Constitutional Convention of 1820.

⁵ Hallowell, *The Nature and Function of Property as a Social Institution*, 1 *Journal of Legal and Political Sociology* 115 (1943), quoted in Howard R. Williams, *Cases and Materials on the Law of Property*. Brooklyn, New York: The Foundation Press, Inc., 1954, 4.

⁶ *Ibid.*, 5.

⁷ Benjamin Leigh, Speech on November 3, 1829, *Proceedings and debates of the Virginia State Convention of 1829-1830, Volume 1*, New York: DeCapo Press, 1971, 156.

⁸ Pius XI, *Divini Redemptoris* ("On Atheistic Communism"), 1937, § 29.

⁹http://www.vatican.va/holy_father/leo_xiii/encyclicals/documents/hf_l-xiii_enc_15051891_rerum-novarum_en.html.

¹⁰ Compare with Keynes: "I see, therefore, the rentier [small owner] aspect of capitalism as a transitional phase which will disappear when it has done its work. And with the disappearance of its rentier aspect much else in it besides will suffer a sea-change. It will be, moreover, a great advantage of the order of events which I am advocating, that the euthanasia of the rentier, of the functionless investor, will be nothing sudden, merely a gradual but prolonged continuance of what we have seen recently in Great Britain, and will need no revolution." *General Theory, op. cit.*, VI.24.ii.

¹¹Wunderlich, the National Socialist Conception of Landed Property, 12 Social Research 60 at 61, 66, 72 (1945), quoted in Howard R. Williams, *Cases and Materials on the Law of Property*. Brooklyn, New York: The Foundation Press, Inc., 1954, 47.

¹²Pius XI, *Quadragesimo Anno* ("On the Restructuring of the Social Order"), 1931, § 120.

¹³John Paul II, *Centesimus Annus* ("On the Hundredth Anniversary of Rerum Novarum"), 1991, § 54.

¹⁴ Fr. Matthew Habiger, Ph.D., O.S.B., *Papal Teachings on Private Property, 1891-1981*. Lanham, Maryland: University Press of America, 1990, 355.

¹⁵Louis O. Kelso, "Karl Marx: the Almost Capitalist" *American Bar Association Journal*, March 1957.

7. The Only True Catholic System? A Critique of Social Credit

(Social Justice Review, May/June 2006)

There is a bewildering array of social and economic systems, each of which is promoted by its adherents as being "the only true Catholic system." In this catch-all category, we have such things as Liberation Theology (particularly when combined with Marxist social and economic theories),[1] the living or family wage as the only just means of generating a living income,[2] capitalism as sanitized by the Acton Institute,[3] Michael Novak,[4] and others as a truly moral system, and socialism deodorized and cleansed of that irritating condemnation by Pius XI in *Quadragesimo Anno*.[5]

One of the "only true Catholic systems" is "social credit," a scheme developed by Major C. H. Douglas in the 1920s. In some circles, "social credit" is presumed to be the only practical means of alleviating poverty and breaking the monopoly of money and credit held by current centers of financial power.[6]

Social credit is based on a disordered understanding of money, credit, banking, and property. These are all necessarily related, and a misunderstanding or misapplication of the principles underlying any of them results in an economic arrangement that is illegitimate and ultimately unjust in some degree.

According to Douglas, the productivity of the nation falls into two categories. The first category relates to what is due to producers. To the laborers go wages, to the owners go profits. Beyond this is a second category, income generated in excess of a "just" return to labor and capital (in classical economics, as Douglas understood, "production = income"). Douglas characterized this as a type of social surplus. In accordance with his principles of social credit, this "surplus" is a "social dividend" which belongs to the nation as a whole, not to those who produced it. The government, in Douglas' proposal, would undertake to monetize this surplus by printing money equal to the value of what was produced in excess of a just return to the producers.

In Douglas' system, whatever the government did not retain for its own use in lieu of direct taxation would be distributed to the people as their share of the social dividend. In this manner, everyone would have an adequate and secure income pegged directly to the national annual production. Direct taxes would also be abolished. Since government debt and borrowing for consumption purposes would be eliminated, usury (charges on non-productive loans) would also disappear, breaking the power of the financial elite. Further, since the amount of new money going into the system would be tied to the amount of production in excess of what was justly due to producers, there would presumably be no inflation.

Rights of Property

There are a number of flaws in Douglas' principles. As they are contrary to the principles of economic and social justice established in the encyclicals, especially those issued by Pius XI, they invalidate the system as a whole. First, monetizing the national surplus is an infringement of the rights of private property and an assumption of State control over the means of production.

To understand this we must first understand the idea of "property." Property is not a thing, but the rights an owner has to and over a thing. One of the most fundamental rights of property is the right to enjoy the fruits of ownership. That is, the owner of a thing has the right to derive the income generated by a productive asset and dispose of it in any way he chooses.

Social credit violates this right by having the collective in the person of the State expropriate a portion of production that someone (else) has determined is in excess of a just return, and distributing it through the mechanism of money creation to others who do not own the means of production.

Justice is violated because the rights of property do not say that an owner is due a *portion* of the fruits of ownership, but *all* of the fruits of ownership, otherwise he is not really the owner.

If some people are denied an adequate and secure income because others have an effective monopoly on the means of production, justice demands that ownership opportunities be opened up to non-owners so that they, too, may participate in the rights of ownership legitimately, without depriving current owners of their due. The guiding principle is that of justice: *suum cuique*, "to each his due." Non-owners as their just due should be enabled to exercise the universal right to property, and the exclusive rights of property once they acquire ownership. They would thereby gain the right to receive and enjoy the fruits of *their* ownership, not that of someone else.

There is also the problem that Major Douglas' system does not expropriate such social surplus *directly*, but by levying the expropriation *indirectly* through the monetary system, a form of hidden taxation. Thus, the collective as a whole bears the cost of the expropriation by an occult *pro rata* levy on everyone who uses the currency or has assets denominated in units of the currency. The problem is that the collective, *per se*, does not own the assets that are being reduced in value in this manner. They are owned by individuals, each of whom takes a "hit" equal to the ratio that the newly issued currency bears to existing currency.

The individuals who make up the collective suffer, not the collective as a whole. The producers of the surplus do not have the whole of the surplus expropriated in this manner, but only a portion of it. The remaining expropriation is levied on holders of currency-denominated assets. Those who produced the social surplus actually retain the greater part of it. In most cases the cost of the greater part of the expropriation would be borne by wage earners and people on fixed incomes. In short, the poor would be forced to pay a hidden tax to finance the social dividend that is then handed back to them after deductions for running the State.

An assumption underlying social credit is that taxation is an exercise of property by the collective in the person of the State in the productive wealth and production of the nation. This was the theory of Thomas Hobbes, detailed in his manual on totalitarian political philosophy, *Leviathan*.[7] According to Hobbes, each citizen can only defend his sacred rights of property[8] against other citizens — not against the State. This orientation deifies the State that becomes in this manner the ultimate owner of everything, including the lives of the citizens. As Karl Marx put it, the State is God, and God is the State.

In contrast to this is the traditional Judeo-Christian orientation, which assumes that the State is a tool instituted for the good of society. As such, any sovereignty held by the State comes to it from God transmitted through the people (individually, not the collective). This was probably best expressed with respect to taxation by the political philosopher John Locke in his responses to Sir Robert Filmer's *Patriarcha*, and which have come down to us as his *Two Treatises on Civil Government*: According to Locke, governments are allowed to levy taxes to defray the legitimate costs of running the State, and are unjust without the consent of the people being taxed. Taxes are not an exercise of property by the State in the goods of the citizens.[9]

There is another aspect of "abolishing taxes" which rarely occurs to the proponents of social credit and similar programs. Cutting people off in that manner from the only control they exercise over government is a sure road to tyranny, as noted by Henry C. Adams in his book, *Public Debts, An Essay in the Science of Finance*.[10] Through their consent to taxation, the people have a direct control over the financing of activities and thus the power of the State.

When politicians can borrow the money they need rather than raise it through taxation, they remove themselves from direct public control over their activities and become unaccountable to the very people they govern. When they can raise the money they need or want without any recourse whatsoever to the public (*e.g.*, by printing what they need and spending it into circulation, whether or not the new money is backed by the general productive capacity of the nation), they establish themselves as an independent force within the nation, over which the great mass of people have no control whatsoever.

Money Creation

Legend has it that Mayer Rothschild declared, "Give me control over money and credit, and I care not who makes the laws." While probably apocryphal, this assertion is a concise statement of the power of money and credit in both the economy and the body politic. Whoever has control over the creation of money, as well as how it is created, ultimately has control over the lives of everyone. Who determines how money is created determines patterns of ownership of productive assets throughout society, the degree of concentration of ownership, and, thus, has control over everyone's income. Putting this power completely into the hands of the State, with no input from individual people via the ability to monetize productive assets individually, puts all power over the lives and fortunes of its citizens into the hands of the State. Instead of being a good servant, the State, like fire, turns into a bad master.

The only sound method of money creation is for citizens to have the ability to monetize their productive projects privately, either individually or in free association with others. When the banking system is purely reactive, that is, it can only create money when such projects are brought to it for financing, then the initial power and ultimate control continues to rest with the people, not the State.

Charged with the care of the common good, the State has the duty to regulate and control the value of the currency. This duty, however, does not include absolute control over the amount of currency (which is determined by the productive capacity of the nation and is thus self-regulating if all financially feasible projects are financed through the creation of new money). Nor does it include the right to initiate the process of money creation, either unilaterally through printing the money it needs backed by productive capacity or actual production owned by others (causing an involuntary and indiscriminate transfer of value from owners to whoever receives the new money as a social dividend), or by selling government debt to banks of issue or the central bank in return for newly created money.

When the process of money creation also includes a provision that favors productive projects structured in such a way as to encourage or mandate widespread ownership of the means of production, then the process of money creation becomes not only as sound as possible, but just as well. It is by this means that ownership opportunities can be opened up for the mass of people who are currently without access to the means of owning and possessing private, productive property of their own. Such a system of money creation would give people control over the means of making a living, maximizing the possibility of gaining an adequate and secure income through their own efforts, not by receiving a distribution through a social dividend of wealth expropriated from the efforts of others.

Credit

The only truly just form of "social credit" is capital credit (that is, credit used to purchase productive assets that are self-liquidating; that pay for themselves) made available to everyone on the basis of the feasibility of the project they wish to finance or the asset they wish to acquire. That is, credit is a social good, and should be made available to everyone in society. Credit is not something that only an elite may employ, whether that elite consists of the State exercising credit presumably on behalf of the citizens, or of a coterie of rich capitalists benefiting society by investing in additional capital and "creating jobs" for others who then become their dependents.

Inflation

With respect to the manner of creation of money, it would, contrary to Douglas' claims, be purely inflationary. This is because, contrary to classic central banking or bank of issue

A Critique of Social Credit — 213

theory, there is no provision for retiring the money created after it has been issued and has done its job. As Dr. Harold G. Moulton explained Douglas' argument in his 1935 classic, *The Formation of Capital*,

> If the payments made by a given business under A amounted to one dollar and the payments made under B amounted to another dollar, the price of the commodity produced would be two dollars; but there would be only the A dollar available with which to buy it.
>
> The fallacy in Major Douglas' analysis is that he concentrates attention upon a single business rather than upon the national economy as a whole. These "external" payments to other organizations do not involve sending the money outside the country, and hence their disbursement is a part of the national income as a whole. That is to say, the payments for raw materials, bank charges, etc., are also disbursed to individuals by raw material producing industries and "other organizations" in the form of wages, salaries, and dividends. Taking the national economy as a whole the aggregate prices of goods and services simply cover the aggregate disbursements of wages, salaries, rents, commissions, and profits to individuals engaged in the processes of production.
>
> The analysis which we have made in *America's Capacity to Consume*, revealing a demand for consumption goods insufficient to call forth the full output of our productive establishment, is not to be regarded as supporting either the position of Major Douglas or of Foster and Catchings. Our analysis did not show that the aggregate disbursements of national income to individuals were less than the aggregate prices of the goods and services turned out; on the contrary, we contended that they were virtu-

ally identical. We were concerned with the allocation of the national income as between savings for investment and expenditures for consumptive purposes; and we showed merely that the proportion of the total income received by individuals which found its way into consumptive channels was inadequate to induce full capacity production.[11]

If Major Douglas' proposal were put into effect, the money would remain in circulation after the production that backed it was consumed. True, this is not *inflation* classically defined, but currency *depreciation*. The effect, however, is the same, only worse. The difference is that the increase in the price level that results from classic inflation, that is, the State printing unbacked money, has a natural check on it in the speed with which government can run a printing press. There is no such check on the increase in the price level that results from removing the backing from a currency. This means, effectively, determining the price level by dividing the money supply by zero. This results in a potentially infinite price level, the phenomenon called "hyperinflation." It becomes impossible for the State to print money fast enough to catch up to the price level, instead of causing a rising price level by printing too much money.

Hyperinflation

This was the situation with the infamous hyperinflation in Germany, Austria and Hungary in the early 1920s. The collapse did not happen all at once. During the war, the German population had patriotically turned in the predominantly gold currency and even personal gold jewelry in exchange for paper notes of the Loan Bank and the Reichsbank. To finance the war, the government issued additional paper currency, keeping the lid on inflation by implementing rationing and price controls.

Controls were abolished at the end of the war, along with the government that had imposed them. As a result, there were shortages of the necessities of life, and a super-

A Critique of Social Credit — 215

abundance of paper money backed only by the former government's promise to pay. Prices doubled before the Allied blockade was lifted, and again before the end of 1919. With her productive capacity in ruins, Germany was forced to import goods as fast as possible as soon as the blockade was lifted just to keep people alive. With no tax base, the government chose to pay off its war debt with newly-printed notes of the Reichsbank. The ensuing inflation effectively repudiated the debts by paying them off in near-worthless currency. Then came the demands for reparations, which finished off the Reichsmark completely by expropriating what remained of Germany's gold reserves as well as virtually the entire portable productive capacity of the nation.

During the rest of 1922, the Reichsmark fell steadily and rapidly against other currencies. In April 1923, prices began rising at an unbelievable rate. Transporting enough currency to purchase a single item became a serious problem. Printing presses began working day and night to turn out enough high-denomination notes to make transactions easier to carry out, but the task was hopeless. The inflation rate was rising so fast that it was impossible to provide enough currency to match the prices.

Adding to the problem of mere quantity of currency was the almost infinite "Velocity of Money." The "Velocity of Money," the rate at which money is spent, went to the maximum as people rushed to spend whatever currency they had before it lost any more value. This effectively multiplied the amount of currency in circulation immensely, adding to the rate of inflation like pouring gasoline on a fire. The price level actually began to rise faster than the rate at which currency could be printed.[12]

Stores refused to sell what little stock they could acquire except for hard foreign currency. Farmers refused to bring food into the city. While foreigners were buying everything in sight at a pittance with hard currency, ordinary people were starving to death. As the *London Daily Mail* reported on August 6, 1923 in an interview, "Villagers who used to send butter to Berlin are no longer troubling to do so. They already have crates in their cottages packed with worthless paper money. 'Why get more'? A workingman said to me: 'We used to talk about the stupid peasants, but now they are laughing at us'."

The Magic of the "Old Wizard"

Finally, on November 13, 1923, Hjalmar Horace Greeley Schacht — the "Old Wizard" — was appointed Commissioner of National Currency. He was given a free hand in all questions of money and credit. His sole priority was to halt the inflation that by this time had become an inferno. Doctor Schacht's first step was to "freeze" the inflation rate on November 20, 1923, when the Reichsmark hit 4.2 trillion to the US Dollar at the official exchange rate (the black market rate had by this time reached more than 14 trillion Reichsmarks to the Dollar). At the official exchange rate, one cent in US money would have repaid the entire German National Debt in 1914 several times over.

Doctor Schacht introduced a parallel currency, the Rentenmark. The new Rentenmark was backed by four *per cent*. of public lands, including the railroads, and pegged at 4.2 to the US Dollar, the pre-war exchange rate for the gold Reichsmark. Issues in excess of the value of the land backing the currency were absolutely forbidden. The Rentenmark was not legal tender, but was convertible on demand at face value into the legal tender Reichsmark.

Actually, as hard assets provided the backing for the Rentenmark, it was effectively the legal tender Reichsmark that was convertible into the non-legal tender Rentenmark. That, however, is not the usual meaning of "convertible currency," generally construed as meaning that the currency is convertible into "lawful money," that is, legal tender. However construed, Dr. Schacht's plan worked. Rentenmarks remained in circulation until 1948 and served to stabilize the currency until demonetized by the Allies when the Deutschmark was introduced.

The idea that hard assets can be used to back the currency when there is insufficient (or non-existent) specie — gold and silver — to supply an adequate money supply is similar to a plan proposed by John Law for Scotland and England in 1705.[13] Law was also the author of the "Mississippi Scheme," the misapplication of which nearly destroyed France in the early eighteenth century.[14] In Germany's case, however, the system worked.

Some people credit the confidence that Doctor Schacht personally exuded in his new system with halting the hyperinflation. This, however, ignores the effect of having a solid, asset-backed currency making up at least part of the money supply and fully convertible at face value with the rest of the money supply.

Doctor Schacht was appointed "President for Life" of the Reichsbank on December 22, 1923. He served the Weimar Republic until stepping down in 1930 over some issues regarding the handling of certain reparations payments. He was Finance Minister of the Third Reich until implicated in a plot to assassinate Hitler. As "the Old Wizard" who had stopped the hyperinflation, Schacht was possibly the one man in the world Hitler dared not kill, but he spent the rest of the war in a concentration camp.

The potential of hyperinflation is endemic with social credit, because the new money is backed exclusively by production, that is, consumer goods. These, obviously, disappear once they are consumed and thus the backing is removed from the currency. Backing the currency with productive assets by means of monetizing the productive capacity of the nation through the commercial banking system by means of loans discounted at the central bank would eliminate this danger. In such a system, new money would be issued to finance new capital formation, that is, to finance projects that pay for themselves.

As the projects were established and began to generate income, a portion of that income would be used for "debt service," that is, to repay the loan that financed the project. As the loan was repaid, the currency that was used to repay the loan would be "destroyed" by the issuing authority (whether a traditional bank of issue, or the central bank through the commercial banking system). Thus, as the backing of the currency "disappeared" (in the form of the depreciating value of the asset(s) as they were "used up" to generate production), the currency that was backed by the present value of the assets would also "disappear," being removed from circulation through debt service payments.[15]

Conclusion

This discussion is not a condemnation of the goals of social credit, but a critique of the means employed to achieve those goals. The end does not justify the means. Means must be carefully examined to ensure that they are consistent with universal moral principles, and that no violation of human dignity occurs. While Major Douglas was a profound thinker with the good of humanity at heart, he allowed certain misconceptions to creep into his work which resulted in a system, unbeknownst to him, that was a perfect recipe for tyranny and absolute control of the broad mass of people by the State.

As Daniel Webster stated, "power naturally and inevitably follows property." Major Douglas' social credit scheme represents the potential destruction of the institution of private property, rather than its democratization. The principles of Major Douglas' social credit are therefore fundamentally inconsistent with the teachings in the social encyclicals. It cannot be considered a "Catholic" system, much less the "only true" Catholic system for establishing and maintaining economic and social justice.

Notes

[1] See, *e.g.*, Rev. Philip S. Land, S.J., *Catholic Social Teaching as I Have Lived, Loathed and Loved It*. Chicago, Illinois: Loyola University Press, 1994.

[2] See the discussion on this issue in Michael D. Greaney, "Social Justice and the Living Wage" an occasional paper published by the Center for Economic and Social Justice, Washington, DC, 1998, as well as "The Living Wage (And Child Care)" *Social Justice Review*, September/October 1998.

[3] "In the story of the Great Northern [Railroad], we see another facet of the moral and practical superiority of capitalism: It promotes social cooperation and mutual aid. [James J.] Hill's success as an entrepreneur was directly linked to the welfare of others; he therefore did what he could to help them succeed. Our future religious leaders need to understand this aspect of capitalism's morality." Rev. Robert A. Sirico, "President's Message" *Acton Notes, The Newsletter of the Acton Institute for the Study of Religion and Liberty*, August 1999, Volume 9, Number 8.

[4] "Democratic capitalism is a system most highly valuing wit, invention, discovery — capitalism (*caput*) being the mind-centered system." Michael Novak, "Saving Distributism" Introduction to G. K. Chesterton, *Collected Works*, Volume V., San Francisco, California: Ignatius Press, 1987, 15.

[5] ". . . it is clear from the encyclical that Pius had a very narrow definition of socialism in mind. For him, socialism was a strictly economic system concerned solely with the material needs of humans.. . . He dismisses without comment the possibility of a Christian Socialism, even [that] such a form did and does exist." Personal communication with the author in response to the reminder, stated by Pius XI in *Quadragesimo Anno*, that "no one can claim to be both a socialist and a good Catholic."

[6] George-Henri Levesque, *Social Credit and Catholicism*, Hawthorne, California: The Christian Book Club of America (ND).

[7] Thomas Hobbes, *Leviathan, or The Matter, Forme and Power of A Common-wealth Ecclesiasticall and Civil*. London: Penguin Books, 1985, 367-8.

[8] Leo XIII, *Rerum Novarum* ("On the Conditions of the Working Classes"), 1891, § 65.

[9] John Locke, *Treatise of Civil Government*. New York: Appleton, Century, Crofts, 1965, 94-95.

[10] Henry C. Adams, *Public Debts, An Essay in the Science of Finance*, New York: D. Appleton and Company, 1898.

[11] Harold G. Moulton, *The Formation of Capital*. Washington, DC: The Brookings Institution, 1935, 180-181.

[12] Ever ingenious, the German and Austrian people tried many expedients to provide circulating media, most notably the series of "notgeld" ("non-money") issues by states, municipalities, and individuals. Overprinting the currency was tried, as was countermarking imperial silver coinage, but it simply could not be

done fast enough. Cardboard "coins," company scrip, even tokens made of rubber were pressed into service at one time or another.

[13] John Law, *Money and Trade Considered, with a Proposal for Supplying the Nation with Money.* Edinburgh: Andrew Anderson, 1705.

[14] See "The Mississippi Scheme," Charles Mackay, *Extraordinary Popular Delusions and the Madness of Crowds.* New York: Farrar, Straus and Giroux, 1932.

[15] In practice, however, the currency would tend to appreciate, that is, increase in value. This is because commercial loans are extended based on the most conservative valuation of the capital to be formed, but capital tends to produce at a much higher rate. Due to the inherently conservative nature of corporate finance, capital tends to remain productive long after it has been paid for, while the value of the currency adjusts upward to allow for the fact that each unit can purchase more goods and services. Absent State money creation to finance its deficits or a rise in prices to accommodate scarcity of an input to production, money becomes worth more.

8. Is Distributism Socialism?

(*Social Justice Review*, May/June 2007
to July/August 2007)

Part I

An Issue of Understanding

> Since the modern world began in the sixteenth century, nobody's system of philosophy has really corresponded to everybody's sense of reality; to what, if left to themselves, common men would call common sense. Each started with a paradox; a peculiar point of view demanding the sacrifice of what they would call a sane point of view. That is the one thing common to Hobbes and Hegel, to Kant and Bergson, to Berkeley and William James. A man had to believe something that no normal man would believe, if it were suddenly propounded to his simplicity; as that law is above right, or right is outside reason, or things are only as we think them, or everything is relative to a reality that is not there. The modern philosopher claims, like a sort of confidence man, that if once we will grant him this, the rest will be easy; he will straighten out the world, if once he is allowed to give this one twist to the mind.[1]

Discussion on the internet, particularly in the com boxes of blogs, ranges from the absurd to the ridiculous. Occasionally, however, serious issues are raised. Even more occasionally they are treated with the respect they deserve.

In my capacity as Director of Research for the interfaith Center for Economic and Social Justice, "CESJ" I regularly review various chat rooms, discussion groups and, of course, blogs. Naturally enough I concentrate on forums in which particulars of economic and social justice are discussed. Most frequently this is on Catholic blogs.

Recently I came across a comment that distributism, a loose set of economic ideas developed by G. K. Chesterton and Hilaire Belloc, is often confused with socialism because distributism is opposed to capitalism. The writer of the comment was obviously ridiculing people who presumably make such a mistake, for both Chesterton and Belloc were adamant in their opposition to both socialism and capitalism. Does, however, simply opposing what you call "socialism" and "capitalism" make you, *ipso facto*, a "distributist"? or is there something more, something deeper involved in the matter?

Let's Define Our Terms

A large measure of misunderstanding is rooted in the fact that quite a large number of people have no idea what they are talking about. Ordinarily this would not be an issue; nobody can be expected to know everything. A distributist, however, inasmuch as distributism is based on private property, should have a working knowledge of the institution. We must, therefore (to avoid similar confusion), be clear on what we mean by "socialism," "capitalism," "distributism," and, especially, "private property."

By "capitalism" we mean an arrangement of the economic order such that a relatively small private elite own or control the means of production, and the great mass of people only gain income through the mechanism of wages.

By "socialism" we mean an arrangement of the economic order such that a relatively small State bureaucracy own or controls the means of production, and the great mass of people only gain income through the mechanism of wages. (By "relatively small State bureaucracy" we do not mean that the bureaucracy under socialism is small, but that the bureaucratic elite that holds actual power is small in comparison to the size of the general population or even the numbers of State employees.)

By "distributism," we mean an arrangement of the economic order such that a relatively large number of private citizens own — and own directly (meaning they have the full traditional rights of private property) — the means of production, and the great mass of people gain income through the mechanism of profits. "Classic" distributism adds that accumulations of capital (productive assets) must be within "human scale," a rather meaningless stipulation. Every human creation is within "human scale" when it is democratically owned and the full rights of private property are passed through to the owner or owners.

So far we have no problem. A little thought will convince the most dedicated capitalist, socialist, or distributist that these definitions are accurate. The problem is that much of what is said by some modern distributists appears to take for granted that the definition of private property has changed. Instead of being a natural and sacred right (as maintained by Leo XIII[2]), private property is to be regarded as prudential matter.

A Slight Digression

Before we begin, we should point out that distributists are not alone in their confusion. "Georgists," as followers of the thought of Henry George are called, are sometimes taken aback when anyone points out that George advocated State ownership or control of land and natural resources — "agrarian socialism." Yet, as stated in George's own words —

> What I, therefore, propose, as the simple yet sovereign remedy, which will raise wages, increase the earnings of capital, extirpate pauperism, abolish poverty, give remunerative employment to whoever wishes it, afford free scope to human powers, lessen crime, elevate morals, and taste, and intelligence, purify government and carry civilization to yet nobler heights, is — *to appropriate rent by taxation.*
>
> In this way the State may become the universal landlord without calling herself so, and without assuming a single new function. In form, the ownership of land would remain just as now. No owner of land need be dispossessed, and no restriction need be placed upon the amount of land any one could hold.

> For, rent being taken by the State in taxes, land, no matter in whose name it stood, or in what parcels it was held, would be really common property, and every member of the community would participate in the advantages of its ownership.[3] [Emphasis in original.]

The issue with the Georgists becomes whether George's goals can be achieved by means other than what he specifically recommended, or if the goals are to be subordinated to the mechanism — a constant danger in today's world. (For the record, CESJ believes that there is a way to respect Henry George's goals, though not the specific mechanism, that also takes into consideration the importance of the free market, a limited role for the State, the rights of private property, and the universal right to private property.)

Karl Marx and Friedrich Engels didn't fiddle with legal technicalities or the difference between form and substance. They went straight to the point in *The Communist Manifesto*:

> The distinguishing feature of Communism is not the abolition of property generally, but the abolition of bourgeois property. But modern bourgeois private property is the final and most complete expression of the system of producing and appropriating products, that is based on class antagonisms, on the exploitation of the many by the few.
>
> In this sense, the theory of the Communists may be summed up in the single sentence: the abolition of property.[4]

Certain disciples of Father Heinrich Pesch, S.J., calling themselves "solidarists" become rather upset if anyone points out that the statement "private property is prudential matter" has nothing in common with the work of Father Pesch. Putting private property under the virtue of prudence effectively abolishes private property as a natural right — not to mention directly contradicting explicit papal pronouncements on the matter.

As for Father Pesch's teachings, he described private property as one of the "three institutional 'pillars' of economic society."[5] The others are "marriage and the family" and "the State as guardian of the positive legal order required by the value and rights of man."[6] The insistence of Austrian and German Catholic socialists at the time Father Pesch wrote, that property was merely prudential, was simply a restatement of their traditional dogma that private property should be abolished. It was also, in part, a direct reaction to Father Pesch's adamantine stance on the sacredness of private property:

> Because man was the center of the social system, he also was at the center of economic activity. Therefore, Pesch accepted the principle of wage labor and of the separation of labor and capital. (*Lehrbuch der Nationalökonomie*, 1, 17 – 18) He demanded, however, that the community, acting through the state, interfere to prevent capitalist excesses which might threaten the economic status of individuals, and especially their private property which they must have to be able to fulfill their function in society. (*Ibid.*, 1, 188, 206 – 207)[7]

These people unfortunately fail to realize that there has never been a society that, having redefined the institution of private property, avoided a similar redefinition of life and liberty, and thereby undermined the dignity of the human person. By striking at the primary means designed by God to sustain human life and liberty and support the dignity of the human person in the temporal sphere, they effectively redefine what it means to be human . . . and what it means to be alive or free.

What is "Property"?

Ask almost anyone to define "property" and he will do so in terms of a thing, tangible or intangible. He will say, "That house is mine; it is my property." Nearly everyone would agree with him . . . and he would be completely wrong.

"Property" is not a thing, but the rights that you, the owner, have *to* and *over* a thing. That is, the rights of property are divided into two parts. The first part is the right to be an owner at all. The second part is the bundle of rights that define what you, the owner, may do with the thing you own. These are, respectively, the right "to" property, and the rights "of" property. In neither case does "property" describe the thing owned, but the rights that relate to the thing owned.

This is an important distinction. Not too long ago one commentator declared that he was for human rights, not property rights. This begs the question, for "property" *is* a human right. It is the rights that a human person has to and over a thing, not the rights that a thing has to or over people or other things. Pius XII clarified the importance of this distinction when he wrote,

> When God blessed our first parents He said to them: "Increase and multiply and fill the earth and subdue it." And to the first father of a human family He said later: "In the sweat of thy brow thou shalt eat bread." Therefore the dignity of the human person normally demands the right to the use of earthly goods as the natural foundation for a livelihood; and to that right corresponds the fundamental obligation to grant private property, as far as possible, to all. The positive laws regulating private property may change and may grant a more or less restricted use of it; but if such legal provisions are to contribute to the peaceful state of the community, they must save the worker, who is or will be the father of a family, from being condemned to an economic dependence or slavery irreconcilable with his rights as a person.[8]

What is a "Person"?

This makes sense only if we know what a "person" is. A person is legally defined as that which has rights: "A man considered according to the rank he holds in society, with all the right to which the place he holds entitles him, and the duties which it imposes. (People v. R. Co., 134 N.Y. 506, 31 N.E. 873.) The word in its natural and usual signification includes women as well as men. (Commonwealth v. Welosky, 276 Mass. 398, 177 N.W. 656.)"[9]

"Things," on the other hand, are something that a "person" has rights to and over. A "thing with rights" is, *ipso facto*, either not a "thing," or is an oxymoron. The legal definition of "things" makes this clear: "The objects of dominion or property as contradistinguished from 'persons.' (Western Union Telegraph Co. v. Bush, 191 Ark, 1085, 89 S.W. 2d 723, 725, 103 A.L.R. 367; Gayer v. Whelan, 59 Cal. App. 2d 255, 138 P. 2d 763, 768.) The object of a right; *i.e.*, whatever is treated by the law as the object over which one person exercises a right, and with reference to which another person lies under a duty. (Holl. Jur. 83.)"[10]

What is a "Right"?

We've made a number of references to "rights." It will be useful to know what this term signifies as well.

> As a noun, and taken in a concrete sense, a power, privilege, faculty, or demand, inherent in one person and incident upon another. "Rights" are defined generally as "powers of free action." And the primal rights pertaining to men are undoubtedly enjoyed by human beings purely as such, being grounded in personality, and existing antecedently to their recognition by positive law. But leaving the abstract moral sphere, and giving to the term a juristic content, a "right" is well defined as "a capacity residing in one man of controlling, with the assent and assistance of the state, the actions of others." (Holl. Jur. 69.)[11]

For the purposes of our discussion, there are two kinds of rights. The first and by far the most important are "natural rights." Natural rights are, as we might expect from the label, part of the natural law. They are an inalienable, that is, "absolute" aspect of human nature. You cannot take such rights away without somehow asserting that the individual or group from which you took them is less than human.

The second are manmade rights ("positive law"). To be legitimate, these must conform to the natural law. That is, a manmade right must define the exercise of, be derived from, or clarify a natural right. It may in no way oppose any natural right, among the most important of which are life, liberty and access to the means of acquiring and possessing private property. As Heinrich Rommen, a student of Fr. Pesch, clarified the issue,

> The Christian philosophy of law, however, absolutely demands the positive law. And if it declares reasonableness to be an essential note of the concept of law, it can still, with St. Thomas, characterize only the absolutely unreasonable law, *i.e.*, one that is at variance with the natural law, as savoring of lawlessness rather than of law. But since order is a very great good, just as is the will of the state which realizes and preserves this order, so along with the demand, addressed to the lawmaker, for the reasonableness of laws goes a demand addressed to the subjects to preserve the great good of order even when a particular law cannot be entirely justified before the bar of reason. The continuance of any order at all, however mixed it may be with injustice and arbitrariness, is of greater value than the utter lack of order, than total disorder. The Christian philosophy of law can demand this because in its eyes the nature of the state is not exhausted in the legal order, although the state must be essentially a constitutional state: it must be in the law. But the state is more than

that, for it does not live by law alone; it also lives by the acts of all the social virtues through which the idea of man is perfected.[12]

The State — the agency most often charged with defining the explicit exercise of rights (two others are custom and tradition) — must never define the exercise of any natural right in any way that effectively negates that right. Neither may the State define the exercise of any manmade right in any way that effectively negates any natural right.

Is Private Property Prudential Matter?

Were the people involved in discussing the issue of private property thinking logically, the above would be more than enough to satisfy that private property is both a natural and a sacred right, just as Leo XIII declared, and must not be tampered with. Unfortunately, so great is the anxiety, even frustration many people feel over the injustices rampant in society that they begin to believe that any remedy is acceptable; that the end justifies any means.

Thus (so the thinking evidently goes), private property is only to be considered inviolate as long as other people are not in need. It then ceases to be a right, and becomes prudential matter. The efficient cause of the act of prudence in granting individuals rights to and of private property is, naturally enough, the State, the guardian of the common good.

The problem is that this line of reasoning is so shoddy and twisted as to constitute unreason. It overlooks one little thing, a fact so glaringly obvious that it is incredible that anyone could miss it except as a deliberate act. To pontificate on property and yet ignore this one small yet painfully obvious fact is so egregious an error as to be breathtaking in its magnitude. It is the sort of profound, fundamental, yet extremely simple mistake of which G. K. Chesterton wrote in *The Dumb Ox*, his brief biography of Saint Thomas Aquinas, in the selection with which we prefaced this article. As Heinrich Rommen observed,

> It follows from the fact of *natura vulnerata* as well as from the ethical character and goal of community life, and of the state in particular, that positive human laws are absolutely necessary for determining the further inferences from the first principles in the interest of a more exact and readily discernible establishment of order and for the setting up of institutions needed for community life. The natural-law prohibition of adultery implies at the same time an affirmation of marriage and of the general norms that are most needed for its functioning as an institution. "Thou shalt not steal" presupposes the institution of private property as pertaining to the natural law; but not, for example, the feudal property arrangements of the Middle Ages or the modern capitalist system. Since the natural law lays down general norms only, it is the function of the positive law to undertake the concrete, detailed regulation of real and personal property and to prescribe the formalities for conveyance of ownership.[13]

Some might not even consider it a mistake at all, regarding it simply as a different perspective. It is, however, so huge an error that the mind boggles at it; it is akin not just to trying to add apples and oranges, but to a belief that an apple *is* an orange. Taken to its logical conclusion, we end with a belief that there is no difference between black and white, up and down, or even good and evil. This last is not hyperbole, for evil consists in twisting what is good — and changing a basic definition such as calling a thing that which it is not (even in pursuit of the highest good) is so profoundly evil that it can never be justified.

So what is this almost cosmic lacuna? Simply this: property is found not under the virtue of *prudence*, but *justice*. Every reference to property in the *Summa* of Saint Thomas Aquinas — even those articles that discuss whether, under extreme circumstances, expedience demands that a measure of what is ordinarily private property be construed as common property — places property under *justice*. Why this is so important will be covered in the second part of this article.

Notes

[1] Gilbert Keith Chesterton, *Saint Thomas Aquinas, "The Dumb Ox."* New York: Doubleday Image, 1956, 145-146.

[2] "Every man has by nature the right to possess property as his own." Leo XIII, *Rerum Novarum* ("On Capital and Labor"), 1891, § 6; "We have seen that this great labor question cannot be solved save by assuming as a principle that private ownership must be held sacred and inviolable." *Ibid.*, § 46.

[3] Henry George, *Progress and Poverty.* New York: Robert Schalkenbach Foundation, 1935, 405-406.

[4] Karl Marx and Friedrich Engels, *The Communist Manifesto.* New York: Penguin Books, 1967, 96.

[5] Gustav Gundlach, S.J., "Solidarist Economics, Philosophy and Socio-economic Theory in Pesch" *Social Order*, April 1951, 185.

[6] *Ibid.*

[7] Alfred Diamant, *Austrian Catholics and the Social Question, 1918-1933.* Gainesville, Florida: University of Florida Press, 1959, 21.

[8] Pius XII, *Christmas Broadcast* ("The Rights of Man"), 1942, § II.

[9] "Person," *Black's Law Dictionary.* St. Paul, Minn., West Publishing Co., 1951.

[10] "Things," *Ibid.*

[11] "Right," *Ibid.*

[12] Heinrich Rommen, *The Natural Law, A Study in Legal and Social History and Philosophy.* Indianapolis, Indiana: Liberty Fund, Inc., 1998, 176.

[13] *Ibid.*, 59.

Part II

An Issue of Human Dignity

In the first part of this article we examined the definitions of terms at some length, concentrating on the meaning of such things as *capitalism, socialism, distributism* and (more to the point) of *person, thing, right* and, of course, *private property*. We concluded that — based on these definitions — private property is not "prudential matter" for the pure and simple reason that it is not classified under the virtue of *prudence*, but of *justice*.

Private property is a natural right, with all that implies, and may not be redefined or violated for any reason without offending against the dignity of the human person. The issue that faces us now is understanding why human dignity is offended if we attack the institution of private property through theft — even if the desired goal is to alleviate the lot of the poor and to rectify the many economic injustices that permeate our society as presently ordered. Don't the needs of the poor override concern for mere rights that others might have in their material possessions?

Concern for the Poor

First off, we should note that, even in the case of dire need (which can sometimes excuse what would otherwise be considered theft), there are stringent requirements that must be met to avoid moral guilt for theft. Even then, it is almost a certainty that, in the interests of order, unilateral redistribution must be punished as a civil crime — even if the individual or group who carried it out incurs no moral guilt. As Heinrich Rommen observed in a passage quoted in the first part of this article,

> . . . since order is a very great good, just as is the will of the state which realizes and preserves this order, so along with the demand, addressed to the lawmaker, for the reasonableness of laws goes a de-

mand addressed to the subjects to preserve the great good of order even when a particular law cannot be entirely justified before the bar of reason. The continuance of any order at all, however mixed it may be with injustice and arbitrariness, is of greater value than the utter lack of order, than total disorder.[1]

There are in general four requirements to be met before anyone can be deprived of life, liberty, or property, whether or not due process is observed. We must, of course, always keep in mind that what may be morally *allowed* is not necessarily *recommended* or even permissible in the civil order. Anyone doing these things must — in the interest of maintaining order — be subject to punishment, whether or not he has incurred any moral guilt.

Perhaps a graphic illustration will help here. Herman Melville's novel, *Billy Budd, Foretopman,* is a fictional attempt to demonstrate the importance of order, even if the cost is very high. The outstandingly innocent Billy Budd must be executed for the accidental killing of the profoundly evil Claggart. This, it is made clear, is solely to maintain discipline and order in society by adhering to the strict letter of the law.

Claggart, while portrayed as the virtual personification of evil, had committed no crime or infraction of the Articles of War, nor had he physically or verbally threatened Billy Budd in any way contrary to that typically associated with maintaining military discipline in the admittedly brutal 18th century. Billy Budd could not, therefore, claim self-defense. The circumstances were such that, legally, the death could not even be termed accidental, but murder. The judge is Captain Vere ("Truth"), who is fully aware that Billy Budd is innocent of any crime — but that even the accidental and utterly guiltless slaying must be punished, or he risks a mutiny as had just happened at Spithead and the Nore. Vere — Truth — is only preserved by Billy Budd's final words just before he is hanged, "God bless Captain Vere," which forestalls a mutiny.

Overriding Private Property

The first requirement that must be met before we can even think of justifying taking goods that belong to another is that the need must truly be *dire*, that is, someone or his dependents must be in danger of death or permanent disability unless succor is received *immediately*. That is, no one may take what would normally be considered the inviolate private property of another without there being a specific and identifiable need. Simply improving "quality of life" for a generalized other ("the poor") is not sufficient justification. Neither may someone take what belongs to another today to relieve tomorrow's anticipated distress.

The second requirement is that all other recourse must be exhausted, including begging on one's hands and knees if it comes to that. Yes, this would be "degrading," but not so degrading as violating the human dignity of an owner by simply taking without asking, or by intimidating through threats. Within a Christian framework, of course, the one doing the begging is not degraded at all, however much the individual or group being solicited is degraded for forcing someone to resort to such tactics. Giving only when one is asked is considered the lowest form of charity.

The third requirement is that the one whose goods are taken must not be left in a situation similar to the one being relieved. That is, if you are starving, you may not take the bread that will keep its current possessor from starvation. More than that, Saint Thomas states quite clearly that what is taken may only come out of another's "*super*abundance," not "abundance." That is, if people are in dire need and someone has what is clearly far, far more than he needs to maintain himself and his dependents in a manner befitting his state in life, *some* of that superabundance may be redistributed to relieve dire necessity. This must, if at all possible and to maintain order, be done by duly constituted authority and only through due process of law.

The fourth requirement is the one most often overlooked. That is, after the emergency is over, the one who took the goods must make an honest effort to restore the equivalent value of what was taken. Reminding welfare recipients or receivers of a living wage or family allowance that they are morally bound to repay what they have received or supply labor at some future date to the value of anything in excess of their due in strict justice without additional compensation would be regarded as ludicrous in today's society.

The Fifth Requirement

There is a fifth requirement in social justice. That is, immediate relief in an emergency situation is well and good, but we are not permitted to rest there. We must make constant and effective efforts, consistent with the laws and characteristics of social justice, to restructure the social order so that similar emergencies do not happen again. With respect to the condition of the poor, this may be summed up in Leo XIII's application of these principles given in *Rerum Novarum*:

> If a workman's wages be sufficient to enable him comfortably to support himself, his wife, and his children, he will find it easy, if he be a sensible man, to practice thrift, and he will not fail, by cutting down expenses, to put by some little savings and thus secure a modest source of income. Nature itself would urge him to this. We have seen that this great labor question cannot be solved save by assuming as a principle that private ownership must be held sacred and inviolable. The law, therefore, should favor ownership, and its policy should be to induce as many as possible of the people to become owners.[2]

Note that the only "prudential matter" in the above selection is the means by which people are to become owners: sufficient wages, out of which he can save enough to purchase assets to generate an adequate and secure income. If another, better means presents itself (such as the capital homesteading program proposed by the interfaith Center for

Economic and Social Justice), the way is clear for its adoption.

Capital homesteading is a particularly moral alternative to redistribution when we consider that it offers a legitimate and essentially painless way to meet the fourth requirement. As capital owners deriving a fully taxable income from their assets, former welfare recipients would be "repaying" what they previously received, and reducing the tax burden on those who were formerly taxed to support the social welfare system. The situation is similar with worker-owners. They "repay" wages they formerly received on the basis of need in excess of the objective, free market value of the labor they supplied by contributing future labor as owners instead of independent contractors or dependents.

Concern for the Rich

Despite all rhetoric, the rich are people, too. If they have committed no crime, then there is no basis to proceed against them. Greed, selfishness, and hard-heartedness may be sinful (though not necessarily sins) but they are not and should never be crimes. Given that, the rich must be as secure as the poor in their lives, liberties, and property. Anything less is an explicit offense against human dignity, which, too, is as valid for the rich as it is for the poor. As William Cobbett pointed out,

> Freedom is not an empty sound; it is not an abstract idea; it is not a thing that nobody can feel. It means, — and it means nothing else, — the full and quiet enjoyment of your own property. If you have not this, if this be not well secured to you, you may call yourself what you will, but you are a slave.[3]

So, why should we consider the redefinition of private property such a colossal error? Don't love and concern for the poor justify any means of relieving their misery? Isn't the life or health of a single human being worth more than all the mountains of wealth devoted to frivolous entertainment, or sitting unused in a rich man's warehouse?

That is a strong argument, as we have seen above. Nevertheless, the argument leaves out the fact that, when we are talking about natural rights, no one may be unjustly deprived of the exercise of life, liberty, or property without due process, that is, in a manner contrary to natural law or positive law. To do anything else is to take away the human dignity — the humanity — of anyone so violated. We make that individual a "non-person" — a slave.

Even worse, if we remove the protection of the law from some people (no matter how good the principle or end we seek), we lose it for ourselves as soon as someone else gains power and decides that *we* are in violation of *their* principles or stand in the way of some desired end. Making the law flexible in this regard is to endanger our own safety, as well as that of the entire common good.

A good illustration of this is seen in the dialogue in Act One of *A Man for All Seasons*, a play by Robert Bolt. The utterly venal Richard Rich, a character drawn from life, is contrasted with the obviously righteous and extremely principled William Roper, a character based on an actual person, but clearly fictional. Both ironically hold that the end justifies the means, the former to obtain a transient personal good, the latter to save society from itself, which many still consider the greatest good of all, temporal or spiritual. In order to obtain worldly advancement, Rich has made it very clear that he is going to betray Sir Thomas More in some fashion. More's wife Alice urges her husband to have Rich arrested. Instead, More explains calmly that Rich hasn't done anything illegal.

> ALICE (Exasperated, pointing after RICH) While you talk, he's gone!
> MORE And go he should, if he was the Devil himself, until he broke the law!
> ROPER So now you'd give the Devil benefit of law!

MORE Yes. What would you do? Cut a great road through the law to get after the Devil?
ROPER I'd cut down every law in England to do that!
MORE (Roused and excited) Oh? (Advances on ROPER) And when the last law was down, and the Devil turned round on you — where would you hide, Roper, the laws all being flat? (He leaves him) This country's planted thick with laws from coast to coast — man's laws, not God's — and if you cut them down — and you're just the man to do it — d'you really think you could stand upright in the winds that would blow then? (Quietly) Yes, I'd give the Devil benefit of law, for my own safety's sake.

Similarly, the judges at the war crimes trials at Nürnberg following the Second World War made it clear that simply changing the definition of a right, or making something a crime contrary to the principles of the natural law, or even claiming or believing that the content of the natural law is other than it is, did not lessen the guilt of the defendants. There was a higher law, the natural law based on God's Nature, not human opinion of divine revelation or the *Volksgeist*, against which all human law must be measured, and which cannot be set aside without destroying the whole concept of right and wrong.

This is precisely as Heinrich Rommen pointed out in his book on the natural law, written in part to explain how the German judiciary of the Third Reich ever managed to participate in such crimes against humanity. The Tribunal at Nürnberg agreed that the German nation had been in terrible danger in the chaos following the First World War, and even that the Allies bore some responsibility for the state of affairs that existed. Nothing, however, excused the fact that innocent people had been condemned by changing basic definitions of rights, and in many cases by the removal of the whole concept of natural rights, especially the natural rights to life, liberty, and private property.

The Problem of Natural Law

All of this leads to a much deeper problem. This is another aspect of the situation so glaringly obvious that many people seem to miss it completely. It is the source of the justification of the violation of human dignity so common today that a failure to participate in this basic injustice is frequently termed a violation of social justice.

The social teachings of the Catholic Church, virtually the whole of its theology in fact, is built on the philosophy of Saint Thomas Aquinas. This point is so important that both Leo XIII and Pius XI issued encyclicals declaring that the philosophy of Saint Thomas is to be taken as normative in understanding and interpreting the teachings of the Catholic Church.

The problem is that many interpreters tacitly or explicitly *reject* Thomism, and declare that their personal insights or private revelations enable them to reach new definitions of essential terms — terms such as life, liberty, and property. Seemingly inevitably the philosophy they substitute (often not realizing that they are doing so) is derived from William of Occam's distortions of the philosophy of Duns Scotus, the "Subtle Doctor." It is not based on that of Thomas Aquinas, the "Angelic Doctor." In effect, they revive an argument that, as far as the Catholic Church is concerned, was settled eight centuries ago.

Will or Nature?

This argument, which may strike most people today as esoteric and unimportant, revolved around whether the natural law is based on God's Will, or God's Nature. The school of Duns Scotus ended by basing the natural law on human interpretation of what they believed to be God's expressed Will. The school of Saint Thomas ended by basing the natural law on human interpretation of what they believed to be God's Nature (Intellect).

This is the critical issue covered by Doctor Heinrich Rommen in his book, *The Natural Law: A Study in Legal and Social History and Philosophy*. His conclusion was that

God's Nature remained the basis of natural law within the Catholic Church, while Will was the origin of the revolt against the Church which led, ultimately, to the rise of positivism as the prevailing legal and social philosophy of our day.

The advantage to positivism, and the thing that renders it so amenable to today's intellectuals and even the general run of the population, is that it allows you to get whatever you want. Truth itself becomes untrue; there is no absolute standard against which to measure one's actions or desires. Everything becomes relative.

"The Triumph of the Will"

Basing the natural law on someone's interpretation of God's Will instead of what we understand of His Nature allows anyone who can scream loud enough or has sufficient power at his disposal, to force his interpretation on others. This renders the entire second tablet of the Law of Moses mutable. Everything becomes relative to the needs or wants of the moment. The concept of an inalienable or natural right disappears. As Rommen observed,

> For Duns Scotus morality depends on the will of God. A thing is good not because it corresponds to the nature of God or, analogically, to the nature of man, but because God so wills. Hence the *lex naturalis* could be other than it is even materially or as to content, because it has no intrinsic connection with God's essence, which is self-conscious in His intellect. For Scotus, therefore, the laws of the second table of the Decalogue were no longer unalterable. The crux of theology, namely, the problem of the apparent dispensations from the natural law mentioned in the Old Testament and thus seemingly granted by God (the command to sacrifice Isaac, Raphael's apparent lie, Osee's alleged adultery, the polygamy of the patriarchs, and so on), was now readily solved. Yet St. Thomas, too, had been able to

> solve such cases. Now, however, an evolution set in which, in the doctrine of William of Occam (d. *cir.* 1349) on the natural moral law, would lead to pure moral positivism, indeed to nihilism.[4]

Thus, despite the clear instructions of the popes to interpret and understand Catholic social teaching in light of the philosophy of Saint Thomas Aquinas, there has been not only acquiescence in, but a deliberate undermining of our understanding of what it means to be human. It is an almost cosmic irony that many of today's distributists reject the very philosophy that Chesterton used to support his ideas of distributism.

Perhaps driven by frustration as much as lack of understanding of the social doctrine developed by Pius XI (although that frustration may be said, ultimately, to be caused by that same lack of understanding), their rejection of Thomism — whether tacit or explicit — forces them into a hopeless situation. They may loudly proclaim the ideals of distributism . . . but they have no way of achieving them (or so they must assume) without doing what, under a Thomist understanding of natural law, must be regarded as contrary to the good, that is, the natural law. That is, they are faced with violating the natural rights of other human beings or disrupting the social order at its deepest level — usually both.

The Double Mind of Man

The solution, from their positivist perspective, is — to change the definition of the rights of life, liberty, and property! This cannot be done under the Thomist orientation that bases the natural law on God's Nature, but it is simplicity itself using William of Occam's reformulation of Duns Scotus' doctrine of the primacy of the Will. An otherwise natural right becomes transformed into prudential matter simply because a commentator has found a passage somewhere that (in his opinion) appears to contradict or abolish the right as a right.

Under positivism, consistency with other teachings or even common sense isn't necessary. All that is necessary is to be able to get a determinant number of people to accept the new interpretation. What is true in one field of study or at one particular time and place is no longer necessarily as "true" or is "true" in a different way. Ultimately, truth is no longer true.

This "Double Mind of Man" was a theory first propounded by Siger of Brabant, the infamous opponent of Saint Thomas. A development of the theory of the primacy of the Will, it opens up the world to complete chaos. As Chesterton analyzes the situation in his short biography of Saint Thomas,

> He had returned victorious from his last combat with Siger of Brabant; returned and retired. This particular quarrel was the one point, as we may say, in which his outer and his inner life had crossed and coincided; he realized how he had longed from childhood to call up all allies in the battle for Christ; how he had only long afterwards called up Aristotle as an ally; and now in that last nightmare of sophistry, he had for the first time truly realized that some might really wish Christ to go down before Aristotle. He never recovered from the shock. He won his battle, because he was the best brain of his time, but he could not forget such an inversion of the whole idea and purpose of his life. He was the sort of man who hates hating people. He had not been used to hating even their hateful ideas, beyond a certain point. But in the abyss of anarchy opened by Siger's sophistry of the Double Mind of Man, he had seen the possibility of the perishing of all idea of religion, and even of all idea of truth.[5]

The end result of what Saint Thomas had seen was his declaration, "I can write no more. I have seen things which make all my writings like straw."[6] It seems reasonable to assume that what Saint Thomas saw was the apparent victory of his opponents and the virtual abandonment of the philosophy of common sense, even of reason itself. To such a man as Aquinas, the moral and philosophical chaos of our day would have been indistinguishable from Hell.

In conclusion, and to return to the original comment that began this examination of whether or not private property may be regarded as "prudential matter," we restate the question: is distributism simply another form of socialism? Absolutely not. Given the understanding of private property by G. K. Chesterton and Hilaire Belloc, the founders of distributism, nothing could be further from the truth.

The problem, however, is that a determinant number of distributists have abandoned (if they ever had) Chesterton and Belloc's understanding of private property. Given their reliance on a philosophical orientation directly at odds with the Thomism that underpins distributism, they are, to all intents and purposes, socialists, whatever they may call themselves. They refuse to argue fairly, although they may argue endlessly about everything except the issue under discussion.

Critics of CESJ in general and of this writer in particular are fond of complaining that we write so much as we try to explain our position. Little, however, is said about the *content* of the writing, and whether or not the arguments are valid or sound. The best of the critics simply abandon the discussion. The worst continue to make vague accusations, but without offering an argument. This is only to be expected. As Chesterton remarked in analyzing Saint Thomas' methods,

> There is always time to argue unfairly; not least in a time like ours. Being himself resolved to argue, to argue honestly, to answer everybody, to deal with everything, he produced books enough to sink a ship or stock a library; though he died in comparatively early middle age. Probably he could not have done it at all, if he had not been thinking even when he was not writing; but above all thinking *combatively*. This, in his case, certainly did not mean bitterly or

spitefully or uncharitably; but it did mean combatively. As a matter of fact, it is generally the man who is not ready to argue, who is ready to sneer. That is why, in recent literature, there has been so little argument and so much sneering.[7]

Notes

[1] Rommen, *The Natural Law, A Study in Legal and Social History and Philosophy*. Indianapolis, Indiana: Liberty Fund, Inc., 1998, 176.

[2] Leo XIII, *Rerum Novarum* ("On Capital and Labor"), 1891, § 46.

[3] William Cobbett, *A History of the Protestant Reformation in England and Ireland*, 1827, §456.

[4] Rommen, *op. cit.*, 51-52.

[5] Gilbert Keith Chesterton, *Saint Thomas Aquinas, "The Dumb Ox."* New York: Doubleday Image, 1956, 140-141.

[6] *Ibid.*, 141.

[7] *Ibid.*, 126.

9. Subsidiarity and Private Property: A Catholic View

The following essay was written in January through April 2004 at the request of the late Father John H. Miller, C.S.C., S.T.D., head of the Central Bureau, Catholic Central Union of America in St. Louis for inclusion in a book on the Catholic view of subsidiarity. As the project never came to fruition, the work has not been previously published, and appears here for the first time.

Part I

The Idea of Subsidiarity

In the movie, *The Secret of Santa Vittoria* (1969), someone had painted on the side of the town's water tower, "Mussolini Is Always Right." For some odd reason, this was in English, although the action presumably took place in a small village in Italy.

The slogan adequately summarizes the idea that many people have about the role of the State and the principle of subsidiarity. That is, subsidiarity consists of the State doing whatever the individual or "lower" orders of society cannot or will not do for himself or themselves.[1]

Others, in a more populist and less State-oriented view, declare that subsidiarity consists of doing everything at the lowest possible level, even if the proposed act isn't appropriate to that particular level.[2] As Father William J. Ferree, S.M., Ph.D.,[3] related,

> This leads to such outlandish formulations as one I ran into personally in trying to dialogue with some students in the hectic passage from the Sixties to the Seventies. This earnest young man was even condescending in the patience with which he tried to explain to me that "the lower level was always right!"[4]

Obviously these two opposing views are evidence of more than a little confusion. Each understanding flatly contradicts the other. The latter belief assumes an automatic conflict between sovereignty and subsidiarity, while the former makes these two concepts virtually identical in a distorted fashion. Both assume that the State — created by man for man — is somehow "sovereign" in and of itself, and that "*the* people" (never people) are necessarily alienated from the very institutions they create.[5]

We shouldn't be surprised to learn that the truth about subsidiarity lies somewhere between these two extremes. They are, as Father Ferree points out, two halves of the concept developed by Pius XI in *Quadragesimo Anno* (1931) and *Divini Redemptoris* (1937), and elaborated by Pius XII in *Summi Pontificatus* (1939). "Perhaps the best way to handle the idea is to think of a single 'Law of Subsidiarity' that has both a 'Subsidiary Function' and a 'Sovereign Function'."[6] Father Ferree's orientation assumes as a matter of course that the human person under God is endowed with an individual and personal sovereignty, but also adds a social — political — sovereignty vested not directly in man's institutions, but in man, individually and personally.[7]

A Necessary Digression

It's a little unusual to digress from the main argument almost before you've started. With all due respect to the commentators and writers who have labored so intensely for decades to get it wrong, however, Catholic social teaching is both more highly "nuanced" (a word I generally try to avoid) and much clearer than many of today's experts suppose. Briefly, we need only keep in mind what both Leo XIII[8] and Pius XI[9] announced at the beginning of their pontificates.

That is, the appropriate framework for understanding Catholic social teaching is a Thomism based firmly on the philosophy of Aristotle. Proper understanding and analysis require some specialized terms and concepts that modern (and modernist) writers and commentators have become adept at twisting into some marvelous shapes. As a result, we're not yet into the discussion on subsidiarity and already we're running into the principal difficulty — and opportunity — represented by what Father Ferree called "the language of Catholic Action." I will try and define these specialized terms as we go along, but it illustrates one of the chief difficulties with Catholic social teaching: the subject is extremely complex. This is in part because Catholic social teaching is directed at the whole of the common good.

The Idea of Subsidiarity — 253

Here begins our first difficulty with ideas and terminology. The common good is not a vague concept as Aristotle supposed and many people continue to believe.[10] It is something specific: that vast network of relationships and institutions within which we subsist as social creatures.[11]

The common good is like a vast and immensely complicated tapestry. Individuals by themselves or even in association with others simply cannot discern the pattern that ties the entire complex weave together. We can only perceive the basic design principles on which the whole of the pattern is based — imperfectly, it is true, but that does not excuse us from the task. The best we can do is to accommodate to that portion of the tapestry that surrounds us, and ensure that whatever we do conforms as closely as possible to the principles that underlie the pattern. The worst we can do is oversimplify and assume that those portions of the pattern that surround us constitute the whole pattern, and then compound the error by mistaking the pattern for the basic design principles.

Oversimplifications, such as declaring that this or that statement or topic represents the quintessence of Catholic social teaching, are almost inevitably wrong or only partially correct, and therefore wrong by being misleading. A single relationship is infinitely complex, yet many authorities declare without a moment of hesitation that they have distilled the cosmically complex network of the common good and our relationship to it — a system of relationships between an almost infinite number of relationships — into a single statement!

Almost as bad is to assume, with Aristotle, that we have no direct access to the common good. Many people still believe that if we individually do the right thing, then everything will work out for the best. The common good will take care of itself somehow. "He who would do good to another must do it in Minute Particulars: general Good is the plea of the scoundrel, hypocrite, and flatterer, for Art and Science cannot exist but in minutely organized Particulars."[12] At first this famous quote from William Blake seems the quintessence of subsidiarity. It ignores the common good in all its vital complexity, however, and thereby manages to become the very antithesis of subsidiarity.

What I'm saying is, don't be too surprised if we can't grasp everything about even the "minor" subject of subsidiarity immediately. On the contrary — we should be suspicious of our conclusions if we do. Paradoxically, the whole thing becomes simple once we understand — really understand — that social virtue, a personal responsibility, is directed at the common good, not any individual's good — no matter how many individuals are involved. In spite of this obstacle, I'll try to be as clear as possible.

To put it plainly then, "subsidiarity" has two elements. The first is that power subsists within people, genuine, actual human beings, individually and in association with others.[13] The second is that people subsist within formal and informal "milieux" (the plural of "milieu"), those levels of the common good that constitute their "natural medium of life." Pius XI makes this clear in a brief and often-overlooked passage in *Divini Redemptoris*: "Only man, the human person, and not society in any form is endowed with reason and a morally free will."[14] This is perhaps one of the most lucid, most profound, and most straightforward statements of individual and personal sovereignty ever made. It also provides a solid sociological context for understanding subsidiarity within the framework of social virtue.

Sovereignty of the Human Person under God

The essence of subsidiarity is control by the human person, individually or in association with others, of the "medium of life" within which he finds himself. The whole theory of specialization, inquiry method, and cell technique that underpins the mechanics and organization of "Catholic Action" is directed toward control of each one's own natural medium of life.[15] These are basic techniques that apply to all effective social movements, such as the civil rights movement in Mississippi, anti-Apartheid in South Africa, and Solidarity in Poland. People who are engaged in this work are therefore engaged in acts of social charity and social justice within their own natural "medium of life."

This "natural medium" or "milieu" within which each individual operates and exists has an extraordinary influence on those who subsist within it. The milieu in this context often consists of "more fluid" organizations. (The temptation here is to describe these organizations as "informal," but — because they are necessarily organized — they have "form." Use of the term "formal" in its colloquial sense, while more or less accurate, would be confusing in this context and should be avoided.) The makeup of the natural medium of life can, therefore, be obscure and confused, not easily defined, causing many writers and commentators to ignore it.[16] They assume that the environment within which each of us exists is effectively of no importance, or is fixed and unchangeable.

This is true whether the organization is more obviously fluid, or less fluid. An organization by its very nature constitutes an institution. What makes discernment more difficult is the fact the more and less fluid organizations that make up the common good are so intertwined as to make specific identification sometimes an almost impossible task. This does not mean, however, that organizations of whatever degree of fluidity have no effect on us simply because we have a hard time identifying them.

On the contrary, while it does not rule us, the natural medium within which we subsist has a very real and very definite influence on each of us. In some cases, where the common good at our particular level is malformed or flawed, that influence can be for the worse, sometimes disastrous. In that case, we may need to practice heroic virtue to overcome the influence of the milieu. In other cases, where the common good at our particular level is properly structured, the milieu within which we subsist can help each of us attain whatever degree of perfection we are able to reach in the temporal sphere.

Further, our environment is far from being fixed and unchangeable. It is, in fact, so fluid and in such a state of flux that Pius XI termed it "radically unstable." Society is constantly changing to an incredible degree. Hence we have the constant and ongoing need to observe, maintain and restructure our institutions. "The fact is that precisely in those social elements which seem fundamental, and most exempt from change, such as property, capital, labor; a constant change . . . is not only possible, but is real, and an accomplished fact."[17] It is because of this "radical instability" that restructuring of the social order becomes necessary — and possible.

Subsidiarity and the Common Good

The principle of subsidiarity demands that each of us have a direct and discernible connection with the milieux within which we subsist, indeed, with the common good in its entirety at our level. The complexity of the common good even at a single level is so great, however, that we cannot hope that a single mechanism will provide that connection in its entirety. The least we can hope for is a solid and life-enhancing connection with the particular milieux within which we subsist, but hardly the whole of the common good. Even the common good at our level of the moment, our milieu, is composed of "sub" milieux, which may themselves consist of institutions and informal organizations — of "sub-sub" milieux, *ad infinitum*. Put in less esoteric terms, the common good consists of an almost unbelievable diversity of more and less fluid organizations and relationships among them.

Again, I define the common good in the way Pius XI used the term — that network of organizations, both more and less fluid, within which we carry out the business of living. The complexity of the common good, even at a single level, is so great that a single individual cannot hope to exercise the required direct control over it alone.

> The natural medium of life is in itself too informal,[18] too complex, too vast, too fluid and changing, too much subject to the will and shortcomings of

thoughtless people, ever to be controlled directly by individual persons in it; for these individuals are helpless when, standing alone, they face its vast collective weight and pressure.[19]

Thus, association with others (and the right of free association itself) is an absolute necessity to the principle of subsidiarity — yet we have writers claiming that free association is irrelevant or, in some instances, a positive evil.[20] More often, though, commentators and other experts identify the right of free association exclusively with the right of labor to organize.[21] This is an extremely shortsighted and limiting understanding of the right of free association, and leads to ideas directly opposed to the intent of Pius XI.

When, therefore, someone claims that the State is to do whatever the individual cannot do for himself, he contradicts the essence of subsidiarity: free association with others for the purpose of connecting with the common good at one's own level directly through one's own powers.

The Personal Exercise of Power

Subsidiarity is, in this sense, an exercise and an aspect of the individual and personal sovereignty with which the Creator endows each person.[22] Sovereignty consists in large measure of those inalienable rights and free will each person has by nature, that is, of the personal power each of us possesses. "Power" is formally defined as "the ability for doing." The principle of subsidiarity commands that each of us exercise a direct and immediate power over the environment within which each of us subsists.

That is, we are intended to have direct control of our milieux, that complex of more and less fluid organizations that make up our natural medium of life at our own particular level of the common good.[23] The urge to create order and discern our pattern of life is a part of human nature. Control over that pattern is a necessary adjunct to that urge, or we become mere slaves to circumstance, as well as, in a very real sense, slaves to other men as well as to sin.

Each of us thus has a mandate to control his own milieux directly through acts of social justice.[24] Control requires power, and power subsists in our individual and personal sovereignty that has been granted to us by our Creator. For this reason, we must delegate our capacity to acquire and develop legal justice (the power to pass and enforce laws) to the State. It is, however, extraordinarily inappropriate for the individual to delegate any of his direct personal and individual sovereignty (which manifests largely as our capacity to acquire and develop social justice) to any other agency, especially the State.

The State's role is restricted to acts of legal, not social justice. We should not delegate any of our capacity to acquire and develop social justice even if the aim is to reform or restructure the common good at his own level, and he finds himself unable to do it alone. This was the temptation that so many people gave in to in Germany in the 1930s. A strong leader with vision might be able to impose order — but the cost is usually unbearably high, and the result is inevitably slavery of one variety or another.

What we delegate to the State is our capacity to acquire and develop legal justice. Unlike social justice that has a direct act, legal justice can only act on the common good indirectly. By means of its delegated capacity to carry out indirect "acts" of legal justice, the State carries out its task as caretaker of the common good.

The principle of subsidiarity requires each of us to take responsibility for his own environment — for the common good at our level.[25] It often turns out, however, that I am incapable of carrying out the necessary direct control by myself.[26] The complexity of the common good virtually ensures that I will be unable to do so. In that case I have the responsibility to join with like-minded others to carry out this mandate.

> The Holy Father [*i.e.*, Pius XI] points out a threefold duty to these institutions or organizations: to organize, to promote, and to support. These are spe-

cific acts of Social Justice; anyone who would refuse to perform them at his level of the institutional structure would thereby fail against Social Justice; for institutions are, as the Pope so clearly points out, "necessary instruments, enabling men to fulfill their obligations." Without them the individual is "helpless to insure justice" and his natural medium of life, his level of society, is in disorder, is socially unjust. When this disorder reaches up into higher and higher levels of society, it becomes world disorder, a true crisis of civilization, such as we are experiencing in modern times.[27]

The formal definition of subsidiarity is simple, but takes a number of things for granted. There are two postulates of overriding importance. First, the principle of subsidiarity states that 1) no "higher" organization may take over a function that a "lower" organization can adequately perform, and 2) no lower organization may "capture" a "higher" one for its own particular purpose.

These two elements are interdependent to such an extent that it becomes virtually impossible to consider them separately. Fortunately, however, we can take Pius XI's discussion of the role of the corporation and get a good grasp of what he meant by subsidiarity in its entirety. Therein, however, lies another one of those problems I discussed earlier.

The Role of the Corporation

Enthusiasm for State action *über alles* has resulted in confusion over what, exactly, Pius XI meant when he referred to "corporation." Because of the intrusiveness of Mussolini's (and, later, Franco's) "corporate state" when *Quadragesimo Anno* was written, many writers just assumed that the pope's phrase, "Which has been called the corporation," somehow referred to Mussolini's establishment. This confusion not only affects the understanding of subsidiarity, but also of the concept that has been translated into English as "vocational groups."[28] Ironically, as Father Ferree points out, the word "corporation" does not even appear in the Latin text.

This link with fascism was expressly disclaimed in paragraph 95 of *Quadragesimo Anno*.[29] Nevertheless, the idea that "corporation" meant a corporate state on the fascist model found its way into Reverend Eamon Cahill's *The Framework of a Christian State, An Introduction to Social Science*.[30] The book, while it contains many otherwise sound principles and interpretations of the social encyclicals up to the time of writing (1932), declared that an authoritarian fascism was the only acceptable Catholic form of government. Father Cahill's book may have furnished the philosophical and religious justification and support for General Duffy's "Blueshirts," the Irish fascist party.

The possibility has escaped many writers, *welche wonne*, that — in addition to all organized human activity in free association stigmatized by Thomas Hobbes as "corporations" in *Leviathan* — Pius XI referred to business corporations. These are institutions (organizations) designed to expedite the process of making a living. This is a function perhaps at the lowest level of human endeavor, but certainly one of the most immediate. As Father Ferree notes,

> A digression may perhaps be made necessary by the occurrence of the word "Corporation" at the end of the above passage. It does not occur in the Latin text, but has received considerable currency in translations. It does *not* mean the "Corporative State" on the Fascist model. In *Quadragesimo Anno*, describing what he does mean, at least in the preparatory stages, the Holy Father succeeds in using the word "free" seven times in less than a dozen lines, and with a few synonymous expressions thrown in for good measure; though as we have seen earlier this very freedom of organization, directed by social justice, is to establish a *juridical* order as well as a social one. Of the Fascist experiment, while granting

that it has "obvious advantages" he expresses a discreet but unmistakable distrust.³¹ [Emphasis in original.]

If by "corporation" Pius XI meant something other than Mussolini's corporate State, then "subsidiarity" has a fundamentally different meaning than that the State does whatever an individual cannot do for himself. Since Pius XI did indeed mean something other than the corporate State, it can only have been such intermediate organizations as the business corporation, an "artificial" person recognized under law in order to encourage and enable commercial activity.

Pius XI clearly referred to a means which allowed individuals to join together to carry out the process of production in the most efficient and equitable manner — and, more importantly, to own a meaningful amount of productive capital without having to be the sole owner. Pius XI understood that the business corporation has the capacity to be an important vehicle of economic subsidiarity, just as the vote is in the political realm.³² The business corporation operates to bring otherwise inhumanly scaled projects down to human scale through the institution of widely owned private property.

Subsidiarity in America

As chronicled by de Tocqueville, subsidiarity was a characteristic of American life.³³ After the ratification of the new Constitution of 1789,³⁴ the Federal government attempted to assert control over the process of incorporation, but to no avail. The American people had become so used to taking care of things themselves that such action by the central government seemed an unwarranted act of tyranny and a violation of personal and individual sovereignty. The vehicle chosen, by and large, to connect people to the productive milieu within the common good at their particular level was the business corporation.³⁵ This resulted in a condition of civil society in America that received a virtual endorsement from Leo XIII, even as he warned against the application of American political principles to religious society.³⁶

Unfortunately, reliance on the business corporation also created a serious problem that remains with us today, and which Leo XIII began addressing in *Rerum Novarum* (1891). The corporation as it evolved was and is a mechanism to connect people with the means of production — with the process of making a living. The corporation, however, was and remains a very imperfect mechanism. This is true to such an extent that a number of otherwise astute commentators and a great many people make the automatic assumption that the corporation itself must be objectively evil.

The corporation, however, is not evil. It is a tool, nothing more. It can bring about good or evil, depending on the orientation of its owners, its agents, and its intrinsic institutional structures. The modern form of the corporation owes itself to some historic accidents. These have resulted in it being primarily a means of disconnecting people from the means of production, rather than a means of connecting them to it in keeping with the principle of subsidiarity.[37]

Ownership and the Formation of Capital

Alienation from the economic process resulted from the way new technologies of production were financed during the Industrial Revolution. As Hilaire Belloc pointed out, there is nothing in the form of the corporation or of economic and social development, Keynes' assertions to the contrary,[38] that preclude widespread ownership of the means of production by the workers themselves.

> Had property been well distributed, protected by cooperative guilds, fenced round and supported by custom and by the autonomy of great artisan corporations, those accumulations of wealth, necessary for the launching of each new method of production and for each new perfection of it, would have been discovered in the mass of small owners. *Their* corporations, *their* little parcels of wealth combined would have furnished the capitalization required for the new processes, and men already owners would, as

one invention succeeded another, have increased the total wealth of the community without disturbing the balance of distribution. <u>There is no conceivable link in reason or in experience which binds the capitalization of a new process with the idea of a few employing owners and a mass of employed nonowners working at a wage.</u>[39] [underline added]

Thus the primary means of connecting people with the way they make a living, private and individual ownership of the means of production, was negated by the means chosen to bring those productive instruments into being. The assumption that capital could only be formed out of past savings, and that savings could only come from the already-wealthy effectively prevented acquisition of a meaningful ownership stake by the ordinary worker.[40]

The corporation as it evolved was not by its nature a means of concentrating ownership of the means of production in the hands of a few. On the contrary, the corporation was custom-designed to be able to break up the ownership of a single large productive enterprise among many owners.[41] Thus, as Pius XI hinted, a reformed corporation is the perfect vehicle for providing the necessary connection within the productive milieu for the great mass of people mandated under the principle of subsidiarity.

As Pius XI noted, "Bodily labor, which Providence decreed is to be performed for the perfection of man's body and soul, is being everywhere changed into an instrument of perversion; for dead matter comes forth from the factory ennobled, while men are there corrupted and degraded."[42] The disconnection of the human person from the milieu within which he subsists became egregious as more and more people came to rely solely on wages to gain a living income. The wage system provides at best an indirect connection with a person's economic or productive milieu.

The Effect of Technology

Now even the tenuous connection provided by the wage system was broken as the alienation of the worker from the means of production increased. This began with the economic disenfranchisement of the working classes through loss of all or nearly all ownership stakes in the means of production. It was completed by the replacement of workers by machines as advancing technology made the use of human labor in the production process both more expensive and less efficient. This was due to the evolving unreformed intrinsic structure of the corporation and traditional methods of corporate finance.[43]

> It was in this roundabout and off-hand way that what was to become the principal implementation of the ownership of capital tools in production, the corporation, drifted into being set up as 'the President and the Board of Trustees' representing largely absent stockholders, while the going concern, the enterprise, was made up of physically present wageworkers and salaried supervisors who were legally 'outside contractors' for their wages, commissions, or salaries.[44]

This alienation has been expressed to the point of redundancy by modern writers and artists, perhaps most amusingly by Charlie Chaplin in *Modern Times* (1955). Nothing has been done to alleviate the situation other than to suggest, in common with the Unabomber, that the only remedy is the complete destruction of the current order. This alone, they assume, will allow the building of a completely new order on the ruins of the old.[45]

In short, the only remedy people could see to the distorted and unreformed institution of the corporation was the old solution of "destroy now, build later."[46]

Notes

[1] "[The State] is to function both positively and negatively to promote the common good, with its own limits established according to the principle of subsidiarity. This means that it intervenes where individuals and the lower social bodies which people have a natural right to establish cannot (or will not!) do the job." Rupert J. Ederer, "Solidaristic Economics" *Fidelity*, July/August 1994, 13.

[2] See Rev. John J. Kelley, S.M., *Freedom in the Church*. Dayton, Ohio: Peter Li, Inc., 2000.

[3] Father William J. Ferree, S.M., Ph.D. was the co-founder of CESJ, and at his death in 1985 was described as the greatest social philosopher in the United States by the Belgian philosopher Father Andrew F. Morlion, O.P., Ph.D., founder and first president of the International University of Social Studies in Rome.

[4] William J. Ferree, S.M., Ph.D., *Forty Years After . . . A Second Call to Battle*, unpublished manuscript, c. 1984.

[5] It is, by the way, these institutions — not the individuals within them — that are the directed object of social virtue. Social justice, for example, does not consist in paying a just wage. A just wage is an individual good. Social justice consists in organizing with others to arrange things so that it becomes possible to pay a just wage — an entirely different concept. Social charity does not mean loving the people within an institution or being in solidarity with them, but in loving that institution as you love yourself — and consequently being ready to restructure the institution (as you would yourself) to conform to universal moral values.

[6] *Forty Years After, op. cit.*

[7] This is based on Pius XI's discernment of a particular type of *social* virtue, inherent in individuals, but only able to be exercised by individuals as members of groups. See Fr. Ferree, *The Act of Social Justice*. Washington, DC: The Catholic University of America Press, 1942.

[8] Leo XIII, *Æterni Patris* ("On the Restoration of Scholastic Philosophy"), 1879.

[9] Pius XI, *Studiorem Ducem* ("On St. Thomas Aquinas"), 1923.

[10] *Ethics*, Book I.vii.

[11] William J. Ferree, *The Act of Social Justice*. Washington, DC: The Catholic University of America Press, 1942, 21.

[12] William Blake, *Jerusalem*.

[13] This was the whole point (politically) of *Quas Primas*, Pius XI's 1925 encyclical that initiated the Feast of Christ the King.

[14] *Divini Redemptoris* ("On Atheistic Communism"), 1937, § 29.

[15] See Msgr. Luigi Civardi, *A Manual of Catholic Action*. New York: Sheed & Ward, Inc., 1936, 40. According to Father Ferree, the overriding concern of Pius XI throughout the whole of his pontificate was his reorientation of "Catholic Action" into a vehicle for the restructuring of the social order in conformity with universal moral values.

[16] Even Igino Giordani, one of the premier commentators on the social teaching of the Church, almost completely ignores the specifically social aspects of the matter. He mentions groups only briefly (*The Social Message of Jesus*. Boston, Massachusetts: Daughters of St. Paul, 1977, 19), and concentrates on the behavior of the human person within the group — not the relationship of the human person to the group or of the group to other groups. Part of this may be the fault of the translator, and the difficulty of understanding a concept at odds with the traditional individualistic interpretation of the social teachings of the Church. The result, however, is the same — a subordination or subsumation of the idea of true social virtue to individual virtue. Thus, while Giordani performs a valuable service in forwarding what Pius XI saw as the foundation of Catholic social teaching — individual reformation of the human person — he does very little to advance or explain the goal of Pius XI, the restructuring of the social order.

[17] Pius XI, *Discourse Commemorating the Thirty-Fifth Anniversary of Rerum Novarum*, May 15, 1926. This idea was echoed in § 132 of *Quadragesimo Anno*, ". . . *the instability of economic life*, and especially of its structure, exacts of those engaged in it most intense and unceasing effort. . . " [emphasis added].

[18] Father Ferree here uses "informal" in an informal sense.

[19] Ferree, *Forty Years After, op. cit.*

[20] See W. H. Hutt, *The Strike-Threat System, The Economic Consequences of Collective Bargaining*. New Rochelle, New York: Arlington House, 1973, for an attack on purely economic association.

[21] There is a broad diversity of these. A short list includes William F. Drummond, S.J. (*Social Justice*. Milwaukee, Wisconsin: The Bruce Publishing Company, 1955); Dom Virgil Michel, O.S.B. (*Christian Social Reconstruction*. Milwaukee, Wisconsin: The Bruce Publishing Company, 1938); Henry S. Spalding, S.J.

(*Social Problems and Agencies*. New York: Benziger Brothers, 1929); Father Cuthbert (*Catholic Ideals in Social Life*. New York: Benziger Brothers, 1904); Rev. Eamon Cahill (*The Framework of the Christian State*. Dublin, Ireland: M. H. Gill and Son, Ltd., 1932); John A. Ryan (*A Living Wage*. New York: Grosset and Dunlap, 1906); Valère Fallon, S.J. (*Principles of Social Economy*. New York: Benziger Brothers, 1933); Rupert J. Ederer (*Economics as if God Matters*. South Bend, Indiana: Fidelity Press, 1995); Raymond J. Miller, C.Ss.R. (*Forty Years After: Pius XI and the Social Order*. St. Paul, Minnesota: Radio Replies Press, 1947); Thomas J. Higgins, S.J. (*Man as Man: The Science and Art of Ethics*. Rockford, Illinois: TAN Books and Publishers, Inc., 1992); Mary Lois Eberdt, C.H.M., Ph.D., and Gerald Schnepp, S.M., Ph.D. (*Industrialism and the Popes*. New York: P. J. Kenedy and Sons, 1953); Amintore Fanfani (*Catechism of Catholic Social Teaching*. Westminster, Maryland: The Newman Press, 1960). This list represents a statistically invalid random sample from my own library. Of the books that I pulled off the shelves, only two made no connection between the right of free association and labor unions, and they made no mention of the right of free association at all. This does not, of course, mean that organized labor is not a valid object or directed end of some of our efforts. The problem is to mistake organized labor as the sole or most important application of the right of free association.

[22] According to St. Robert Cardinal Bellarmine, this sovereignty is granted to the collective (*De Laicis, or, the Treatise on Civil Government*, Westport Connecticut: Hyperion Press, Inc., 1979, Ch. VI). Pius XI corrected this by pointing out (see above) that only the human person, and not society in any form is endowed with reason and a morally free will (*Divini Redemptoris*, § 29).

[23] If we wanted to complicate the discussion at this point, we could observe that each of us is constantly shifting milieux as we carry out the business of living. None of us exists permanently or unchangeably within any set milieu.

[24] See Rev. John Francis Murphy, S.T.L., *The Moral Obligation of the Individual to Participate in Catholic Action*. Washington, DC: The Catholic University of America Press, 1958.

[25] Giordani considers this responsibility one of the principal characteristics of Christianity. "Thus every Christian carries the burden of a tremendous duty, that of winning his battle in view of its eternal sanction. He possesses within himself an immortal value — the soul — and he must respect it without end. This

respect must be understood not in a formalistic but a Christian sense, as an inner thing, not as a source of pride. Personal responsibility is an impulse that sets in motion all the resources of the individual and therefore generates initiative, which produces that enrichment of spiritual and material well-being that the American philosophers call the more abundant life. It is an inexhaustible dynamo of social energy. And to be convinced of this it is sufficient to compare the civilization of Christian peoples, stimulated by this sense of personal responsibility, with that of the Moslems, frozen by fatalism." *The Social Message of Jesus, op. cit.,* 126.

[26] *Divini Redemptoris,* § 53.

[27] Ferree, *Forty Years After, op. cit.*

[28] Briefly, "vocational groups" were not to be construed as labor unions. Pius XI characterized them as not primarily economic in nature in § 32 of *Quadragesimo Anno,* and reiterated this in *Divini Redemptoris,* § 32. Neither were the workers associations to be an authoritarian means of controlling production via the so-called "Industry Council Plan" (See Mary Lois Eberdt and Gerald J. Schnepp, *Industrialism and the Popes.* New York: P. J. Kenedy & Sons, 1953). On the contrary, "vocational groups" (a poor translation), were to be Catholic Action groups organized along lines consistent with each particular milieu, with the aim of restructuring the social order — not attempting to duplicate the economic role of the guild or labor union. Their primary purpose was the spiritual perfection of the individual to prepare him for the restructuring of the social order.

[29] "We are compelled to say that to Our certain knowledge there are not wanting some who fear that the State, instead of confining itself as it ought to the furnishing of necessary and adequate assistance, is substituting itself for free activity; that the new syndical and corporative order savors too much of an involved and political system of administration; and that (in spite of those more general advantages mentioned above, which are of course fully admitted) it rather serves particular political ends than leads to the reconstruction and promotion of a better social order."

[30] Dublin: M. H. Gill and Son, Ltd., 1932.

[31] Fr. William J. Ferree, *The Act of Social Justice.* Washington, DC: The Catholic University of America Press, 1942, 129.

[32] If the reader will indulge me, a good example of the sort of confusion rampant today in interpreting Catholic social teaching is illustrated by an amusing, if inherently very sad anecdote.

When CESJ — the Center for Economic and Social Justice — sent out pre-publication review copies of its 1994 book, *Curing World Poverty* (referenced below), one critic took exception to the statement by Dr. Norman G. Kurland that, "Next to the State itself, the modern corporation is our most important social tool." (157) Obviously misunderstanding that Catholic social teaching applies specifically and particularly to civil society, the critic snarled, "Wow! What happened to Church and school?" The answer, of course, is that nothing "happened to Church and school." Human society is divided into three "types." These are civil (the State), religious (the Church), and domestic (the family). The social teachings of the Church are directed toward civil society, not religious society or domestic society. The Church does not come under civil society at all. Education ("school") is the responsibility of the family (domestic society), and is only delegated to Church or State as a matter of expedience.

[33] "The Principle of the Sovereignty of the People of America," Book I, Chapter iv. Alexis de Tocqueville, *Democracy in America*. New York: Alfred A. Knoph, 1994. We also must not overlook the contributions of Orestes A. Brownson, regarding the embodiment of Catholic principles in American life, especially *The American Republic* (1865).

[34] It appears that, primarily through the agency of George Mason of Gunston Hall, the American structures of government embody "Catholic" political principles. George Mason was the principal author of the Virginia Declaration of Rights (June 12, 1776), which affirmed the right to the means to acquire and possess private property as a natural right, as well as the "Father of the Bill of Rights," the first ten amendments to the Constitution. Whether Mr. Mason acquired his knowledge of Catholic principles directly through the writings of St. Robert Cardinal Bellarmine or indirectly via Algernon Sidney's *Discourses Concerning Government* remains an open question. See Rev. John Clement Rager, S.T.D., *The Political Philosophy of St. Robert Bellarmine*. Spokane, Washington: The Apostolate of Our Lady of Siluva, 1995.

[35] When the same "frenzy" to form corporations hit England during the early 18th century, so little were the people used to depending on their own efforts that they allowed the corporation movement to evolve into the infamous "South Sea Bubble." See Charles Mackay, "The South Sea Bubble," *Extraordinary Popular*

Delusions and the Madness of Crowds. New York: Crown Publishers, 1995.

[36] *Testem Benevolentia Nostra* ("On Americanism in Religion"), 1899. This "apostolic letter" (frequently misidentified as an encyclical) has, despite its overt praise for American civil institutions, somehow been understood as a condemnation of democracy and the United States in general. On the contrary, the document condemns the application of democratic principles to the faith, morals and administrative structure of the Catholic Church, not to American civil society.

[37] An in-depth analysis of the flaws of the corporation as it evolved and the effect of this on society is found in a number of articles by Judge Peter Stenger Grosscup in the early twentieth century. See "How to Save the Corporation," *McClure's Magazine*, February, 1905; "Who Shall Own America?" *American Illustrated Magazine*, December 1905, and its sequel, "The Rebirth of the Corporation," *American Illustrated Magazine*, June 1906, as well as a number of other articles. Judge Grosscup described his approach as a process of "people-ization," his version of subsidiarity.

[38] "The immense accumulations of fixed capital which, to the great benefit of mankind, were built up before the war, could never have come about in a Society where wealth was divided equitably." John Maynard Keynes, *The Economic Consequences of the Peace*. London: Penguin Books, 1988, 19. This is more than an isolated statement taken out of context. It is the central thought in the pivotal chapter, "Europe Before the War," of a book that economists have come to realize represents a statement of the major orientation and direction of all Keynes' subsequent work. The war itself, and the contrast between pre-war and post-war conditions color the totality of Keynes' economic thought, and directed his efforts toward developing a system that would explain what the war had done, and provide a means for restoring the pre-war *status quo*. It is now considered impossible to understand Keynes' *General Theory* without first reading *The Economic Consequences of the Peace*, just as Adam Smith's *The Wealth of Nations* puzzles or misleads those who have not read *The Theory of Moral Sentiments*. The effect of the First World War on the consciousness of an entire epoch of thought is frequently ignored today, but should not be, if we are to understand what people were talking about. See the introduction

by Robert Lekachman to the above-cited edition of *The Economic Consequences of the Peace*.

[39] Hilaire Belloc, *The Servile State*. Section 4, "How the Distributive State Failed." Indianapolis, Indiana: Liberty Fund, Inc., 1977, 100-101.

[40] The falsity of the idea that capital can only be financed from existing pools of savings was proved by Harold Moulton in his economic classic, *The Formation of Capital*. Washington, DC: The Brookings Institution, 1935.

[41] Limited liability was added centuries after the invention of the corporation. Limited liability ensured the corporation's success and effectiveness as a social tool, but was not originally part of the concept.

[42] *Quadragesimo Anno*, § 135.

[43] An in-depth treatment of this development can be found in two books by Louis O. Kelso and Mortimer J. Adler, *The Capitalist Manifesto* (1958) and *The New Capitalists* (1961).

[44] Ferree, *Forty Years After. . . op. cit.*

[45] Hilaire Belloc, *The Restoration of Property*. New York: Sheed and Ward, 1936, 11-12.

[46] Fr. William J. Ferree, S.M., Ph.D., *Introduction to Economic and Social Development*. Rome: Private Printing, 1966, 15-16.

Part II

The Function of Subsidiarity

The theme of alienation of the worker, indeed, of everybody, captured the popular imagination for the greater part of the twentieth century. You only have to view films from Charlie Chaplin's *Modern Times* (1936), to James Dean's *Rebel Without a Cause* (1955), or just about any modern film, novel or work of art you care to mention to be struck by the overwhelming sense of alienation that — according to Hollywood — pervades modern life. There is sometimes a question as to from what, exactly, all these people are being alienated, but the alienation itself seems beyond dispute.

Almost inevitably, the chosen solution to overcome alienation is violence and destruction. Somehow this is supposed to bring people's attention to the problem. In typical modern fashion, the mere fact of getting people focused on a problem — "raising their consciousness" — will solve everything. In reality, of course, all destruction and violence ever accomplish is more destruction and violence.[1]

A Mere Good Intention

In far distant second place to destruction as a solution is the assumption, particularly popular in Catholic circles, that mere goodwill or a good intention is sufficient to solve all problems.[2] We see this, for example, in another movie, Fritz Lang's *Metropolis* (1925). The basic theme of the film is the assumption that a simple change of heart on the part of the individual capitalists who run the system is the only thing necessary to improve society.[3] "The mediator between brain and muscle must be the heart."

The inadequacy of the individualistic approach can be illustrated with an ironic little twist of fate. Lang's wife, Thea von Harbou, who wrote the novel and adapted the screenplay for *Metropolis*, divorced Lang and became a Nazi. Something of a tribute to the human need to bring order out of chaos at any cost, she was not alone among those in Germany who saw Hitler's tyranny as the only solution to the social and economic disorder precipitated by the First World War.

Adam Smith, considered by many, including Father William J. Ferree,[4] as the supreme individualist, used a similar approach. Smith, however, believed that an individual need merely pursue his own, personal good in order to benefit the whole of society, very nearly inadvertently and, at times, actually in spite of himself. Smith removed even the presumed necessity for a good intention to bring about positive changes in the common good. Only individual acts were necessary, whether or not consciously directed to the common good.

Adam Smith's theory is a near perfect example of Aristotle's assumption that the common good is not directly attainable or to be directly affected by anyone, at any level.[5] Smith assumed that a supremely selfish or "rapacious" act, lacking even a personal good intention, as long as it was in accordance with certain "moral sentiments" was enough to bring about the good of others — indirectly. Smith called the mechanism that brought about this effect the "invisible hand."[6]

The "Invisible Hand" and Subsidiarity

Connecting the average person to the means of production in Smith's system, that is, the mechanism of subsidiarity within the productive milieu, is the wage system. As far as Smith was concerned, actual ownership of the means of production is irrelevant.[7] The "invisible hand" distributes the goods of the earth in as equitable a fashion as if ownership of the means of production were widely distributed.[8] The corporation merely facilitates the functioning of the "invisible hand," enhancing the mechanism and thus the action of subsidiarity.

The problem with Smith's assumptions should be obvious to anyone who understands the institution of private property and the effect of technology.[9] The worker's connection to production under the wage system is intrinsically flawed, for there is no direct connection to production. In Smith's system, a rich man will employ human labor instead of technology to produce the goods and services that meet his wants and needs out of the moral sentiments of beneficence and approbation. Beneficence will ensure that the rich man will employ as many people as possible for the sake of exercising good will toward those people, while he will garner public approbation and approval for being the employer of so many.

That is not the way the system works. In reality, labor is sold for wages, and the transaction ends there.[10] Attempts to alleviate this disconnection via "right to work" laws, or a presumed "right" of the worker to the totality of production always fail in their immediate purpose, which is to reconnect the worker to the means of production.[11] They also make matters worse by increasing class conflict and encouraging acts of injustice against owners of capital. Further, mandating a wage system job as the chief or only means whereby income is gained is very nearly the final step toward the establishment and maintenance of Belloc's "servile state."[12]

The Role of Property

Property, considered irrelevant by Smith, connects the worker to the means of production by its very nature. This is because property is not the thing owned, but the rights that an owner has with regard to what he owns. Property is a direct and inalienable connection, for the right to property is an inalienable right.[13] The form and exercise of the rights of property may differ in response to the needs of society and the common good as well as individuals within society,[14] but the connection cannot be severed without violating an inalienable right that accrues to the human person as a sacred thing.[15] Nowhere is this more evident than in the work of Father Heinrich Pesch, S.J.

> Because man was the center of the social system, he also was at the center of economic activity. There-

fore, Pesch accepted the principle of wage labor and of the separation of labor and capital. (1, 17 – 18) He demanded, however, that the community, acting through the state, interfere to prevent capitalist excesses which might threaten the economic status of individuals, and especially their private property which they must have to be able to fulfill their function in society. (1, 188, 206 – 207)[16]

The conclusion is startling and, inevitably, rejected by a great number of writers. Frequently, especially from Catholic writers, we read that "property as a right is not absolute."[17] Unfortunately, this is only partly correct. The right to own something — the natural right to property — is absolute. That is, it is inalienable. It cannot be taken away without negating the humanity of the one from whom the right is taken. The exercise of property, however, is limited by the demands of the common good and the needs of other individuals.[18] Correctly then we should say that the *exercise* of property as a right is not absolute.[19]

One of the reasons Pius XI insisted on the right of the average worker to own a significant stake of income generating property is that property is the "vehicle" of subsidiarity within the productive milieu — the economic common good. The amount of ownership cannot be token, for that would negate the principle of subsidiarity with respect to that particular milieu.

Neither can individual accumulations of wealth be too large. That would mean an excess of power in the hands of one person, which, inevitably, as Lord Acton stated,[20] would corrupt not only that individual, but, through social transactions, others as well. This is the reason for insisting that the popes have insisted that the ideal ownership stake is "moderate." A property stake should be sufficient to provide the worker and his family with a comfortable income when thrift and frugality are exercised, but not large enough to give the owner control over the lives of others.[21]

The Role of Technology

So much for the alienation inherent in the wage system. How technology disconnects the worker from the means of production is more obvious. In 1776, however, Adam Smith could be excused for not realizing the ultimate effect of technology. The Industrial Revolution was just beginning. Smith saw the fundamental change in the mode of production only in terms of increased specialization of human labor (his famous pin factory).[22] As far as Smith was concerned (and virtually every economist since his time), technology only enhances the productivity of labor. Technology is not, in and of itself, independently productive.[23]

That, however, is not the case. The goal of technology is not to "enhance" or increase the productivity of the worker — but to replace him. Technology is, in fact, independently productive, in the sense that the production equation has two "independent variables" — labor and technology. Technology is not, however, *autonomously* productive. The point, however, is that technology does not simply enhance human labor, but replaces it.

If technology functioned merely to enhance human labor, a machine would, in effect, be a physical part of the human body, paradoxically a part not owned by the person inhabiting the body (another form of slavery)! Anyone using a machine, simple or otherwise, would be — in effect — a cyborg, a blending or joining of man and machine. This is something properly done socially — not physically — through the institution of private property.

While this idea is common enough, and the effect of machinery is almost inevitably described as an extension of the physical capabilities of human beings — as seems obvious, when we look at a hammer or a spear — appearances (and conclusions) can be deceiving. The effect of all machines is not to extend or enhance human capabilities. Machines (even the simplest) do what human beings normally cannot do, or they would not have been invented in the first place.

You might be able to find a martial artist who can drive nails with his hands, but most people drive nails with hammers; the hammer does what the human hand does not ordinarily do. Similarly, a human being can dig holes with his hands, but a shovel under human direction and addition of motive power not only digs holes faster and more efficiently, it does it differently, in a way the human hand cannot ordinarily duplicate. The human hand digs by scraping then scooping, a shovel by *cutting* then scooping. Both dig holes, but do it in different ways. Because it is designed specifically to dig, the shovel is more efficient and faster than the human hand, a "tool" designed for general purposes . . . mostly manipulation of tools designed for specific purposes.

Technology replaces *human* productivity with *non-human* productivity. Ultimately, the human worker becomes redundant, replaced by the non-human worker. The principle of subsidiarity, realized incompletely and tenuously through the wage system, is eliminated entirely when the worker loses his job and has no connection whatsoever with the means of production.

Adam Smith's assumption that human labor would be preferred over technology was also incorrect. He ridiculed the man who preferred to employ technology in preference to living, breathing human beings.[24] He failed to recognize the fact that the immense productive capacity of technology relative to human labor would mean that anyone who employed human labor in competition with hyper-productive technology would quickly go out of business.

Not a Job for "Outsiders"

A critical aspect of subsidiarity is that the act of connection with the particular milieu must be carried out by those within the milieu itself. It cannot be imposed from the outside, from those at other levels of the common good. If subsidiarity were a particular virtue of its own (it is not), then its proper "act" within the economic common good would be the exercise of the rights of property that accompany ownership. Ownership provides the mechanism of subsidiarity, that intrinsic connection so necessary to the proper functioning of the common good at any level, not just within the economic milieu:

> Here we meet Pope Pius XI's great principle: "The first apostles to the workers ought to be workers." This is the principle which in his "Catholic Action" became known as Milieu specialization: specialization according to the "natural medium" of each one's ordinary daily life.
>
> The theory is that each one's own life is so complex and so specialized, that the person alone is a "specialist" in that life. In the same way, each group's own interests are so complex and so particular to it, that only its members are specialists in the needs and aspirations and hopes and fears of that group.
>
> Anyone who would try to run such a group "from outside" would evidently be a rank amateur. The group must be run by those who are in it, and in order to run the group they must get together and decide in common the means they will adopt, in other words they must organize their life.[25]

Thus Pius XI saw the modern business corporation precisely and exactly as the best means to allow ordinary workers — who comprise the bulk of society — to connect themselves to the common good at their particular levels within the economic milieu. There were and remain serious problems with the structure of the corporation. Many presume, however, that the flaws of the corporation are not inadvertent. They firmly believe that the flaws of the modern corporation are the essence of the thing that is the corporation. Hence socialists and fascists strive to abolish the corporation or impose State control, while capitalists and elitists attempt to show that the immorality that results from its flaws is in fact moral.[26]

Reform of the Corporation

Pius XI saw the need for serious and extensive reforms of the modern corporation before it could become an effective agent of subsidiarity. The most important reform consisted, obviously, in restructuring the ownership of the corporation so that those most concerned with the enterprise itself, the workers, would be directly connected to it. Such is the nature of society and, especially, of the economic common good, that the best means of connecting the worker to the corporation was through a significant, if moderate, ownership stake — a defined private property right — in the corporation for which he worked.

This program is obvious, given the principle of subsidiarity. When we add the nature of private property and the demands of modern methods of production, it is astounding that some writers continue to insist that workers have no absolute right to participate in ownership of the business enterprise for which they work. In light of the explicit statements in the encyclicals as to the desirability and, indeed, mandate for worker ownership, the refusal to acknowledge or recognize this right or even the reason for it verges on the pertinacious.

In their narrow focus on their own particular hobbyhorse, these commentators dismiss worker ownership as something restricted to agricultural land, or as mere prudential matter. They inevitably revert to the wage system and the dependency status imposed by subsisting on wages alone as the only just means of gaining a living income. Worker ownership in this orientation becomes prudential matter, something that would be nice, but is by no means necessary. They consider the tenuous connection provided by the wage system sufficient to give the average worker the power necessary to join with others and have a direct effect on his particular milieu.

They couldn't be more wrong. The wage system empowers no one except the currently wealthy and powerful with more wealth and power over others. The wage system requires the coercive power of the State to back it up. Workers

The Function of Subsidiarity — 281

in the wage system can, of course, organize, and, in fact, must if they are to achieve even a modicum of justice through the bargaining power thus gained. The problem is that organizing among themselves is of little benefit in providing a social connection (as provided by ownership) to the means of production. Absent State power to back up union demands, there is nothing to prevent owners from firing every worker who joins a union, and from hiring someone who will work for a lower wage or under poorer conditions.

As an owner, however, the worker has a social as well as a legal right to organize to protect his interests with the management his board of directors has hired to run the business that he owns. In this context it is important to repeat that subsidiarity runs "both ways." That is, higher levels of society are not to interfere with the lower levels of society except as required for the common good — but neither are the lower levels of society permitted to interfere with the higher levels of society, again, except as required for the common good.

Co-ownership does not, therefore, automatically mean co-management. The ordinary worker must, by the principle of subsidiarity, have some say so in matters that directly affect his job. The right to have this say-so is vested in the worker by his property in the business. As a non-owning worker, of course — essentially an outside contractor — the employee has no natural right to demand any satisfaction at all. Of course, the State may step in and back up worker or union demands with its coercive power. Such an act, however, is at the level of a statutory right. This is far inferior to the natural rights bestowed by direct private and personal ownership in the enterprise.

Such action by the State directly violates the principle of subsidiarity. It is directly contrary to the recognized role of the State in Catholic Action. In social justice, the State is to provide the environment that allows ordinary people to organize and affect the common good at their particular level so they can improve and restructure the relevant institutions.

It is not to impose desired conditions by mandate. That would be an egregious violation of subsidiarity, acting outside the State's competence and directly interfering in a lower level of society simply because it has the power and presumably wants the same results as those within the milieu affected.

Pius XI thus assigned the corporation an important role in applying the principle of subsidiarity — connecting the worker directly to the means of production — and provided the aim of corporate reform which would enable it to fulfill this role: ownership by the workers in the enterprise in which they worked. By this means they would acquire the necessary power to affect directly their particular milieu at their level of the economic common good.[27]

A Living Income

The income aspects of ownership were by no means overlooked. It is clear from the language of the encyclicals, however, that income *per se* is secondary to empowering the worker with direct control over his milieu. Significantly, when Pius XI finally mentioned wages in *Quadragesimo Anno*, it was in context of how the ordinary worker is to gain the ownership that Leo XIII declared was the only reason anyone would work for wages.[28]

> This program cannot, however, be realized unless the propertyless wage-earner be placed in such circumstances that by skill and thrift he can acquire a certain moderate ownership, as was already declared by Us, following the footsteps of Our Predecessor. But how can he ever save money, except from his wages and by living sparingly, who has nothing but his labor by which to obtain food and the necessities of life? Let Us turn, therefore, to the question of wage, which Leo XIII held to be "of great importance," stating and explaining where necessary its principles and precepts.[29]

Nevertheless, numberless writers of both the capitalist and the socialist persuasions[30] insist to the point of pertinacity that wages, and the living or family wage in particular, are the be-all and end-all of Catholic social teaching. How they could persist in this view in light of the clear and unequivocal statements of the popes from Leo XIII to John Paul II is a mystery that cannot easily be resolved. Perhaps the best thing to do is simply write it off to human obstinacy and the perversity of fallen man, and work around it.

Without subsidiarity, properly implemented, social justice, and hence Catholic Action, is a dead letter. Too much emphasis should not, however, be placed on the economic aspects of subsidiarity. Empowering the workers with property in the enterprise in which they work is possibly the single most important aspect of the economic common good within that particular milieu. The economic aspect of the common good, however, is not the whole of the common good, nor is an adequate and secure income the ultimate end of social justice or Catholic social teaching. The goal of Catholic Action is and should be restructuring society to conform to universal moral principles so as to establish and maintain the Reign of Christ the King.[31]

The Wage System and Dependency

It is highly unlikely that the condition of dependency forced on workers by the wage system could ever result in their attaining the required status of adulthood upon which that Kingdom is established — but it is possible, however infinitesimally. This realization makes it clear that, despite the belief of a number of commentators, economic justice is merely a part of social justice.[32] The emphasis the popes put on economics is by way of example and the recognition of the immediacy of the need to make a living.[33]

The true end of man is heaven, and attainment of heaven requires a fully adult, free "independent other" in all respects, political, economic and, overwhelmingly, religious.[34] Anything, therefore, that contradicts or contravenes the true end of man by inhibiting or preventing his "independent otherness" — forcing on him a condition of dependency or slavery — in politics, economics or religion, acts against man's true end. It may, therefore, be objectively evil if there is no legitimate justification for maintaining an individual in such a condition.

Subsidiarity can be overlooked for a time, but ignored permanently, never. Expedience may dictate, for example, a dependent condition on the part of some men, as Saint Thomas acknowledged.[35] This condition obviates subsidiarity, for a dependent has no control over his milieu. Instead, the dependent affects his milieu indirectly through the "reflected" virtue of his principal, as Aristotle stated, and as Pius XI affirmed in *Quas Primas* (1925). This dependent condition, however, must never be construed as a permanent or ideal condition of the individual or state of society.

Perhaps the best way to think of subsidiarity is as a species of freedom — the freedom to be completely and fully human, and to work out our salvation within the constraints imposed by the demands of human nature — the common good of all mankind. To close and to emphasize the importance of private property as the vehicle for subsidiarity, we cannot do better than quote William Cobbett, "the Poor Man's Friend,"[36] that astute Protestant commentator who so ably defended the reputation of the Catholic Church in the late eighteenth and early nineteenth centuries.

> Freedom is not an empty sound; it is not an abstract idea; it is not a thing that nobody can feel. It means, — and it means nothing else, — the full and quiet enjoyment of your own property. If you have not this, if this be not well secured to you, you may call yourself what you will, but you are a slave. Now, our Catholic forefathers took special care upon this cardinal point. They suffered neither kings nor parliaments to touch their property without cause clearly shown. They did not read newspapers, they did not talk about debates, they had no taste for "mental enjoyment;" but they thought hunger and

thirst great evils, and they never suffered anybody to put them to board on cold potatoes and water. They looked upon bare bones and rags as indubitable marks of slavery, and they never failed to resist any attempt to affix these marks upon them. You may twist the word freedom as long as you please, but at last it comes to quiet enjoyment of your own property, or it comes to nothing. Why do men want any of those things that are called political rights and privileges? Why do they, for instance, want to vote at elections for members of parliament? Oh! because they shall then have an influence over the conduct of those members. And of what use is that? Oh! then they will prevent the members from doing wrong. What wrong? Why, imposing taxes that ought not to be paid. That is all; that is the use, and the only use, of any right or privilege that men in general can have.[37]

Notes

[1] "The favorite 'social technique' of our own time is the 'peaceful' demonstration, especially when media coverage is likely or can be arranged. Subsidiary aspects of the demonstration are boycotts, sit-ins, organized lobbying pressures, single-issue 'advocacy' and then — crossing an invisible line which is hard to define and harder still to hold — civil disobedience, violent demonstrations, and, ultimately, terrorism!" *Forty Years After, op. cit.* True, destruction and violence, if total, can solve an immediate problem very effectively. Using destruction and violence to solve problems, however, inculcates society and the individuals of society with the habits of destruction and violence, which eventually leads to the destruction of both society and the individuals within it.

[2] Ferree, "Saint Thomas' Analysis of Legal Justice," *The Act of Social Justice. op. cit.*, 9-35.

[3] Giordani counters the "mere goodwill" assumption by stressing the importance of individual and personal responsibility (*loc. cit.*), but, in my opinion, fails to apply this to our individual responsibility to restructure the social order. In part, this is due to Giordani's concern that people not take the prescriptions in

scripture in an absolute or literal sense, but discern the principles and learn to apply them. As he says, Jesus was a generalist, and did not give specifics for the structure of society (*op. cit.*, 19). It's up to us to apply these principles in a rational way. In other words, it would be foolish of us to seek out some Pharisees or Doctors of the Jewish Law in order to follow their example and ignore their teachings. Jesus gave that as an example of how we are to discern the truth in anyone's teachings, but not model our acts on a teacher's bad behavior.

[4] I believe that Father Ferree, irritated with Adam Smith's individualistic approach, may have been guilty of a "hasty generalization" in regards to Smith. Father Ferree characterized Smith's theories as "destructive" (*Introduction to Social Justice*. Washington, DC: Center for Economic and Social Justice, 1997, 7), but Smith was not so much destructive as indifferent. Destructiveness and indifference can and often do have the same end result, but they are not the same thing.

[5] Aristotle, Book I.v, *The Politics*.

[6] Adam Smith, *The Theory of Moral Sentiments*, IV.I.10.

[7] "They [the rich] are led by an invisible hand to make nearly the same distribution of the necessaries of life, which would have been made, had the earth been divided into equal portions among all its inhabitants." *Ibid.*

[8] *Ibid.*

[9] A good detailing of the material effects of technology (which unfortunately omits the political and social effects) can be found in the works of R. Buckminster Fuller, especially *Utopia or Oblivion: the Prospects for Humanity*. New York: Bantam Books, 1969. Kelso and Adler add the economic, political and social effects of technology (as well as a philosophical justification), while Pius XI provides the idea of social virtue and the means of restructuring the social order to accommodate rather than deny or ignore progress.

[10] Prescient commentators such as Charles Morrison asserted the necessity of worker ownership through the corporation, but recognized that the laws under which the corporation existed at the time in England (the mid-1850s) made this impossible. See *An Essay on the Relations Between Labour and Capital*, London: Longman, Brown, Green, and Longmans, 1854.

[11] See, *e.g.*, William P. Quigley, *Ending Poverty as We Know It: Guaranteeing a Right to a Job at a Living Wage*. Philadelphia, Pennsylvania: Temple University Press, 2003.

[12] Hilaire Belloc, *The Servile State*. Indianapolis, Indiana: Liberty Fund, Inc., 1977, 50, 179-80.

[13] John XXII, *Quia Vir Reprobus* ("That Evil Man"), 1329, §§ 34-35. *Vir Reprobus* was the Bull of Excommunication issued against Michael of Cessena, former Father General of the Franciscans, when he asserted that property was not a natural right and postdated the fall of man.

[14] Pius XII, "On the Rights of Man," Christmas Message, 1942.

[15] *Rerum Novarum*, § 46.

[16] Gustav Gundlach, S.J., "Solidarist Economics, Philosophy and Socio-economic Theory in Pesch" *Social Order*, April 1951, 185.

[17] This belief is as widespread as it is erroneous. Only a few examples are necessary to illustrate this point. "The rights not to be coerced and to private property are rights of great importance, but not so important or precise in scope as to be absolute. Nothing about either right suggests more than *prima facie* status. Accordingly, any more right — such as the right not to be harmed — that is weightier in the circumstances can override the right not to be coerced or the right to hold property." Tom Beauchamp, Department of Philosophy at the Kennedy Institute of Ethics at Georgetown University, *Rights of Health Care*, 1985, 121. "Still others (Rawls 1971) challenge the implicit assumption that our natural talents and skills are our property in the sense that we deserve, and are entitled to benefit from, their use in any way that we can through free exchanges. They argue that such endowments are themselves 'undeserved' and should work to the advantage of everyone, not just their possessors." Norman Daniels, professor of philosophy at Tufts University, *Just Health Care*, 1985, 121. All of these statements, and an almost infinite number of others, merely serve to undermine human nature, of which the right to property is an inherent and inalienable — "absolute" — part. Note also the confusion between the right to property and the exercise of property, a common "logical fallacy of equivocation" that has been used to good effect by socialists. Other socialist distortions have also crept in, particularly a reversal of the traditional idea that ownership creates the right to use. The Nazis, for example, held that use created ownership — that private property was only a social expedient, not a natural right. (Wunderlich, the National Socialist Conception of Landed Property, 12 Social Research 60 at 61, 66, 72 (1945), cited in Howard R. Williams, *Cases and Materials on the Law of Property*. Brooklyn: The Foundation Press, Inc., 1954, 46-47.

[18] Giordani, *op. cit.*, 281-283.
[19] Fr. Thomas J. Higgins, S.J., *Man as Man, the Science and Art of Ethics*. Rockford, Illinois: Tan Books and Publishers, Inc., 1992, §§ 494-573. We see the same sort of over-simplification with respect to the oft-quoted statement by Saint Paul to Timothy (1 Timothy 6:10). It's not that "money is the root of all evil," but that "*love* of money is the root of all evil" — a very different concept indeed.
[20] "Power tends to corrupt; absolute power corrupts absolutely." *Letter to Bishop Mandell Creighton*, 1887.
[21] Kelso and Adler summarized these concepts in their "Three Principles of Economic Justice," 1) Participation, 2) Distribution, and 3) Harmony (which Kelso and Adler expressed as "Limitation"). See Norman G. Kurland, "Economic Justice in the Age of the Robot," *Curing World Poverty: The New Role of Property*, John H. Miller, C.S.C., S.T.D., editor. St. Louis, Missouri: Social Justice Review, 1994, 61-74.
[22] *Wealth of Nations, op. cit.*, Book I, Ch. I.
[23] Many commentators confuse the fact that technology is independently productive with the erroneous assumption that technology is autonomously productive. On the contrary, technology requires human input ("labor") in some form, even if only an original order to begin, but that portion of production due to technology is completely independent of that portion that is due purely to labor. See Kelso and Adler, *op. cit.*
[24] Smith, *The Theory of Moral Sentiments*. Book IV, Chapter I, §6.
[25] Ferree, *Forty Years After. . . op. cit.*, 29.
[26] See Michael D. Greaney, *Social Justice Betrayed*. St. Louis: Catholic Central Union of America, 2001.
[27] "It [worker ownership] is about a new set of power relationships — between workers and management, workers and their unions, and workers and their company." Robert Woodman, President of the Oglebay-Norton Employee Economic Empowerment Association ("ONEEEA"), during the attempt of the employees to purchase the Marine Services division of the Cleveland, Ohio, company. Quoted in "Bidders get grant to probe Oglebay," Alison Grant, *The Plain Dealer*, March 4, 2004.
[28] "It is surely undeniable that, when a man engages in remunerative labor, the impelling reason and motive of his work is to obtain property, and thereafter to hold it as his very own." *Rerum Novarum*, § 5. Undeniable, perhaps, but that has not stopped anyone from denying it.

[29] *Quadragesimo Anno*, § 63.

[30] The underlying assumptions of both schools of thought are so similar that Father Ferree, in company with others, referred to socialism as "absolutist state capitalism." *Introduction to Economic and Social Development, op. cit.*, 15.

[31] I've said it before, but it bears repeating, especially if it serves to correct some of the wilder ideas people have about political and economic theory within the broader framework of Catholic social teaching. Consistent with the teachings of the popes from at least Pius IX on, the "Reign of Christ the King" does not mean either a theocracy or a situation in which the State takes direct orders from Church or pope. The Reign of Christ the King is a condition of society in which the institutions of society are based on universal moral values whose application is consistent with the interpretation and guidance of the Catholic Church through its head, the Vicar of Christ. This maximizes each individual's chance of developing spiritually and attaining his true end of heaven — in the next life, not on earth. Keeping this in mind, it appears that the Reign of Christ the King would be characterized by what CESJ calls "the four pillars of an economically just society. These are, 1) limited economic role for the State, 2) restoration of the rights of private property, especially in corporate equity, 3) free and open markets, and, most particularly, 4) widespread ownership of the means of production. Each of these "pillars" has a specific and precise meaning that frequently differs from popular conceptions. A good analysis and explanation can be found in *Curing World Poverty, op. cit.*

[32] "Social justice can, therefore, be defined as: *a special species of justice, distinct from commutative, legal and distributive, which requires that material goods, even privately owned, shall serve the common use of all men.*" [55] [Emphasis in original.] That is, as the author states elsewhere, social justice and economic justice are to be understood as equivalent terms: "'Social justice' is always proposed as the fundamental guiding principal for the solution of *economic* questions." [22] [Emphasis in original.] William F. Drummond, S.J., *Social Justice*. Milwaukee, Wisconsin: The Bruce Publishing Company, 1955. Drummond's claim contradicts the statement of Pius XI in § 76 of *Quadragesimo Anno*, below.

[33] In § 76 of *Quadragesimo Anno* Pius XI makes it clear that the economic common good is given by way of example, and as a result of a restructured social order — not as social justice itself:

"What We have thus far stated regarding an equitable distribution of property and regarding just wages concerns individual persons and only indirectly touches social order, to the restoration of which according to the principles of sound philosophy and to its perfection according to the sublime precepts of the law of the Gospel, Our Predecessor, Leo XIII, devoted all his thought and care."

[34] Contrast this with the condition of pagan society: "In ancient society such personal liberty with its derivatives, initiative, responsibility, and sanctions, was not understood in so broad a sense but was limited by conditions of time and space and was dependent upon men and upon contingent and mutable causes; nor was it conceded to more than a minority. The persons *sui juris* were few in comparison to those subject to the free head of the family and especially in comparison to the mass of slaves in whom civil law did not recognize a personality at all. Then the liberty even of the free was conditioned by and incorporated into the organism of the State, which fixed its limits and supplied its initiative. Personality was more or less submerged in political collectivity. The person, in short, belonged not to himself but to others." Giordani, *op. cit.*, 127.

[35] IIa IIae q. 57, a. 3.

[36] William Cobbett, *The Poor Man's Friend, or, Essays on the Rights and Duties of the Poor*. London: Printed by William Cobbett, Fleet Street, 1829.

[37] William Cobbett, *A History of the Protestant Reformation in England and Ireland*. Rockford, Illinois: Tan Books and Publishers, Inc., 1988, § 456.

Bibliography

Encyclicals and Other Papal Documents

John XXII, *Quia Vir Reprobus* ("That Evil Man"), 1329. ("Bull of Excommunication" against Michael of Cesena)

Benedict XIV, *Vix Pervenit* ("On Usury and Other Dishonest Profit"), 1746.

Leo XIII, *Æterni Patris* ("On the Restoration of Christian Philosophy"), 1879.

Leo XIII, *Rerum Novarum* ("On the Condition of the Workers"), 1891.

Leo XIII, *Testem Benevolentia Nostra* ("On Americanism in Religion"), 1899. ("Apostolic Letter" to James Cardinal Gibbons)

Pius X, Apostolic Constitution, *Lamentabili Sane* ("Syllabus of Errors Condemning Modernism"), 1907.

Pius X, *Pascendi Dominici Gregis* ("On the Doctrines of the Modernists"), 1907.

Pius XI, *Ubi Arcano Dei Consilio* ("On the Peace of Christ in the Kingdom of Christ"), 1922.

Pius XI, *Studiorum Ducem* ("On Saint Thomas Aquinas"), 1923.

Pius XI, *Quas Primas* ("On the Kingship of Christ"), 1925.

Pius XI, Discourse Commemorating the Thirty-Fifth Anniversary of *Rerum Novarum*, May 15, 1926.

Pius XI, Discourse to Diocesan Congress of Catholic Youth, May 16, 1926.

Pius XI, Discourse to the Ecclesiastical Assistants of the U.C.F.I., July 19, 1928.

Pius XI, *Quadragesimo Anno* ("On the Restructuring of the Social Order") 1931.

Pius XI, *Divini Redemptoris* ("On Atheistic Communism"), 1937.

Pius XII, "The Rights of Man" Christmas Message, 1942.

Pius XII, *Summi Pontificatus* ("On the Unity of Human Society"), 1939.

John XXIII, *Mater et Magistra* ("Christianity and Social Progress"), 1961.
Paul VI, *Populorum Progressio* ("On the Development of Peoples"), 1967.
John Paul II, *Centesimus Annus* ("On the Hundredth Anniversary of Rerum Novarum"), 1991.
Sacred Congregation for the Doctrine of the Faith, *Instruction on Certain Aspects of the "Theology of Liberation,"* 1984.

Articles

Armey, Dick "Review Merits of Flat Tax," *Wall Street Journal*, June 16, 1994, A16.
Ashford, Robert H. A. Ashford, "The Binary Economics of Louis Kelso" *Curing World Poverty, op. cit.*, 112.
Basile, Anthony, Ph.D., "Selling Out Catholic Social Teaching: The Acton Institute's Misleading Message" *Culture Wars*, September 1999.
Beauchamp, Tom, Department of Philosophy at the Kennedy Institute of Ethics at Georgetown University, *Rights of Health Care*, 1985.
Brownson, Orestes A., *Boston Quarterly*, July 1840.
Daniels, Norman, professor of philosophy at Tufts University, *Just Health Care*, 1985, 121.
Ederer, Dr. Rupert J., Letter to Father John H. Miller, C.S.C., S.T.D., August 4, 1993.
Ederer, Rupert J., "Solidaristic Economics" *Fidelity*, July/August 1994, 13.
Grant, Alison, "Bidders get grant to probe Oglebay," *The Plain Dealer*, March 4, 2004.
Greaney, Michael D., "Social Justice and the Living Wage" an occasional paper published by the Center for Economic and Social Justice, Washington, DC, 1998.
Greaney, Michael D., "The Living Wage (and Child Care)" *Social Justice Review*, September/October 1998.
Griswold, Charles L., Jr., "Adam Smith: Conscience of Capitalism" *The Best of the WQ*, 43-51.

Grosscup, Peter Stenger, "How to Save the Corporation," *McClure's Magazine*, February 1905.
Grosscup, Peter Stenger, "The Rebirth of the Corporation," *American Illustrated Magazine*, June 1906.
Grosscup, Peter Stenger, "Who Shall Own America?" *American Illustrated Magazine*, December 1905.
Gundlach, Gustav, S.J., "Solidarist Economics, Philosophy and Socio-economic Theory in Pesch" *Social Order*, April 1951, 185.
International Right to Life Federation, Inc., "The Gates Billions" *Newsletter*, September/October 1999, 1.
James VI/I, *A Speech to the Lords and Commons of the Parliament at White-Hall* (1610).
James VI/I, *The Trew Law of Free Monarchies* (1598).
Kagan, Donald, "Books: Appreciating Acton" *The Wall Street Journal*, January 11, 1988, 24.
Kelso, Louis O., "Karl Marx: the Almost Capitalist" *American Bar Association Journal*, March 1957.
Kurland, Norman G., J.D., *How to Win a Revolution. . . and Enjoy It*. Washington, DC: Center for Economic and Social Justice, 1987.
Kurland, Norman G., J.D., *The Capital Homestead Act: National Infrastructural Reforms to Make Every Citizen a Shareholder*. Washington, DC: Center for Economic and Social Justice, 1999.
McGregor, Deborah, "Growth Fails to Close US Economic Divide" *Financial Times*, January 19, 2000.
Mueller, Franz H., "I Knew Heinrich Pesch, the Formative Influence of a 'Human Scholar'" *Social Order*, April 1951, 149.
Mulcahy, Richard E., S.J., "Economic Freedom in Pesch" *Social Order*, April, 1951.
Mulcahy, Richard E., S.J., "Heinrich Pesch, S.J., 1854-1926" *Social Order*, April, 1951, 146.
Novak ,Michael, "Saving Distributism" Introduction to G. K. Chesterton, *Collected Works*, Volume V., San Francisco, California: Ignatius Press, 1987, 15.

Novak, Michael, "How Christianity Created Capitalism" *The Wall Street Journal.* December 23, 1999.

Schlesinger, Jacob M., Mabry, Tristan and Lueck, Sarah, "Charting the Pain Behind the Gain: Income Is Up, Poverty Down, But Overall, Wages Barely Budged Over the Decade" *The Wall Street Journal.* October 1, 1999, pp. B1, B4.

Sirico, Fr. Robert A., "Free Market Morality" *The Wall Street Journal.* January 29, 1991.

Sirico, Fr. Robert A., "President's Message" *Acton Notes, The Newsletter of the Acton Institute for the Study of Religion and Liberty.* June 1997, p. 1.

Sirico, Fr. Robert A., "President's Message" *Acton Notes, The Newsletter of the Acton Institute for the Study of Religion and Liberty.* August 1999, 1.

Sirico, Fr. Robert A., "President's Message," *Acton Notes,* October 1999, 1.

Sirico, Fr. Robert A., Acton Institute, "Institute's Web Outreach Expanded" *Acton Notes.* December 1999, Volume 9, Number 12, 3.

Storck, Thomas, *Catholic Men's Quarterly,* Fall 2007, 36.

Waters, Dr. Raphael, Ph.D., "Freedom in the Political Order" *Social Justice Review.* November/December, 2002, 165.

Yenni, Jacques, S.J., "Pesch's Goal of the Economy" *Social Order,* April 1951, 175.

Books

Adams, Henry C., *Public Debts, An Essay in the Science of Finance,* New York: D. Appleton and Company, 1898.

Althusius, Johannes, *Politica.* Indianapolis, Indiana: Liberty Fund, Inc., 1995.

Aquinas, Saint Thomas, *On the Governance of Rulers (De Regimine Principum), Translated from the Latin by Gerald B. Phelan, Ph.D.* Toronto, Canada: Saint Michael's College, 1935.

Aquinas, St. Thomas, *Summa Theologica.*

Aristotle, *The Nicomachean Ethics*, Translated by J. E. C. Welldon. Buffalo, New York: Prometheus Books, 1987.

Aristotle, *The Politics, Revised Edition, Translated by T. A. Sinclair*. Bungay, Suffolk, U.K.: Penguin Books, Ltd., 1981.

Ashford Robert H. A. and Shakespeare, Rodney, *Binary Economics, The New Paradigm*. Lanham Maryland: University Press of America, 1999.

Augustine, Saint, *The City of God*. New York: Random House, 1950.

Bales, Kevin, *Disposable People, New Slavery in the Global Economy*. Berkeley and Los Angeles, California: University of California Press, 1999.

Bellarmine, Saint Robert Cardinal, *De Laicis, or, The Treatise on Civil Government*. Westport Connecticut: Hyperion Press, Inc., 1979.

Bellarmine, Saint Robert, *De Ecclesiastica Monarchia*.

Belloc, Hilaire, *The Restoration of Property*. New York: Sheed and Ward, 1936.

Belloc, Hilaire, *The Servile State*. Indianapolis, Indiana: Liberty Fund, Inc., 1977.

Binding and Hoche's *The Release of the Destruction of Life Devoid of Value* (*i.e.*, "Permission to Destroy Useless Life").

Black's Law Dictionary. St. Paul, Minn., West Publishing Co., 1951.

Brennan, William, *Dehumanizing the Vulnerable, When Word Games Take Lives*. Chicago, Illinois: Loyola University Press, 1995.

Brownson, Orestes A., *The American Republic: Its Constitution, Tendencies and Destiny*. New York: P. O'Shea, 1866.

Burckhardt, Jacob, *Reflections on History*. Indianapolis, Indiana: Liberty Fund, Inc., 1979.

Bury, J. B., *The Invasion of Europe by the Barbarians*. New York: W. W. Norton, 1967, 13.

Cahill, Rev. Eamon, *The Framework of a Christian State, An Introduction to Social Science*. Dublin: M. H. Gill and Son, Ltd., 1932.

Cassell's Latin Dictionary, New York: Macmillan Publishing Company, 1968.

Catechism of the Catholic Church. Libreria Editrice Vaticana, 1994.

Chesterton, Gilbert Keith, *Saint Thomas Aquinas, "The Dumb Ox."* New York: Doubleday Image, 1956,

Chesterton, Gilbert Keith, *The Outline of Sanity, G. K. Chesterton, Collected Works, Vol. V.* San Francisco, California: Ignatius Press, 1987.

Chesterton, Gilbert Keith, *What's Wrong With the World. G. K. Chesterton, Collected Works, Volume IV.* San Francisco, California: Ignatius Press, 1987.

Civardi, Msgr. Luigi, *A Manual of Catholic Action.* New York: Sheed & Ward, Inc., 1936.

Clowes, Brian, Ph.D., *Call to Action or Call to Apostasy? How Dissenters Plan to Remake the Catholic Church in their own Image.* Front Royal, Virginia: Human Life International, 1997.

Cobbett, William Cobbett, *The Poor Man's Friend, or, Essays on the Rights and Duties of the Poor.* London: Printed by William Cobbett, Fleet Street, 1829.

Cobbett, William, *A History of the Protestant Reformation in England and Ireland.* Rockford, Illinois: Tan Books and Publishers, Inc., 1988.

Cobbett, William, *The Poor Man's Friend, or, Essays on the Rights and Duties of the Poor.* London: Printed by William Cobbett, Fleet Street, 1829.

Cuthbert, Father, *Catholic Ideals in Social Life.* New York: Benziger Brothers, 1904.

Diamant, Alfred, *Austrian Catholics and the Social Question, 1918 – 1933.* Gainesville, Florida: University of Florida Press, 1959,

Dicey, Albert Venn, *Lectures on the Relation Between Law and Public Opinion in England During the Nineteenth Century.* New Brunswick, Connecticut: Transaction Books, 1981.

Drummond, William F., S.J., *Social Justice.* Milwaukee, Wisconsin: The Bruce Publishing Company, 1955.

Eberdt, Mary Lois, C.H.M., Ph.D., and Schnepp, Gerald J., S.M., Ph.D., *Industrialism and the Popes: A Study Made*

Under the Auspices of the Department of Sociology Saint Louis University with Special Emphasis on the Industry Council Plan. New York: P. J. Kenedy & Sons, 1953.

Ederer, Rupert J., *Economics as if God Matters*. South Bend, Indiana: Fidelity Press, 1995.

Fahey, Rev. Denis, *The Kingship of Christ According to the Principles of St. Thomas Aquinas*. Palmdale, California: Christian Book Club of America, 1990.

Fahey, Rev. Denis, *The Mystical Body of Christ in the Modern World*. Dublin: Regina Publications, 1987.

Fallon, Valère, S.J., *Principles of Social Economy*. New York: Benziger Brothers, 1933.

Fanfani, Amintore, *Catechism of Catholic Social Teaching*. Translated by Reverend Henry J. Yannone. Westminster, Maryland: The Newman Press, 1960.

Fanfani, Amintore, *Catholicism, Protestantism and Capitalism*. New York: Sheed and Ward, 1955.

Fawcett, Henry, *Pauperism, Its Causes and Remedies*. London: Macmillan and Co., 1871.

Ferree, Rev. William J., *A Discourse on Social Charity*. MS., 1966.

Ferree, Rev. William J., *Administration and Social Ethics*. MS., 1984.

Ferree, Rev. William J., *Forty Years After . . . A Second Call to Battle*. MS., 1984.

Ferree, Rev. William J., *Introduction to Catholic Action*. Washington, DC: NCWC, c. 1950.

Ferree, Rev. William J., *Introduction to Social Justice*. Washington, DC: Center for Economic and Social Justice, 1996 (Originally published 1948).

Ferree, Rev. William J., S.M., Ph.D., *An Introduction to Economic and Social Development*. Rome: Private Printing, 1966.

Ferree, Rev. William J., *The Act of Social Justice*. Washington, DC: The Catholic University of America Press, 1942.

Filmer, Sir Robert, *Patriarcha* (1680).

Filmer, Sir Robert, *Observations Upon Aristotle's Politiques* (1652).

Fuller, R. Buckminster, *Utopia or Oblivion: the Prospects for Humanity*. New York: Bantam Books, 1969.

Gardner, Martin, "Introduction to the Dover Edition," G. K. Chesterton, *Four Faultless Felons*, New York: Dover Publications, Inc., 1989

Garnsey, Peter, *Ideas of Slavery from Aristotle to Augustine*. Cambridge, UK: Cambridge University Press, 1996.

Gaskell, Peter, *The Manufacturing Population of England, Its Moral, Social, and Physical Conditions, and the Changes Which Have Arisen from the Use of Steam Machinery; with an Examination of Infant Labour*. London: Baldwin and Cradock, 1833.

George, Henry, *Progress and Poverty, Centennial Edition 1879-1979*. New York: Robert Schalkenbach Foundation, 1979.

Giordani, Igino, *The Social Message of Jesus*. Boston, Massachusetts: Daughters of St. Paul, 1977.

Giordani, Igino, *The Social Message of the Early Church Fathers*. Boston, Massachusetts: Daughters of St. Paul, 1977.

Glenn, Msgr. Paul J., *A Tour of the Summa*. Rockford, Illinois: Tan Books and Publishers, Inc., 1978.

Greaney, Michael D., *Social Justice Betrayed, the Misinterpretation of Catholic Social Teaching*. St. Louis, Missouri: Catholic Central Union of America, 2001.

Habiger, Fr. Matthew, Ph.D., O.S.B., *Papal Teachings on Private Property, 1891-1981*. Lanham, Maryland: University Press of America, 1990.

Hertz, Solange, *The Star-Spangled Heresy: Americanism*. Santa Monica, California: Veritas Press, 1992.

Hertz, Solange, *Utopia: "NOWHERE" — Now Here*. Santa Monica, California: Veritas Press, 1992.

Higgins, Fr. Thomas J., S.J., *Man as Man, the Science and Art of Ethics*. Rockford, Illinois: Tan Books and Publishers, Inc., 1992.

Hobbes, Thomas, *Leviathan, or The Matter, Forme and Power of A Common-wealth Ecclesiasticall and Civil*. London: Penguin Books, 1985.

Hohfeld, Wesley, *Fundamental Legal Conceptions*. Cook's Edition, 1919, 1923.

Humboldt, Wilhelm von, *The Limits of State Action*. Indianapolis, Indiana: Liberty Fund, Inc., 1993.

Hutt, W. H., *The Strike-Threat System, The Economic Consequences of Collective Bargaining*. New Rochelle, New York: Arlington House, 1973.

Jasay, Anthony de, *The State*. Indianapolis, Indiana: Liberty Fund, Inc., 1998.

Kelley, Rev. John J., S.M., *Freedom in the Church: A Documented History of the Principle of Subsidiary Function*. Dayton, Ohio: Peter Li, Inc., 2000.

Kelly, Msgr. George, *The Battle for the American Church*. San Francisco, California: Igatius Press, 1995.

Kelso, Louis O. and Adler, Mortimer J., *The Capitalist Manifesto*. New York: Random House, 1958.

Kelso, Louis O. and Adler, Mortimer J., *The New Capitalists: A Proposal to Free Economic Growth from the Slavery of Savings*. New York: Random House, 1961.

Keynes, John Maynard, *The Economic Consequences of the Peace*. London: Penguin Books, 1988.

Keynes, John Maynard, *The General Theory of Employment, Interest, and Money*. New York: Harcourt Brace Jovanovich, Publishers, 1991.

Khaldûn, Muhammad Ibn, *The Muqaddimah, An Introduction to History*, translated by Franz Rosenthal. Bollingen, 1969.

Kurland, Norman G., Brohawn, Dawn K., and Greaney, Michael D., *Capital Homesteading for Every Citizen: A Just Free Market Solution for Saving Social Security*. Arlington, Virginia: Economic Justice Media, 2004.

Land, Rev. Philip S., S.J., *Catholic Social Teaching as I Have Lived, Loathed and Loved It*. Chicago, Illinois: Loyola University Press, 1994.

Law, John, *Money and Trade Considered, with a Proposal for Supplying the Nation with Money*. Edinburgh: Andrew Anderson, 1705.

Leoni, Bruno, *Freedom and the Law*. Indianapolis, Indiana: Liberty Fund, Inc., 1991.

Levesque, George-Henri, *Social Credit and Catholicism*, Hawthorne, California: The Christian Book Club of America (ND).
Likoudis, Paul, *The Legacy of CHD, A Critical Report and Analysis of the U.S. Bishops' Campaign for Human Development*. Minneapolis, Minnesota: The Wanderer Press, 1990.
Locke, John, *Treatise of Civil Government*. New York: Appleton, Century, Crofts, 1965.
Mackay, Charles, *Extraordinary Popular Delusions and the Madness of Crowds*. New York: Farrar, Straus and Giroux, 1932.
Malthus, Rev. Thomas *Essay on Population* (1797, 1803).
Marx, Karl and Engels, Friedrich, *The Communist Manifesto*. New York: Penguin Books, 1967.
McInerny, Ralph, *What Went Wrong With Vatican II*. Manchester, New Hampshire: Sophia Institute Press, 1998.
Michel, Dom Virgil, O.S.B., Ph.D., *Christian Social Reconstruction, Some Fundamentals of the* Quadragesimo Anno, *Second Printing*. Milwaukee, Wisconsin: The Bruce Publishing Company, 1936.
Miller, John H., editor, *Curing World Poverty: The New Role of Property*. Saint Louis, Missouri: Social Justice Review, 1994.
Miller, Raymond J., C.Ss.R., *Forty Years After: Pius XI and the Social Order, A Commentary*. St. Paul, Minnesota: Radio Replies Press, 1947.
Montesquieu, Charles de, *The Spirit of Laws* (Two Volumes) Littleton, Colorado: Fred B. Rothman & Co., 1991.
Morrison, Charles, *An Essay on the Relations Between Labour and Capital*, London: Longman, Brown, Green, and Longmans, 1854.
Moulton, Harold G., *The Formation of Capital*. Washington, DC: The Brookings Institution, 1935.
Murphy, Rev. John Francis Murphy, S.T.L., *The Moral Obligation of the Individual to Participate in Catholic Action*. Washington, DC: The Catholic University of America Press, 1958.

National Conference of Catholic Bishops, *Economic Justice for All: Pastoral Letter on Catholic Social Teaching and the U.S. Economy*. Washington, DC: United States Catholic Conference, 1986.

Nell-Bruening, Rev. Oswald von, S.J., *Reorganization of Social Economy*. Milwaukee, Wisconsin: Bruce Publishing Company, 1936.

Orel, Anton, *Das Verfassungsmachwerk der "Republik Österreich" von der Warte der immerwährenden Philosophie aus und im Lichte von der Idee, Natur und Geschichte Österreichs geprüft un verworfen*. Vienna: Vogelsan Verlg Gmbh, 1921.

Orel, Anton, *Kirche-Kapitalismus-Proletariat*. Vienna: Vogelsang-Verlag, Gmbh, 1928.

Panzer, Fr. Joel S., *The Popes and Slavery*. New York: Alba House, 1996.

Pesch, Rev. Heinrich, S.J., *Lehrbuch der Nationaloeconomie* (1905).

Phillipe, Rev. A. C.SS.R., *Christ, King of Nations*. Kansas City, Missouri: Instauratio Press, 1992.

Plutarch, *Selected Essays and Dialogues, A New Translation by Donald Russell*, Oxford, UK: Oxford University Press, 1993.

Plutarch, *The Lives of the Noble Grecians and Romans, Translated by John Dryden*. New York: The Modern Library, (ND).

Polybius, *The Rise of the Roman Empire* (Selections from the *Universal History* of Polybius), London: Penguin Books, 1979.

Proceedings and debates of the Virginia State Convention of 1829-1830, Volume 1, New York: DeCapo Press, 1971.

Proudhon, Pierre Joseph, *What is Property? An Inquiry into the Principle of Right and Government* (1841).

Quigley, William P., *Ending Poverty as We Know It: Guaranteeing a Right to a Job at a Living Wage*. Philadelphia, Pennsylvania: Temple University Press, 2003.

Rager, Rev. John Clement, S.T.D., *The Political Philosophy of St. Robert Bellarmine*. Spokane, Washington: The Apostolate of Our Lady of Siluva, 1995.

Ricardo, David, *The Principles of Political Economy and Taxation*. London: Everyman's Library, 1991.

Rommen, Heinrich A., *The Natural Law, A Study in Legal and Social History and Philosophy*. Indianapolis, Indiana: Liberty Fund, Inc., 1998.

Rousseau, Jean-Jacques, *The Basic Political Writings*. Indianapolis, Indiana: Hackett Publishing Company, 1987.

Roussel, Rev. Fr. A., *Liberalism & Catholicism, the Great Betrayal* (Kansas City, Missouri: Angelus Press, 1998)

Ryan, John A., *Distributive Justice*. New York: Grosset and Dunlap, 1942.

Ryan, John A., S.T.D., *A Living Wage: Its Ethical and Economic Aspects*. New York: Grosset & Dunlap, Publishers, 1906.

Ryan, John H., *Distributive Justice*. New York: Macmillan, 1906.

Sacred Congregation for the Doctrine of the Faith, *Instruction on Certain Aspects of the "Theology of Liberation,"* 1984.

Sidney, Algernon, *Discourses Concerning Government*. Indianapolis, Indiana: Liberty Fund, Inc., 1996.

Smith, Adam, *An Inquiry into the Nature and Causes of the Wealth of Nations*. New York: Alfred A. Knopf, 1991.

Smith, Adam, *The Theory of Moral Sentiments*. Indianapolis, Indiana: Liberty Fund, Inc., 1982.

Spalding, Henry S., S.J., *Social Problems and Agencies*. New York: Benziger Brothers, 1929.

Studienrunde katholischer Soziologen, *Katholisch-soziales Manifest*. Mainz: Mathias Grünewald, 1932.

Sumner, William Graham, *On Liberty, Society, and Politics*. Indianapolis, Indiana: Liberty Fund, Inc., 1992.

Thornton, William T., *A Plea for Peasant Proprietors*. London: John Murray, Albemarle Street, 1848

Tocqueville, Alexis de, *Democracy in America*. New York: Alfred A. Knoph, 1994.

Tocqueville, Alexis de, *Memoir on Pauperism*. Chicago, Illinois: Ivan R. Dee, Publisher, 1968

Weber, Max, *The Protestant Ethic and the Spirit of Capitalism*. London: Routledge, 1992.

Williams, Howard R., *Cases and Materials on the Law of Property*. Brooklyn: The Foundation Press, Inc., 1954.

www.ingramcontent.com/pod-product-compliance
Lightning Source LLC
Chambersburg PA
CBHW032034150426
43194CB00006B/269